P9-DVS-427

An Altitude SuperGuide

The Best Hikes of Colorado

The
Best Hikes
of Colorado

An Altitude SuperGuide
by Christina Williams

Publication Information

Altitude Publishing Ltd.

12445 East 39th Ave., Unit 521,
Denver, Colorado 80239

9 8 7 6 5 4

Copyright © 1999 Altitude Publishing Ltd.
Text copyright © 1999 Christina Williams
All rights reserved. No part of this book may be reproduced in any form or by any means, electronic or mechanical, without prior written permission of the publisher.

Extreme care has been taken to ensure that all information presented in this book is accurate and up-to-date, and neither the author nor the publisher can be held responsible for any errors.

Cataloging in Publication Data

Williams, Christina.
The best hikes of Colorado

Includes index.
ISBN 1-55265-006-5
1. Hiking--Colorado--Guidebooks. 2. Colorado--Guidebooks.
I. Title
GV199.42.C6W54 1998   917.8804'33   C98-910775-2

We acknowledge the financial support of the Government of Canada through the Book Publishing Industry Development Program (BPIDP) for our publishing activities.

Front cover photo: Diamond Lake Trail
Insets, front cover: right: Mule deer
left: Heart-leaf arnica
Frontispiece: The valley of Grizzly Creek
Back cover photo: Lost Creek Wilderness

visit Altitude's web site:
www.altitudepublishing.com

Design and Production Team

Concept/Art direction	Stephen Hutchings
Associate publishers	Dan Klinglesmith
	Patrick Soran
Design/layout	Patrick Soran
	Kelly Stauffer
Editor	Sabrina Grobler
Financial management	Laurie Smith
Maps	Scott Manktelow
Index	Elizabeth Bell

A Note from the Publisher

The world described in *Altitude SuperGuides* is a unique and fascinating place. It is a world filled with surprise and discovery, beauty and enjoyment, questions and answers. It is a world of people, cities, landscape, animals and wilderness as seen through the eyes of those who live in, work with, and care for this world. The process of describing this world is also a means of defining ourselves.

It is also a world of relationship, where people derive their meaning from a deep and abiding contact with the land—as well as from each other. And it is this sense of relationship that guides all of us at Altitude to ensure that these places continue to survive and evolve in the decades ahead.

Altitude SuperGuides are books intended to be used, as much as read. Like the world they describe, *Altitude SuperGuides* are evolving, adapting and growing. Please write to us with your comments and observations, and we will do our best to incorporate your ideas into future editions of these books.

Stephen Hutchings
President and Publisher

Altitude Greentree Program

Altitude Publishing will plant twice as many trees as were used in the manufacturing of this product.
Printed and bound in Canada by Friesen Printers

Contents

Maps

At the beginning of each hike is a map that indicates the trailhead and the route. The following is a list of where to find the regional maps:

The Best Hikes of Colorado are organized according to this color scheme:

Introduction

RMNP

The Front Range

Vail

Aspen

Steamboat Springs

San Juans

Sangre de Cristos

Reference

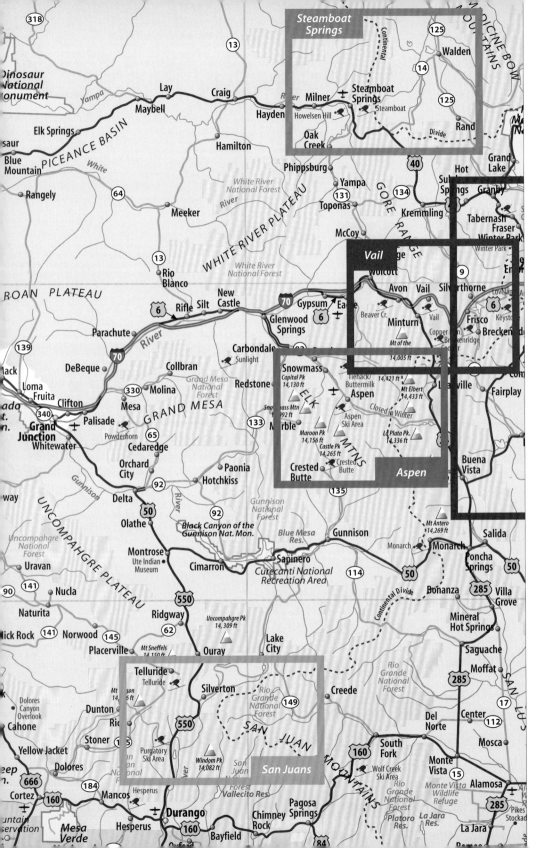

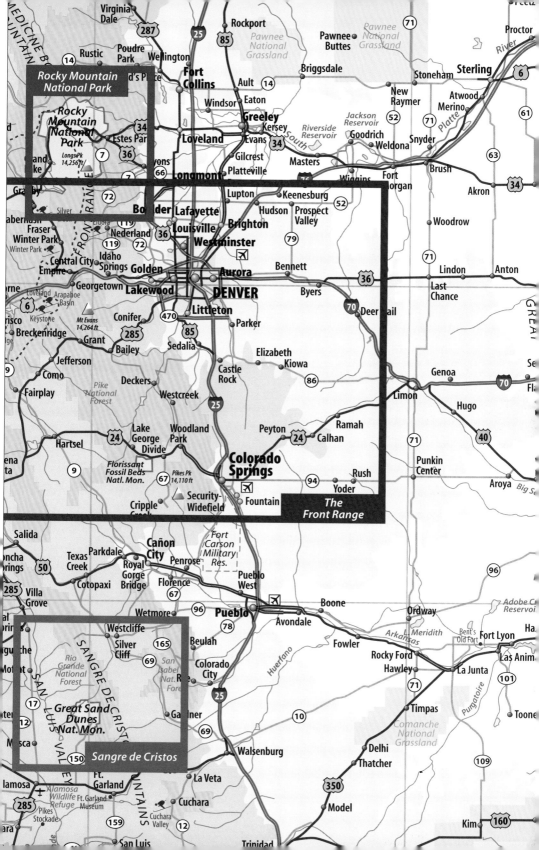

The Best Hikes of Colorado

Hike	Rating	Length	Elev. Gain	Features
① Emerald Lake — Day hike	Easy	1.8 mi. one way	605 ft.	family · vistas · wildflowers · foliage · fee
② Bear & Fern Lakes — Day hike	Moderate	8.5 mi. one way	1,205 ft.	vistas · wildflowers · foliage · horse · fee
③ Flattop Mountain — Day hike	Strenuous	5.0 mi. one way	3,238 ft.	vistas · wildflowers · foliage · Seasonal · fee
④ Black Lake — Day hike	Moderate	4.7 mi. one way	1,380 ft.	family · vistas · wildflowers · foliage · horse · fee
⑤ Sky Pond — Day hike	Moderate	4.6 mi. one way	1,660 ft.	family · vistas · wildflowers · foliage · horse · fee
⑥ Longs Peak — Day hike	Strenuous	8 mi. one way	4,855 ft.	vistas · wildflowers · horse
⑦ Chasm Lake — Day hike	Moderate	4.2 mi. one way	2,400 ft.	vistas · wildflowers · horse
⑧ Estes Cone — Day hike	Moderate	3.3 mi. one way	1,606 ft.	family · vistas · horse
⑨ Bluebird Lake — Day hike	Strenuous	6.3 mi. one way	2,478 ft.	family · vistas · wildflowers · foliage · horse · fee
⑩ Thunder Lake — Day hike	Strenuous	6.8 mi. one way	2,074 ft.	family · vistas · wildflowers · foliage · horse · fee
⑪ Sandbeach Lake — Day hike	Moderate	4.2 mi. one way	1,963 ft.	family · foliage · horse · fee
⑫ Gem Lake — Day hike	Easy	1.8 mi. one way	910 ft.	family · vistas · foliage · horse
⑬ Ypsilon Lake — Day hike	Moderate	4.5 mi. one way	2,000 ft.	vistas · foliage · horse · fee
⑭ Lulu City — Day hike	Easy	3.7 mi. one way	350 ft.	family · vistas · wildflowers · foliage · horse · fee
⑮ Lake Verna — Day hike	Strenuous	6.9 mi. one way	1,889 ft.	family · vistas · wildflowers · foliage
⑯ Gibraltar Lake — Day hike	Strenuous	8.0 mi. one way	2,520 ft.	vistas · wildflowers · foliage · horse · dog
⑰ Mount Audubon — Day hike	Moderate	4 mi. one way	2,743 ft.	vistas · wildflowers · horse · dog · fee
⑱ Diamond Lake — Day hike	Easy	2.5 mi. one way	800 ft.	family · vistas · wildflowers · dog
⑲ Devils Thumb Lake — Day hike	Moderate	5.5 mi. one way	2,140 ft.	vistas · wildflowers · foliage · horse · dog
⑳ Pikes Peak — 1- or 2-day hike	Strenuous	13 mi. one way	7,510 ft.	vistas · wildflowers · foliage · horse · bike · dog

Legend

- 👪 → This hike is suitable for family outings
- 📷 → This hike features spectacular vistas
- 🌾 → This hike features summer wildflowers
- 🍂 → This hike features autumn foliage

The Best Hikes of Colorado

Hike	Rating	Length	Elev. Gain	Features
21 Lost Creek Loop — Backpack	Moderate	24 mi. loop	3,400 ft.	camera, flower, leaf, horse · dog
22 Rock Creek — Day hike	Easy	1.7 mi. one way	700 ft.	family, camera, flower, leaf, horse · dog
23 Pitkin Lake — Day hike	Moderate	5 mi. one way	3,000 ft.	family, camera, flower, leaf · dog
24 Booth Lake — Day hike or overnight	Moderate	6 mi. one way	3,080 ft.	family, camera, flower, leaf · dog
25 Missouri Lakes — Day hike or overnight	Moderate	4.4 mi. one way	1,986 ft.	camera, flower · dog
26 Mount Elbert — Day hike	Strenuous	5 mi. one way	4,373 ft.	camera, flower · dog
27 Lost Man Loop — Shuttle day hike	Moderate	8.8 mi. one way	1,294 ft.	camera, flower, horse · dog
28 Grizzly Lake — Day hike	Moderate	3.6 mi. one way	1,960 ft.	camera, flower, horse · dog
29 Cathedral Lake — Day hike or overnight	Moderate	3.2 mi. one way	1,966 ft.	camera, flower, leaf, horse · dog
30 American Lake — Day hike	Moderate	3.2 mi. one way	1,965 ft.	camera, flower, leaf, horse · dog
31 Conundrum Spgs. — Overnight	Strenuous	8.5 mi. one way	2,500 ft.	camera, flower, leaf, horse · dog
32 Buckskin Pass — Day hike	Strenuous	4.7 mi. one way	2,882 ft.	family, camera, flower, leaf, horse · dog
33 Capitol Lake — Day hike or overnight	Strenuous	7.3 mi. one way	2,600 ft.	camera, flower, leaf, horse · dog
34 Rabbit Ears Peak — Day hike	Easy	3 mi. one way	1,050 ft.	family, camera, flower, horse, bike · dog
35 Fish Creek Falls — Day hike or overnight	Strenuous	6 mi. one way	2,370 ft.	family, flower, leaf, horse · dog, fee
36 Three Island Lake — Day hike	Moderate	3 mi. one way	1,478 ft.	family, flower, leaf, horse · dog
37 Crater Lake — Day hike or overnight	Moderate	5.5 mi. one way	856 ft.	family, camera, flower, horse · dog
38 Chicago Basin — 2+ day backpack	Strenuous	8.0 mi. one way	3,200 ft.	camera, flower, leaf, horse · dog
39 Great Sand Dunes — Day hike	Moderate	1.0 mi. each way	700 ft.	family, camera, leaf · dog, fee
40 Willow Lake — Day hike or overnight	Moderate	3.9 mi. one way	2,364 ft.	camera, flower, leaf, horse · dog

Horses are allowed on this trail

Dogs are allowed on this hike

Bikes are allowed on this trail

A fee is charged to enter this area

Hiking in Colorado

Trail along Lost Man Creek, Aspen

T he majestic ranges of Colorado's Rocky Mountains provide some of the greatest hiking and backpacking opportunities in the world. Within an area six times that of Switzerland, 54 summits rise to a gravity-defying 14,000 feet above sea level and more than 1,000 peaks

are two miles high.

Unlike many mountainous regions in North America, the Colorado Rockies afford a safe wilderness experience for the hiker. Trails penetrate the most scenic areas, limiting the need for difficult cross-country travel. The wildlife presents little danger. While black bears and mountain lions do exist, there have been few reported threats to hikers.

This book describes 40 of the best trails in Colorado. It is divided into seven regional chapters: Rocky Mountain National Park, Indian Peaks Wilderness and the Front Range, the Vail Area, the As-

pen Area, the Steamboat Springs Area, the San Juans and the Sangre de Cristos.

How to Use This Book

The trails described in *The Best Hikes of Colorado* were chosen after extensive consultation with USDA Forest Service and National Park Service rangers, fellow hikers and other experts. The decision to include each of these 40 hikes was based on such criteria as the majestic beauty of the terrain through which the trail passes, the splendor of the destination, an intriguing

regional history, closeness to centers of population and, in some cases, an inviting challenge. All of the hikes follow established, well-maintained trails.

Read the entire text for a hike before you head out onto the trail. This will help you to decide if the hike is right for the interest and ability level of your party. Remember that snow lingers on many of the higher sections of trail well into July, making progress more difficult than this book might imply. Many of the hikes pass waterfalls, lakes or other intermediate features. These provide excellent desti-

left: Trail to Gem Lake

nations when the high country is snowpacked or for those looking for a shorter trip.

Call the appropriate Forest Service or National Park information centers for current conditions, warnings, road and trail closures, and any additional information you may need.

Trails

The word "trail" signifies a designated foot, bicycle or horse route that is maintained by the Forest Service or National Park Service. Because of the popularity of these 40 trails, forest and park rangers generally do an excellent job of trail maintenance. It is important to remember, however, that natural disasters such as landslides, avalanches, fires and blowdowns do occur in the Colorado Rockies, often destroying sections of trail. How quickly these are repaired depends entirely on the extent of the damage.

Maps

The maps that accompany each hike were created especially for this guidebook. They depict the route and surrounding landmarks as precisely as possible. It is advisable to purchase the appropriate United States Geological Survey (USGS) topographic map or maps before venturing into the mountains. Because of their size and scale, these provide much more detailed information than can be included in a book. It is important to note that many topographic maps have not been revised recently and that some of the trails shown on these maps have been rerouted or no longer exist.

Camping

As most of the 40 hikes described in *The Best Hikes of Colorado* start fairly close to Colorado's major towns, plenty of motels, restaurants, grocery stores and other amenities are available.

Designated Forest Service or National Park campgrounds exist in each region of the state. These provide facilities for tents and recreational vehicles. They have outhouses or flushing toilets and cold water for washing and drinking. They do not have showers, cabins, restaurants or grocery stores.

Camping is permitted in most of Colorado's backcountry. Information on this is provided on the boards at each trailhead. Fees and permits are applicable in Rocky Mountain National Park and the Indian Peaks Wilderness Area. While regulations differ from one wilderness to the next, the following general rules apply.

• Follow rules posted at individual trailheads.

• Camp in designated or established campsites whenever possible to avoid damage to the environment.

• If no established campsite is available, camp on hard ground at least 100 feet from streams and lakes. Camp in wooded areas rather than meadows. Trees offer shelter from the wind and provide privacy by hiding your campsite from view.

Assumption of Risk

Safety is a major concern in all outdoor activities, whether it be hiking, backpacking, climbing, cycling, horseback riding or fishing. No guidebook can prepare readers for every danger that could potentially be encountered in the backcountry.

When you follow any of these trails, you take full responsibility for your own safety. Neither the author nor the publisher can be held responsible for any accidents, injuries, property loss or other difficulties that may result from using the information in this book.

Editor's note: The author has hiked every trail in *The Best Hikes of Colorado* at least once, and has taken great care to describe the paths, river crossings and terrain as accurately as possible and with the greatest concern for safety. However, landslides, avalanches, flash floods, fires, tree falls and blowdowns often change the face of the landscape overnight, obliterating bridges and sections of trail. Just because a path or natural feature is described in this book does not mean that it will be the same at the time of your visit or that it is still safe to travel in that region. Consult the information service closest to the trail you wish to hike before you embark on any outing. As with any facet of life, exercising common sense while hiking is essential.

The fall landscape is a riot of golds and browns

Choose a spot where you will have a minimal impact on the environment.

• Always suspend food, trash and perfumed toiletries (such as soap and toothpaste) in a tree at least 10 feet off the ground and four feet out from the trunk.

• Use a backpacking stove instead of a fire for cooking whenever possible.

• If campfires are allowed, do not cut down living trees or shrubs for firewood. Always drown a campfire before leaving the area or going to bed.

• Do not dig trenches around your tent.

• Keep your dog under control at all times.

• Naturalize your campsite after camping by scattering pine duff on worn areas.

Call the local Forest Service or National Park office for information about wilderness regulations, backcountry camping permits and to find out which is the closest campground to your proposed hiking trail.

Climate

Coloradans love to joke, "If you don't like the weather, just wait 10 minutes." And in the Rocky Mountains, this adage can prove to be very,

Lightning Awareness

Lightning kills more people in the United States than tornadoes, hurricanes, floods or any other weather-related hazard. Lightning presents the greatest danger to hikers and climbers in the Colorado Rockies. Blue skies and low humidity characterize summer mornings in the mountains. Around noon, cumulus clouds (fluffy white clouds with flat bases) begin to appear in the western sky. By mid-afternoon, these have developed into thunderstorms which produce lightning, heavy rain, hail and often snow.

Before you venture on a hiking trip, it is important to have a good understanding of mountain weather and of the proper safety procedures to follow if a storm threatens or if you are caught in a storm. Here are some tips to enhance the safety of your trip.

• Get the weather forecast for the region you are going to hike in before starting on the trail. If the forecast is bad, plan your trip for another day.

• If the forecast calls for good weather, begin your hike in the early morning so that you reach your destination by noon at the latest and are on the way down from exposed elevations by the time thunderstorms threaten.

• Watch for cumulus clouds building in the western sky. If they are developing rapidly into cauliflower-shaped towers over a black base, thunderstorms will probably begin within an hour.

• If towering cumulus clouds appear and you are on an exposed peak, ridge or open slope above tree line, head for shelter within a thick growth of trees in a low-lying area. If you have not yet reached the summit of your chosen peak, abort the climb.

• If you are caught in a thunderstorm, remember that lightning strikes the highest object in a landscape. Avoid being that object or standing next to it. Do not take shelter under lone trees, rocks or other features rising above the landscape.

• Crouch in a low-lying spot, keeping your head down. If you choose to continue to move toward the safety of a forest, keep your body as close to the ground as possible.

very true. Low humidity, sunny mornings, stormy afternoons and clear nights characterize summers in Colorado. Nevertheless, mountain weather can be downright unpredictable. Individual mountain ranges frequently create their own weather patterns. Storms can blow in without warning at any time. You can experience all four seasons in one day, so being prepared for any eventuality is an important rule for safe hiking. Despite the fact that summer temperatures in the Colorado Rockies often rise to 80 degrees Farenheit and even to the 90s (necessitating shorts and a T-shirt), always carry extra wool or fleece garments and rain gear.

Night temperatures drop significantly. If you plan to camp, bring a warm sleeping bag. Also, remember that the temperature drops about 3.5 degrees Fahrenheit with each thousand feet of elevation gain.

Hypothermia

Hypothermia is one of the most life-threatening conditions that occurs in the Colorado high country. Left untreated, a victim can die within a few hours. Hypothermia exists when the internal core temperature of the body falls to dangerous levels due

to exposure to cold, wind and wetness. This does not only happen during frigid weather. In fact, most cases develop when air temperatures are between 30 and 50 degrees Fahrenheit. Symptoms include intense shivering, drowsiness, exhaustion, slurred speech, irrational behavior, clumsiness, stumbling and fumbling hands.

The best way to avoid hypothermia is to stay warm and dry. Always carry several layers of spare clothing, including gloves, a hat, long pants and a warm jacket or sweater. If temperatures drop, immediately put on additional layers of clothing. Do not wait until you begin to feel cold. Party members should watch each other as hypothermia victims are often unaware that they have a problem.

If a member of your party develops hypothermia, imme-

Maps Elevation

more than 13000 ft

between 12000 and 13000 ft

between 11000 and 12000 ft

between 10000 and 11000 ft

between 9000 and 10000 ft

between 8000 and 9000 ft

less than 8000 ft

diately do whatever you can to warm him or her up. Get the hypothermic person out of the wind and rain, remove any wet clothes and replace

Trailhead Information

You will find a "Trailhead" box for every hike. This describes how to get to the starting point for the hike from major highways, centers of population or park entrances. All distances are shown in miles.

Route Information

On the first page of each hike is a box entitled "Route." At the top of this box is the total one-way distance for the hike from trailhead to destination. The hike is also identified as a "Day hike," "backpack," "overnight," "loop" or "shuttle" hike. A "day hike" can easily be accomplished in one day. A "backpack" necessitates camping in order to cover the route. The term "overnight" refers to trips of day-hiking length which have destinations suitable for camping. A "loop" is a circular hike that begins and ends at the same spot. A "shuttle" hike begins and ends at different locations, requiring either two vehicles or the use of a bus

or other transportation between the trailheads.

Information is provided on distances from the trailhead to landmarks along the route, such as campgrounds, trail junctions, lakes, stream crossings and passes. The altitude of these points is also indicated. All distances are shown in miles and elevations are in feet.

The USGS topographic map for the hike is listed at the bottom of the box. Hiking times have not been given as these depend entirely on your experience and capability, together with the nature of the terrain and the current weather conditions.

them with several dry layers. If the sufferer is sufficiently alert, provide warm drinks and high-energy food. If a sleeping bag is available, huddle in the bag with the hypothermic person to share body warmth.

Altitude Sickness

As elevation increases, the amount of oxygen in the air decreases. This reduced oxygen can result in a condition known as altitude sickness, which can be fatal if left untreated. The symptoms of altitude sickness include shortness of breath, headaches, dizziness, nausea, heart palpitations, extreme thirst, weakness and loss of appetite.

Altitude affects every hiker differently. Some people happily climb to the top of Four-

teeners with no apparent problem other than increased shortness of breath. Others experience severe headaches when hiking at 10,000 feet. Often, one member of a party will suffer while the others are unaffected. When symptoms of altitude sickness begin to occur:
• Stop and rest
• Hike more slowly
• Drink more water
• Eat high energy foods
• If the problem increases, immediately descend to a lower elevation

The best prevention for altitude sickness is slow acclimatization to high elevations. Do not start the hiking season by climbing a Fourteener. Begin with a lower destination and gradually work upward. If you live at a

low elevation, take a couple of days to get used to to Denver's "mile-high" altitude before hiking in the Colorado Rockies. Sleeping at a high elevation is one of the most efficient ways to give your body plenty of time to adjust to the decreased oxygen level. You can also minimize altitude sickness by drinking plenty of water while hiking and by avoiding alcohol and heavy meals immediately prior to and during the trip.

Sun Exposure

Sunburn is a major concern for anyone hiking in Colorado. Harmful ultraviolet rays grow stronger with increased elevation, so the greatest risk is on Colorado's alpine tundra. Remember, you can get a sunburn at any time of the year—even when the sun does not feel warm on your skin. Following these precautions will help you avoid sunburn.
• Always apply sunscreen to all exposed skin before heading onto the trail. Your face, neck, ears, shoulders and arms are particularly vulnerable. A sweatproof sunblock with an SPF rating of 30 or more is ideal for hiking and climbing in the Rockies.
• Bring lip balm that incorporates sunscreen to prevent dry and chapped lips.
• Use a baseball cap or hat with a brim to protect your face and neck.
• Wear sunglasses or goggles with ultraviolet lenses.
• If you are fair-skinned or have not been out in the sun recently, wear a long-sleeved shirt and long pants.

Suggested First Aid

Always carry a first aid kit when you hike. This lets you treat minor problems such as blisters, headaches and small cuts. While commercially packaged kits are available, it is easy to assemble your own. Many hikers choose to take a first aid course through the American Red Cross or other such agency before venturing into the wilderness. This provides valuable information on what to do in an emergency and the correct use of a first aid kit. Always tell your hiking companions about any allergies or specific conditions that you might have. Store your kit in a sturdy box or waterproof bag. Your kit should include the following items:

• Swiss army knife with tweezers and scissors
• Band-Aids for minor wounds
• Sterile gauze pads (4 x 4 inches) for larger wounds
• A roll of adhesive tape to attach dressings
• Butterfly bandages for closing minor lacerations
• Triangle bandage for slings
• Ibuprofen for pain relief
• Antibiotic ointment to reduce the risk of infection in wounds
• Alcohol swabs for cleansing skin
• Moleskin for blisters
• Latex gloves to reduce the risk of infection
• Insect repellent containing DEET
• Paper and pencil
• First aid instruction booklet
• Personal prescription drugs

North Maroon and Maroon Peaks, reflected in the crystal-clear lake, is the most photographed scene in Colorado

Insects & Parasites

While mosquitos are common pests in the Colorado Rockies, they do not carry malaria or any other infectious disease. On the other hand, Rocky Mountain ticks can be dangerous, as they can transmit such illnesses as Colorado tick fever and Rocky Mountain spotted fever. A tick usually has to be attached to its host for a number of hours before infection occurs. Therefore, tick-borne diseases can generally be prevented by quick removal of the parasite. Ticks look like tiny, flattened spiders and are usually found in low shrubs and grass in montane regions during spring and early summer.

The following measures will help minimize problems with insects.

• Wear light-weight clothing that covers as much of your body as possible.

• Tight-fitting collars, sleeves and pant-leg cuffs may help to keep bugs from crawling onto your body.

• Use an insect repellent containing DEET. Spray it onto your clothing as well as exposed body parts.

• Check frequently for ticks on your clothing, scalp and exposed areas of skin.

• At night, thoroughly inspect your body for ticks. Carefully check your armpits, scalp, neck, under your socks and any place constricted by

Author's Favorite Picnic Spots

Emerald Lake Viewpoint

(Hike 3.) Flattop Mountain and Hallett Peak
From this lofty perch, 3.0 miles into the Flattop Mountain and Hallett Peak climb, the gargantuan vista extends over the east side of Rocky Mountain National Park.

Diamond Lake

(Hike 18. Diamond Lake)
Rocks scattered among shady conifers provide family picnic benches with a view of Diamond Lake (2.5 miles) and the ice-streaked gray cliffs looming behind the tarn.

Lost Man Pass

(Hike 27. Lost Man Loop)
Lost Man Pass is a good vantage point 2.6 miles from the trailhead, with nearly unparalleled views for the 1,294 feet of elevation gained.

Upper Fish Creek Falls

(Hike 35. Fish Creek Falls and Long Lake)
Upper Fish Creek Falls, 3.0 miles along the trail, is a destination for many hikers. Plentiful rocky ledges provide perfect seats for spectators at the foot of this magnificent cascade.

South-facing slope overlooking Willow Creek Park

(Hike 40. Willow Lake)
A sunny hillside, 1.5 miles into the hike to Willow Lake, is just the spot to rest and enjoy the wonderful panorama east to the Willow Creek drainage and west over the San Luis Valley.

elastic or tight straps.

• Avoid camping near stagnant water or lakes.

• Avoid going off the trail and rubbing against low bushes or walking in long grass. This is where you are most likely to encounter ticks.

Drinking Water and *Giardia*

Day-hikers should always start out with at least two quarts of safe drinking water to prevent dehydration caused by the ultra-dry Colorado atmosphere. Backpack-

ers will need to use some method of water treatment. *Giardia lamblia* has become so widespread in the Rocky Mountains that you should never drink from streams or lakes however clean the water may appear.

Giardia is caused by a microscopic organism, carried by human and animal feces, which can cause severe diarrhea, gas, cramps, abdominal distension and vomiting several weeks after it gets into your digestive system.

Boiling is always the best method to purify water. Stores that specialize in hiking and camping equipment stock a variety of filters and water-treatment chemicals such as iodine, some of which are more effective than others. Before purchasing a filter or other treatment system, read the label to make sure that it kills or screens out *giardia*. The amount of chemical to use and length of time it takes to kill microorganisms depends on the temperature of the water. Wait at least 30 minutes to an hour before drinking iodine-treated water.

Personal Sanitation

The following rules will help you to avoid polluting water sources in the wilderness.

• Wash, do dishes and brush your teeth at least 100 feet from streams and lakes.

• Do not rinse off soap in water sources. Even biodegradable soaps are pollutants.

• Throw out dirty water at least 100 feet from water sources.

• In the backcountry,

Author's Five Favorite Hikes

The evening light enhances the dunes of Great Sand Dunes National Monument

The Great Sand Dunes Hike No. 39

The unique environment of the 700-foot-high sand dunes heaped against the base of the Sangre de Cristo Mountains provides one of the best year-round hiking opportunities Colorado has to offer.

Longs Peak Hike No. 6

Longs Peak, rising to 14,255 feet, reigns like a monarch over Rocky Mountain National Park. The climb to its summit offers the greatest challenge in this book because of the distance, elevation gain and exposure during the last mile.

Missouri Lakes Hike No. 25

The Missouri Lakes Trail leads to

an expansive alpine basin dotted with 14 lakes and ponds. This serene landscape provides plenty of terrain to explore as well as extensive hiking possibilities.

Cathedral Lake Hike No. 29

The half-day trip to Cathedral Lake, starting only a half-hour's drive from Aspen, takes the hiker to one of the most easily accessible tarns in the Colorado Rockies.

Bear Lake-Fern Lake Shuttle Hike No. 2

Expansive panoramas over Rocky Mountain National Park, minimal elevation gain, varied terrain and a string of picturesque lakes are hallmarks of this fascinating shuttle hike.

defecate in individual "cat holes" at least 100 feet away from streams and lakes and a good distance from your tent and cooking area. Dig the hole at least 10 inches deep in the topsoil and, after use, re-fill the hole with the soil you removed.

• Urinate on hard, rocky surfaces whenever possible. This will prevent animals, which are attracted by the salt in your urine, from digging holes and destroying the frag-ile alpine soil.

• Do not bury toilet paper as animals may dig it up. Put it with your trash and pack it out.

Clothing

For maximum enjoyment, it is important to have appropri-ate clothing when hiking. While many companies mar-ket excellent (and often ex-pensive) items such as jackets and vests, it is unnecessary to spend an exorbitant amount of money to provide yourself with suitable equipment.

There are certain rules that you should follow when choosing clothing for the trail.

• Well-fitting light- or medium-weight boots with sturdy Vibram® soles are es-sential for hiking in Colorado. It is a good idea to break your boots in by wearing them around the house or on short walks before you head out on a long trip. Sneakers provide little support on rough, rocky trails.

• Wear heavy wool or wool-blend socks with thin, polypropylene liners. This combination will keep you warm even if the socks get wet and will reduce your risk of

Colorado Blue Columbine

The Colorado blue columbine is one of the most majestic of all wildflowers. It is so lovely that, in 1899, Colorado law de-creed it to be the state flower. The columbine's favorite habitat is aspen groves in the montane zone, although it thrives in many different locations, includ-ing talus slopes and mountain meadows up to an elevation of 12,000 feet. Nine species of columbine, including red, yel-low and dwarf varieties, grow in the Rockies. In 1971, Colorado passed the Recreation Land Preservation Act, making it ille-gal to pick any wildflower grow-ing on government property.

The columbine can grow up to three feet tall while display-ing several stems and many di-vided leaves. Its delicate blos-som consists of five white inner petals surrounded by five deep-blue or lavender outer sepals. Its most distinctive feature, however, is its backward-pro-jecting spurs, which act as re-ceptacles for plant-produced nectar. In the process of obtain-ing this sweet secretion, hum-mingbirds and insects transfer pollen from flower to flower.

Essentials for Survival

Use this checklist before start-ing on a hike. It includes the "Ten Essentials" recommended for comfort and safety by the Colorado Mountain Club. Carry-ing these items prepares you for unforeseen emergencies due to accident, injury or weather.

❑ Day pack or backpack
❑ Map and compass
❑ Pocket knife
❑ Two quarts of water
❑ Lunch, plus extra food
❑ Extra layers of clothing (in-cluding rain gear)
❑ Waterproof matches, lighter and other fire starters

❑ Flashlight or head lamp (with spare batteries and bulb)
❑ Bivouac gear (space blanket, large plastic bags, insulating pad)
❑ Sunglasses, sunscreen and lip balm
❑ First aid kit
❑ Toilet paper in a waterproof bag; Ziploc® bag to carry TP out
❑ Whistle, signal mirror
❑ Metal cup to melt snow and boil water
❑ Duct tape for general repairs

Maroon Bells

getting blisters.

• Use gaiters to keep rain, snow, mud and scree out of your boots.

• Polypropylene long underwear is ideal for wicking sweat away from your body. Many people find polypropylene bottoms ideal for wearing under shorts while on the trail.

• Never wear jeans for hiking, as cotton dries slowly and feels very uncomfortable when it gets wet.

• Always bring several insulation layers for your upper body. Jackets, parkas, vests and sweaters made of wool, fleece and down are best.

• Carry a wool or fleece hat and warm mittens. Water-proof overmitts will keep your hands warm and dry in the wind and snow.

• Don't forget to pack a rain jacket and pants. It is not necessary to own breathable Gore-Tex® garments. Any waterproof jacket and pants will keep the rain from penetrating your clothing. These items can also double as wind gear.

Leave No Trace

"A thing is right when it tends to preserve the integrity, stability and beauty of the biotic community. It is wrong when it tends otherwise." So said forester and philosopher Aldo Leopold in the 1930s. Today, as more hikers than ever are seeking the simple living, adventure and solitude in Colorado's backcountry, there is a growing concern about the way this use is impacting the environment.

During your hike, it is crucial that you use the land in an ethical manner and that you do your utmost to ensure the survival of the wilderness for future generations. "Leave No Trace" is an education program, pioneered by the National Outdoor Leadership School, dedicated to teaching the practical conservation techniques involved in minimum-impact backcountry use. The following is a list of the program's "Leave No Trace Principles."

Principles of Leave No Trace:
- Plan ahead and prepare
- Concentrate impacts in high use areas
- Spread use and impact in pristine areas
- Avoid places where impact is just beginning
- Pack it in, pack it out
- Properly dispose of what you cannot pack out
- Leave what you find
- Use fire responsibly

Rocky Mountain National Park

The Loch is a popular hiking destination

Attracting more than three million visitors each year, 415-square-mile Rocky Mountain National Park encompasses some of the most diverse and spectacular mountain scenery in the United States. One hundred fourteen named peaks rise above 10,000 feet. The highest, Longs Peak, tops out at 14,255 feet.

With more than 355 miles of trails, the park offers hikes for people of every age and ability. Trails, ranging from level paths to vertical ascents, provide access to serene alpine lakes, tumbling waterfalls and breathtaking views from overlooks and mountain summits.

Trail Ridge Road, the highest continuous paved highway in the United States, crosses the Continental Divide, linking the two sides of the park. On its 50-mile journey, it winds above tree line for 11 miles of magnificent scenery, allowing the traveler to experience the alpine tundra environment.

The two main population centers nearby are Estes Park on the east side and Grand Lake on the west side. Both of these towns have motels, campgrounds, restaurants, supermarkets and other tourist facilities.

The nearest major airport, Denver International Airport, is near Denver, 70 miles to the southeast of the park. The fastest route to Rocky Mountain National Park from Denver is north along Interstate 25 to US Highway 36, and northwest on US Highway 36 through Boulder, Lyons and Estes Park.

Park information is available at Visitor Center Headquarters, Moraine Park Museum, Longs Peak and Wild Basin ranger stations, and Lily Lake, Kawuneeche and Alpine visitor centers.

Within the park are five drive-in campgrounds with a total of 589 campsites. Backpackers must obtain a permit to pitch a tent in one of the 267 backcountry campsites. Call the backcountry office at (970) 586-1242.

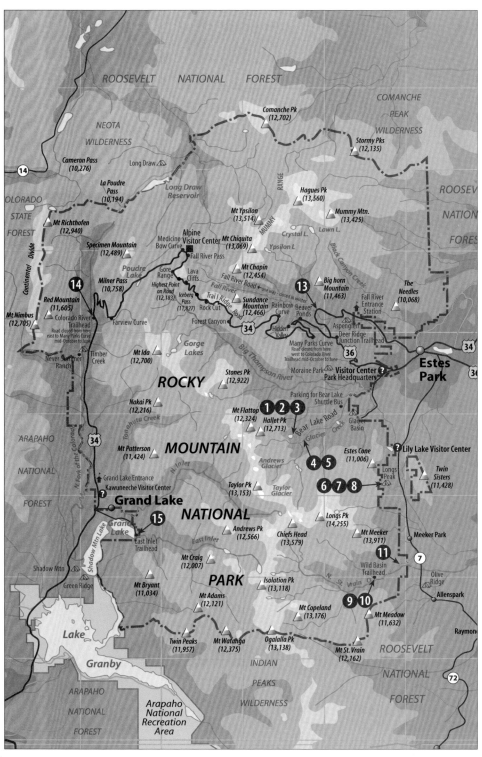

Dream Lake sprawls in glacier-gouged Tyndall Gorge

~ 1 ~ Emerald Lake

The trail to Emerald Lake is the most popular in Rocky Mountain National Park. In a distance of 1.8 miles and with an elevation gain of only 605 feet,

it climbs from shady subalpine forest to a majestic landscape of stark, barren rock. Each of the three tarns along the way is a worthy destination in itself, with its own individual character and beauty, and offering plenty of picnic spots with magnificent views of Hallett Peak and Flattop Mountain towering above.

Trailhead

Follow US Highway 36 for 0.2 mile west of the Beaver Meadows Entrance Station to Rocky Mountain National Park. Head south for 9.2 miles along Bear Lake Road to the Bear Lake parking area where the road ends. As gateway to the most popular hiking area in the park, this lot fills quickly during the summer. The Park Service recommends using the free and frequent shuttle bus from the shuttle bus parking area 5.0 miles south of US 36 on Bear Lake Road. An early start will help you avoid the summer crowds. The Bear Lake Trailhead, ranger information kiosk and restrooms are at the west end of the parking area.

Trailhead to Nymph Lake
Bridge a stream and take an immediate left, following signs for Nymph, Dream and Emerald lakes. Stay right at the intersection, avoiding the path that descends to Glacier Gorge Junction.

Route		
Day hike; 1.8 miles one way; easy		
Route	Elevation (ft.)	Distance (mi.)
Bear Lake Trailhead	9,475	0
Nymph Lake	9,700	0.5
Lake Haiyaha Jct	9,900	1.0
Dream Lake	9,900	1.1
Emerald Lake	10,080	1.8
USGS Topographic map: McHenrys Peak, Colo.		

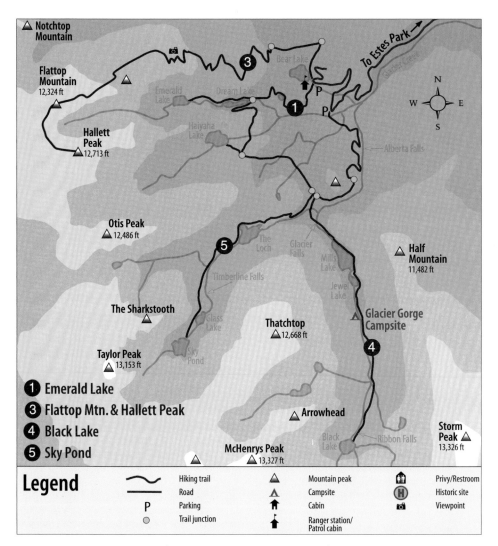

△ Notchtop
Mountain

Flattop
Mountain
12,324 ft

📷

Bear Lake

❸

To Estes Park →

△

N
W ⊕ E
S

Emerald
Lake

Dream Lake

🏕 P

Hallett
Peak
△ 12,713 ft

Haiyaha
Lake

❶

P

Alberta Falls

Otis Peak
△ 12,486 ft

The
Loch

Glacier
Falls

❺

Mills
Lake

Half
Mountain △
11,482 ft

Timberline Falls

Jewel
Lake

The Sharkstooth
△

Glass
Lake

Thatchtop
△ 12,668 ft

Glacier Gorge
Campsite ▲

❹

Taylor Peak
△ 13,153 ft

Sky
Pond

❶ Emerald Lake

❸ Flattop Mtn. & Hallett Peak

Arrowhead
△

Storm
Peak △
13,326 ft

❹ Black Lake

Black
Lake

Ribbon Falls

❺ Sky Pond

McHenrys Peak
△ △ 13,327 ft

Legend

〜	Hiking trail	△	Mountain peak	🏛	Privy/Restroom
▬	Road	▲	Campsite	Ⓗ	Historic site
P	Parking	🏠	Cabin	📷	Viewpoint
○	Trail junction	🏴	Ranger station/ Patrol cabin		

As the broad and well-constructed trail ascends gently through the forest, En-gelmann spruce and sub-alpine fir gradually make way for tall, skinny lodgepole pines. Periodic openings in the trees to the left frame the gray, snub-nosed summit of Longs Peak looming over Glacier Gorge. Rising to a lofty 14,255 feet, this is the highest mountain in the park and the fifteenth tallest in Colorado.

Watch for chipmunks (striped face) and golden-mantled ground squirrels (slightly larger with no stripes on the face) scurrying by the trail, and listen for the chatter of red squirrels in the trees. Remember, even though these tiny creatures may look as if they expect a free hand-out, it is against park regula-tions to feed them. An animal that depends on humans for food is no longer wild and may starve during the winter.

A half mile into the hike, the trail veers to the right, levels and arrives at Nymph Lake. This little tree-encir-cled pool gained its name from the bright yellow pond lilies dotting its surface dur-ing the summer. *Nymphaea polysepala* was at one time the flower's scientific name, although botanists have since changed it to *Nuphar polysepalum*.

The trail to Lake Haiyaha offers marvelous views of the Longs Peak massif and Glacier Gorge

Nymph Lake to Dream Lake

Nymph Lake reflects lofty Hallett Peak and Flattop Mountain among the lily pads as the trail skirts its northeastern shoreline. Then it is Longs Peak that appears in the dark green water as the path angles west and steepens toward Dream Lake.

The tenacious limber pine begins to make an appearance. This is easy to identify as it is the only conifer in the park with needles growing in bundles of five.

Vistas improve as you gain altitude. An overlook above Nymph Lake affords an extensive panorama northeastward over the park. Directly below, Bear Lake glistens like a sapphire amid the verdant conifers. The forested ridge of Bierstadt Moraine leads toward Sprague Lake and the cliffs of Teddys Teeth on Rams Horn Mountain. This lake is an artificial pond constructed for fishing by early innkeeper Abner Sprague. Early campers at the YMCA of the Rockies named Teddy's Teeth for its similarity to Theodore Roosevelt's smile as

Park Regulations

In order to preserve and protect the natural environment and to ensure the visitor's maximum enjoyment, the Park Service has formulated a list of rules.

These are included in the "Official Map and Guide" which visitors receive upon entry into Rocky Mountain National Park. Rules are also generally posted at trailheads. Park regulations include the following:

• Camping is allowed only in designated campsites. Backcountry campers are required to purchase a permit.

• Pets are not allowed on trails. Leashed pets are permitted in campgrounds, parking areas and in other places that are accessible by car.

• Build campfires only in established fireplaces. Purchase bundles of firewood in campgrounds or nearby stores. Do not gather dead wood or cut down trees within the park.

• Bicycles are only allowed on roads, never on trails.

• It is illegal to feed, hunt, capture or otherwise harass any wild creature. Always observe wildlife from a distance.

• Do not remove, vandalize or disturb any flower, tree, shrub, rock or other natural object.

• Purchase a Colorado State fishing license before fishing in the park. Check on current regulations for possession limits and catch-and-release areas.

it was drawn in cartoons just after the turn of the century.

Abundant aspens along the next section of the trip make for an excellent fall hike. Slim whitish-green trunks topped by a mass of shimmering golden leaves sprout from fissures in rocky outcroppings, seemingly without benefit of soil. Wild blueberries carpet the ground, their leaves turning copper-red in September. Indian paintbrush, mountain harebells and pearly everlasting add specks of color during the summer months.

The trail rounds a craggy promontory and traverses a sunny south-facing slope.

Photographers will delight in the breathtaking view across the broad gash of Glacier Gorge to Longs Peak and the jagged series of spires called the Keyboard of the Winds. In the fall, strands of yellow aspens intermingle with the dark green evergreens blanketing the moraine-choked valley. Far below, Tyndall Creek roars its way down from Dream Lake toward Glacier Creek.

Veering directly toward Tyndall Gorge, the trail curves around a final rocky protrusion and crosses Tyndall Creek via a sturdy log bridge. A junction provides two hiking options. Lake Haiyaha lies 1.1 miles to the left (see pg. 28); Nymph and Emerald lakes are to the right.

To continue to Nymph and Emerald lakes, recross the stream as it meanders through a small meadow and hook left onto some rocks. Dream Lake stretches ahead, long and narrow in the glac-

ier-gouged gorge.

The majestic setting is a tantalizing invitation to linger and to take in as much of the scene as possible. During June, July and August, many choose to do just that. Outcrops among the wind-tortured and twisted limber pines make for excellent picnic spots if they are not already occupied by the summer hordes. The formidable bulks of Hallett Peak (to the left) and Flattop Mountain (to the right) loom over the water, their reflections grander and more impressive than those seen in Nymph Lake.

Dream Lake to Emerald Lake

The trail to Emerald Lake follows the forested north shore of Dream Lake.

Marsh marigolds and elephant's head flourish in boggy areas along the route.

The path then climbs steeply through a shady tunnel of mature subalpine fir and Engelmann spruce, on several occasions necessitating rocky scrambles.

Tyndall Creek cuts through the bedrock to the left. This moist environment sustains a profusion of wildflowers. Mountain figwort, chimingbells, Jacob's ladder, fireweed and ragwort thrive

Please Don't Feed the Animals

Hundreds of thousands of people flock to Rocky Mountain National Park each year to view the abundant birds and animals and to capture them on film. Unfortunately, well-meaning visitors often offer handouts to these creatures in order to encourage them to come close enough to be photographed. At picnic spots, campgrounds, along trails and at pullouts on the highways, Clark's nutcrackers, chipmunks and squirrels brazenly beg for food.

Park regulations prohibit the feeding, harassing or touching of wildlife. There are a number of reasons why this is detrimental. First, animals that depend on people for sustenance cease to be wild and cannot adapt to natural conditions when the number of park visitors dwindles during the winter. Second, animals

generally breed in relation to the amount of food available. Frequent handouts often create an unhealthy population level much in excess of the natural food supply, causing possible winter starvation. Third, the snacks commonly offered to wildlife contain little nutritional value and can cause malnourishment and disease. Fourth, cute little squirrels and chipmunks have sharp teeth, and a nip to your finger hurts. Also, the park's small mammals have been known to be infected with rabies, which humans can contract from a bite.

Always look at animals from a distance. If they appear nervous, you are too near. Use binoculars for viewing and a telephoto lens for photographing. Let the wildlife remain wild.

Golden-mantled Ground Squirrel

Slightly larger than its relative, the chipmunk, the golden-mantled ground squirrel is often seen in campgrounds, picnic areas and along popular trails begging for handouts. Feeding these creatures violates park regulations because it results in over-population and starvation when the summer crowds have gone.

With similar coloring to the chipmunk, the golden-mantled ground squirrel lacks the chipmunk's characteristic facial stripes and has a less bushy tail. A true hibernator, it needs to acquire a sufficient amount of body fat to see it through the winter.

You will often see a ground squirrel sitting up on its hind legs like a begging dog. If it senses danger, it will freeze and, if need be, will make a lightning dash to the safety of its burrow.

Chipmunks

The chipmunk is one of the most commonly seen mammals in Rocky Mountain National Park. Active during the day, this inquisitive, fast-moving rodent often scampers away at your approach, only to reappear quickly so it can keep a watchful eye on you.

Measuring four to six inches in length, with a somewhat shorter and slightly bushy tail, chipmunks are chestnut or yellowish-gray, with dark and white stripes down the back and face. They eat seeds, nuts, insects and berries, which they carry in their spacious cheek pouches and store in large quantities. During the winter hibernation, they often awaken to feed on this hoard.

Chipmunks live in moss- or grass-lined nests beneath rocks, roots or fallen tree stumps in coniferous woodlands. Four to six young are born in spring, are weaned in six weeks and are able to breed the following year.

Of the 15 species of chipmunks found in North America, five live in Colorado. Only subtle differences in size, behavior, color and habitat identify one from the other, and the same general description applies to them all.

by the trail, enjoying the mist generated by the dancing stream.

The trail levels and then, 1.8 miles from the trailhead, descends slightly to Emerald Lake.

Emerald Lake, which is indeed an incandescent green, nestles in a gray cirque be-neath the saddle separating Hallett Peak and Flattop Mountain. Barren, talus-clad slopes rise sheer from the frigid water's edge. The official trail ends here, but rock climbers often scramble over the carelessly strewn boulders along a terrace above the left shore and up the rough slope to the col. This is the starting point for a number of technical routes up the massive north face of Hallett Peak.

This environment is home to a variety of birds and animals, including Clark's nutcrackers, Steller's jays and marmots.

Lake Haiyaha Loop Option

While the trail to Nymph, Dream and Emerald lakes resounds with the laughter of children and the groans of sneaker-clad aunts and uncles, Lake Haiyaha enjoys relative peace and quiet. Its musical name comes from an Indian word meaning "rocks."

To visit this gem of a tarn, backtrack to Dream Lake, cross Tyndall Creek and fork right, following the sign for Lake Haiyaha.

The trail climbs gradually through the subalpine forest that cloaks the flank of Hallett Peak above Dream Lake. A little way up the slope it switchbacks sharply to the left and then, after another 300 yards, it turns sharply, cresting the ridge and leaving Tyndall Gorge. An overlook offers marvelous views of the Longs Peak massif and Glacier Gorge.

Now the path sweeps down into Chaos Canyon and, as the trail bridges the outlet stream from Lake Haiyaha, good views open up to the boulder-strewn valley to the snowfield hanging between Hallett and Otis peaks.

Continuing through the forest, the trail crosses a second stream and reaches an intersection. Glacier Gorge Parking Area, the final destination for this side trip, is signed as being 3.6 miles down to the right. Lake Haiyaha lies several hundred yards farther on.

During its final approach to the tarn, the trail fades away. Take care as you clamber over the field of boulders littering the shore. A few ancient limber pines, thick-trunked and dwarfed, cling tenaciously to the huge stone blocks.

Chaos Canyon rises above the lake in a jumble of glacial debris, with the white icefield glistening at its head, suspended between Hallett and Otis peaks. Travel in this rock-choked landscape is next to impossible. Only the most determined of fishermen succeed in boulder-hopping around the tarn in search of the best fishing holes.

To continue the loop, return to the fork and meander downhill, round the flank of Otis Mountain and hike between the two Glacier Knobs to a four-way junction. From this point, the ambitious hiker can choose to turn right and trek the 0.6 mile to Mills Lake. Alternatively, you can take a left and then an immediate right and climb for 0.8 mile to The Loch. For those who wish to complete the loop, staying left will lead to Glacier Gorge Junction after 1.9 miles.

The wide, heavily traveled pathway exits Glacier Gorge by the splendid Alberta Falls. At Glacier Gorge Junction you have the choice of climbing the half mile back up to the Bear Lake Trailhead or, in summer, using the free shuttle bus to make the ascent.

Route

Distances are from Bear Lake Trailhead

Route	Elevation (ft.)	Distance (mi.)
Lake Haiyaha	10,220	2.1
Loch Vale-Glacier Gorge Jct	9,780	3.7
North Longs Peak Trail Jct	9,740	4.2
Alberta Falls	9,400	5.0
Glacier Gorge Jct	9,240	5.6

USGS Topographic map: McHenrys Peak, Colo.

Odessa Lake lies snug within the embrace of the mighty peaks of the Continental Divide

~ 2 ~ Bear Lake-Fern Lake Shuttle

You can tackle this scenic hike from either of the two trailheads. It makes sense, however, to start from the Bear Lake Trailhead as it is 1,320 feet

Trailhead

To reach the Bear Lake trailhead, follow US Highway 36 for 0.2 mile west of the Beaver Meadows Entrance Station. Head southwest on Bear Lake Road for 9.2 miles until it dead ends at the multiacre Bear Lake parking area. The trailhead, restrooms and ranger information kiosk are at the west end of the lot.

During the summer, it is advisable to leave your car at the shuttle bus parking area 5.0 miles from the beginning of Bear Lake Road and to make use of the free shuttle. Ask for a current bus schedule at the entrance station or call park headquarters in advance.

To get to the Fern Lake Trailhead, take Bear Lake Road for 1.3 miles from US 36 and go right (west) for Moraine Park Campground. After 0.6 mile, turn left (south) and continue until the road ends after another 2.0 miles.

Route

Shuttle day hike or overnight; 8.5 mi. one way; moderate

Route	Elevation (ft.)	Distance (mi.)
Bear Lake Trailhead	9,475	0
Bierstadt Lake Jct	9,700	0.4
Flattop Mountain Jct	9,960	0.8
Sourdough Campsite	10,600	2.5
Lake Helene	10,600	2.9
Odessa Lake and Campsite	10,020	4.1
Fern Lake and Campsite	9,530	4.7
Fern Falls	8,800	5.8
Old Forest Inn Campsite	8,400	6.8
The Pool	8,400	6.8
Arch Rocks	8,300	7.0
Fern Lake Trailhead	8,155	8.5

USGS Topographic map: McHenrys Peak, Colo.

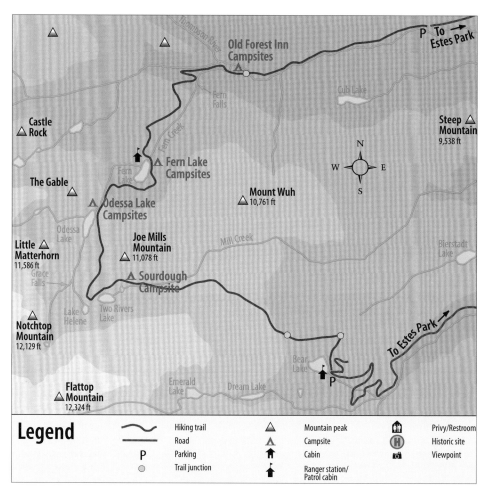

Old Forest Inn
Campsites

P To
Estes Park

Thompson River

Cub Lake

Fern
Falls

Fern Creek

Castle
Rock

Steep
Mountain
9,538 ft

Fern Lake
Campsites

Fern
Lake

The Gable

Odessa Lake
Campsites

Mount Wuh
10,761 ft

N
W E
S

Odessa
Lake

Joe Mills
Mountain
11,078 ft

Mill Creek

Bierstadt
Lake

Little
Matterhorn
11,586 ft

Grace
Falls

Sourdough
Campsite

To Estes Park

Lake
Helene

Two Rivers
Lake

Notchtop
Mountain
12,129 ft

Bear
Lake
P

Flattop
Mountain
12,324 ft

Emerald
Lake

Dream Lake

Legend

~	Hiking trail	△	Mountain peak	🏚	Privy/Restroom
—	Road	⚠	Campsite	Ⓗ	Historic site
P	Parking	♠	Cabin	📷	Viewpoint
○	Trail junction	♣	Ranger station/ Patrol cabin		

higher than the Fern Lake Trailhead, and only involves a steady 1,205-foot elevation gain. Also, the views of Odessa Gorge are more dramatic when approached from the east.

Each of the lakes along the route makes for an excellent destination in itself. Therefore, shorter excursions are possible without the need for a car or bus shuttle.

Most of the hike passes through shady conifers, although gaps in the trees offer excellent viewpoints along the first half of the route.

Bear Lake Trailhead to Bierstadt Lake Junction

Proceed around Bear Lake in a counter-clockwise direction. With an early start, you can avoid the crowds that travel the broad, paved 256-foot-long path from the parking lot to Bear Lake. Also, getting going early will ensure that you reach the lake before the day's breezes start to ripple the perfect reflection of Hallett Peak in the water's glassy surface.

Because this glacial tarn is one of the most popular at-

tractions in the park, many of the birds and small mammals have become habituated to people and are blatant beggars. Remember, park regulations prohibit the feeding of these creatures as it results in an artificially high population and starvation during the winter when there is not enough natural food to sustain them. Enjoy the wildlife from a distance.

With bold manners and often-raucous voices, jays are natural opportunists. Three kinds of jays live around Bear Lake. The foot-long gray bird with black and white wing and tail feathers and a long bill is the Clark's nutcracker. About the same size, the fluffy gray jay or "camp robber" has a short beak and a long tail. The blue Steller's jay is handsomely decked out with a long black crest.

Also look for chipmunks, golden-mantled ground squirrels, snowshoe hares, cottontail rabbits and red squirrels among the subalpine firs and Engelmann spruce by the lake.

A private contractor built the first road to Bear Lake in 1921 to harvest dead timber from the forest fire of 1900. Shortly after, the Bear Lake Lodge was constructed to provide accommodation for the massive influx of tourists. The park service dismantled this and revegetated the area in 1960.

Follow signs for Odessa and Fern lakes and veer right. The beautifully maintained trail climbs gently through a boulder-strewn corridor of aspens. In September, the shimmering leaves gradually take on their characteristic golden fall hues.

After 0.4 mile, there is an intersection with the trail to Bierstadt Lake.

Bierstadt Lake Junction to Sourdough Campsite

Take a sharp left for Fern Lake (on the Flattop Mountain Trail) and ascend to a promontory overlooking Bear Lake. Square-topped Longs Peak rises in bold relief against the sky, with the jagged Keyboard of the Winds leading to aptly named

Pagoda Peak to the right. This series of rocky spires was called the Keyboard of the Winds because gales howling across the ridge seem to play a mournful tune.

At a second junction, 0.8 mile from the trailhead, continue straight on for Odessa and Fern lakes. A moderate but steady traverse leads just below tree line along the northern flank of Flattop Mountain. Gaps in the spruce and firs to the right offer ever-increasing vistas across Bierstadt Moraine to Bierstadt Lake, glistening like a gem amid the dark conifers, and to the mountains to the north and east across the park.

A blanket of mist often hangs in the low-lying regions or "parks" within the park during the early morning. Photographers will enjoy the magnificent sight of mountain peaks protruding from a sea of fog tinged by low-angle sunlight.

A couple of miles into the hike, the trail crosses Mill Creek and begins its long loop around Joe Mills Mountain which, together with Mount Wuh, forms the eastern flank of Odessa Gorge. Joe Mills Mountain was named for Enoch Josiah Mills, who ran the Crags Hotel in Estes Park and helped his brother, Enos Mills, create Rocky Mountain National Park.

With Mill Creek flowing off to the left, the trail leaves the thick subalpine forest and traverses the open talus slope that falls from the summit of Joe Mills Mountain. From here, you get an excellent view of Notchtop Mountain jutting near the head of

Odessa Gorge. A distinct cleft divides the main bulk of the peak from a sheer buttress, which drops into the valley. Ragged snowfields glisten between talus-strewn ramps and weathered gray walls.

After 2.5 miles, the trail passes Sourdough backcountry campsite off to the right, the first of several well-placed spots to pitch a tent along this route.

Sourdough Campsite to Odessa Lake

The deep rift of Odessa Gorge yawns below as you crest the ridge separating the Mill and Fern creek drainages. Steep slopes plunge into the glacier-gouged depths. Fern Creek, squeezed from a residual glacier hanging between Flattop and Notchtop mountains, tumbles over Grace Falls. The striking pyramid-shaped tower of Little Matterhorn, actually the abrupt end of a ridge that extends east from Knobtop Mountain, looms 1,500 feet above Odessa Lake sprawling in the valley bottom. To the north, Odessa Gorge dwindles toward its merger with Forest Canyon and its journey into the heart of the park. Picturesque Lake Helene lies a couple of hundred feet to your left along a faint track.

A vertiginous ledge blasted from sheer rock defines the trail as it hastens its 600-foot descent along the sheer western side of Joe Mills Mountain toward Odessa Lake. The rumble of Fern Creek gains in volume as you lose altitude.

Upon passing a hitchrack in the valley bottom, take a

sharp left-hand detour for Odessa Lake. Backtrack a short distance by the stream, crossing a one-plank bridge along the way and passing the turnoff to Odessa Lake Campsite.

It is hard to imagine a more dramatic setting for a lake. Snug within the embrace of the mighty peaks of the Continental Divide, Odessa Lake is a study in tranquillity. Its peaceful waters reflect the ice-filled cirques and shattered rocks soaring from its tree-fringed shoreline. The Little Matterhorn towering above now looks very much like its more famous Swiss relative. This is the perfect place for a leisurely snack and a bit of a rest while you watch the large trout swimming just below the surface of the tarn.

Odessa Lake to Fern Lake

Return to the intersection and get back on the path for Fern Lake and The Pool. The trail briefly parallels Fern Creek as it cascades through a narrow rocky cleft. Wild blueberry interspersed with a variety of mushrooms cover the floor under the thick growth of subalpine forest.

When the valley widens, the trail veers to the right and makes a swerving descent to Fern Lake. The forest grows thicker, taller and more luxuriant with a profusion of undergrowth, mosses and lichens as the ground becomes wetter and richer. Good views of Fern Lake open to the left and Fern Lake Group Campsite is to the right. A sign indicating a restoration area prohibits clambering down to the shore.

Meeting the lake near its outlet, the trail crosses a lengthy, heavy-duty log bridge. Willows and red-osier dogwood spill into the stream and marsh-loving grasses thrive along the waterside. Notchtop Mountain and Little Matterhorn rise behind the forested glacial shelf beneath Odessa Lake.

Fern Lake Lodge, once situated by the lake, provided a base for snowshoeing, skiing and other outdoor activities.

Fern Lake Lodge

Fern Lake Lodge once stood on the shore of Fern Lake, a beautiful spot in Rocky Mountain National Park. Despite the four-mile hike or horseback ride from the nearest road, it was, at one time, an important center for winter activities.

Dr. William Workman first came to Colorado from Knobnoster, Missouri, in 1898. He purchased land in Moraine Park and, in order to spend his summers there, he established a practice in Denver.

He explored the canyons to the west of Moraine Park and named many of the mountains, lakes, streams and waterfalls in the area, including Knobtop Mountain, Little Matterhorn, Grace Falls, Odessa Lake, Lake Helene, Fern Lake and Fern Creek.

Around 1910, he built Fern Lake Lodge, using it first as his private summer residence and then as a resort hotel. The *Estes Park Trail* of July 27, 1912, advertised accommodation at a rate of $2.50 per day or $14 a week.

A unique feature of the lodge was the living room floor—a mosaic of circular log cross sections, with compacted dirt in between. The dining room contained a table, seating maybe 20 guests, decorated with a homemade, six-foot-wide Lazy Susan mounted on a section of tree stump which held all the serving dishes. Dr. Workman sold the lodge in 1915 and the Higby brothers, Frank W. Byerly, his wife Edna B. Bishop and her son James were among its later owners.

During the years immediately following the establishment of the park, Fern Lake Lodge was the region's center of winter activity. In February, 1917, a "winter sports carnival" proved so successful that nearby toboggan slides and ski runs were improved. The members of the Colorado Mountain Club used this as the location for their annual winter outings until 1934. Their activities included snowshoeing, skiing and listening to presentations by local notables.

Due to the remoteness of the property and the development of other more accessible resorts around Estes Park, the popularity of Fern Lake Lodge gradually dwindled. By 1939 it had ceased to offer overnight lodging, only opening sporadically for light noon-time refreshments until the late 1950s, when the lease ownership reverted to the park.

The park service recently dismantled the lodge, and the property is now being allowed to return to its natural condition.

In autumn, the leaves turn golden in this corridor of aspen

The building has been dismantled and the site is now being revegetated. A patrol cabin stands near the tarn and a privy is just past the outlet.

Fern Lake to Fern Falls

At an intersection, signs point left for Fern Lake Campsite and Spruce Lake unimproved trail, and right for Fern Lake Trailhead.

Veering right, you head down the left side of the valley with Fern Creek babbling among the trees to your right. The presence of aspen and tall lodgepole pines indicates the transition from the subalpine to the montane life zone. As the trail drops down the broadening valley, panoramas extend toward Estes Park.

You hear the crashing of Fern Falls long before you see the cascades. In a couple of spectacular 40-foot chutes, Fern Creek plunges into a catch basin choked with wet logs and boulders. This is the destination for many hikers starting from the Fern Lake Trailhead. Rocks scattered around this pleasant grotto provide excellent rest spots.

Fern Falls to The Pool

The trail hastens downhill through an increasingly lush forest, with aspens and Rocky Mountain maples making an appearance. Cross the bridge over Fern Creek and pass an outhouse and Old Forest Inn Campsite.

The sculpting forces of nature are evident in The Pool, a deep basin carved in the bedrock by the vigorous churning of the Big Thompson River. A huge outcropping overlooking the stream offers plenty of space for picnicking and relaxation.

The Pool to Fern Lake Trailhead

At a junction, the Cub Lake Trail forks to the right. The route to Fern Lake Trailhead crosses the Big Thompson River via an elaborate wooden bridge. Continue straight ahead.

For the final 1.7 miles, the trail meanders in the base of the valley along the north side of the Big Thompson River, losing only 245 feet of elevation. Rocky Mountain maple, willow, birch and alder choke the banks of the stream. Such a wealth of pteridium ferns thrive in this moist environment that the falls and lake were named after them.

After 0.7 mile from the last intersection, the immense red boulders of Arch Rocks loom over the trail. This interesting formation was created by a rockfall from the cliffs above at the end of the last ice age.

The hike ends at Fern Lake Trailhead. If you are doing this excursion in the early fall, watch for herds of elk congregating in Moraine Park. This is one of their favorite meadows and a prime location to hear the bulls bugle during the evening and early morning hours.

North American Elk

The bull elk's antlers help it compete with its rivals for cows during the annual fall rut

The eerie bugling of lovesick bull elk draws crowds to Rocky Mountain National Park during the annual fall rut. At the end of summer, elk descend from the high country and congregate in the grassy meadows. Prime bulls compete for the right to breed with a herd of cows. While they may clash their racks of antlers in mating jousts, this rarely causes injury. Generally, competition is played out in postural displays, the emission of a musky odor and by bugling.

The elk is the largest animal in the park. Bulls average about 700 pounds, although they can weigh up to 1,100 pounds and stand five feet tall at the shoulder. Females are considerably smaller. This slender-legged, thick-necked member of the deer family relies on camouflage for protection from predators. During the summer, the brown head, neck, stomach and legs contrast with the gray-brown body and tawny rump.

In winter, the entire coat becomes lighter.

Bulls shed their antlers every year between January and April and new ones begin to grow almost immediately. As the elk matures, its antlers develop more points up to an average maximum of six on each side.

In past centuries, the area around Rocky Mountain National Park was home to numerous elk. The Ute and Arapaho hunted them in the summer, but caused little impact on the total population levels. In the 1860s, settlers flocked to the Estes Valley. In an effort to make a living, pioneers hunted the wild game and sold it in Denver markets. By the end of the century, the elk herd was entirely eliminated.

Conservationists such as Enos Mills began to campaign for the preservation of the region's wildlife and natural beauty. In 1913, the Estes Park Protective and Improvement Association brought 49 elk

from Yellowstone National Park to replace the obliterated native herds. At the same time, a concerted attempt was made to rid the area of predators such as the grizzly bear and gray wolf. Since then, the elk population has gradually risen to its current summer concentration of over 3,000. Most of these are descended from the transplanted animals.

The fall rut is at its height from mid-September to mid-October. The best places to spot elk at this time are Moraine Park, Horseshoe Park, Upper Beaver Meadows and the Kawuneeche Valley. Dawn and dusk are good times to hear the bulls' piercing bugling.

Emerald Lake shimmers in bleak Tyndall Gorge

~ 3 ~ Flattop Mountain and Hallett Peak

The strenuous ascent of two prominent peaks on the Continental Divide rewards the hiker with some of the most sensational views in the park.

The lofty 3,238-foot elevation gain is accomplished by means of a steady climb along a smooth, well-constructed trail. In its transition from thick subalpine forest to open alpine tundra, the trail passes through a variety of ecosystems, offering the opportunity to spot many kinds of flowers, birds and animals.

Trailhead

Follow US Highway 36 for 0.2 mile west of the Beaver Meadows Entrance Station to Rocky Mountain National Park. Head south for 9.2 miles along Bear Lake Road to the Bear Lake parking area where the road ends. As gateway to the most popular hiking area in the park, this lot fills quickly during the summer. The Park Service recommends using the free and frequent shuttle bus from the shuttle bus parking area 5.0 miles south of US 36 on Bear Lake Road. An early start will help you avoid the summer crowds. The Bear Lake Trailhead, ranger information kiosk and restrooms are at the west end of the parking area.

Route

Day hike; 4.4 miles one way to Flattop Mountain, 5.0 miles to Hallett Peak; strenuous

Route	Elevation (ft.)	Distance (mi.)
Bear Lake Trailhead	9,475	0
Bierstadt Lake Jct	9,700	0.4
Odessa Lake Jct	9,960	0.8
Emerald Lake Viewpoint	11,300	3.0
Flattop Mountain	12,324	4.4
Top of Tyndall Glacier	12,300	4.7
Hallett Peak	12,713	5.0

USGS Topographic map: McHenrys Peak, Colo.

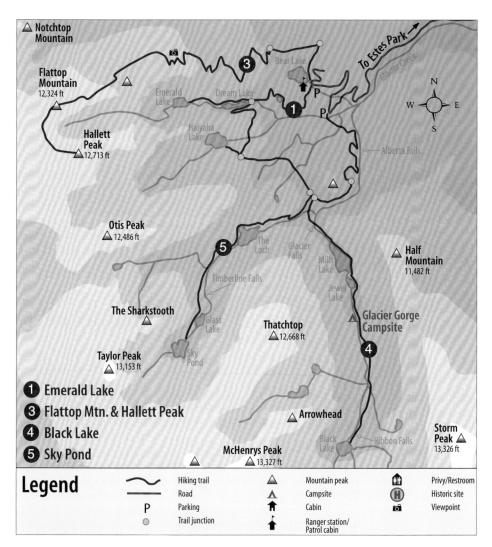

△ Notchtop Mountain

Flattop Mountain
12,324 ft

Hallett Peak
△ 12,713 ft

Bear Lake

Emerald Lake

Dream Lake

Haiyaha Lake

To Estes Park →

Glacier Creek

N
W · E
S

Alberta Falls

Otis Peak
△ 12,486 ft

The Loch

Glacier Falls

Mills Lake

Half Mountain
11,482 ft

Timberline Falls

Jewel Lake

The Sharkstooth
△

Glass Lake

Thatchtop
△ 12,668 ft

Glacier Gorge Campsite

Taylor Peak
△ 13,153 ft

Sky Pond

Arrowhead

Storm Peak △
13,326 ft

1 Emerald Lake

3 Flattop Mtn. & Hallett Peak

4 Black Lake

5 Sky Pond

Black Lake

Ribbon Falls

McHenrys Peak
△ 13,327 ft

Legend

∿ Hiking trail	△ Mountain peak	Privy/Restroom
— Road	◬ Campsite	Ⓗ Historic site
P Parking	⌂ Cabin	📷 Viewpoint
○ Trail junction	Ranger station/Patrol cabin	

Trailhead to Bierstadt Lake Junction

After crossing a wooden footbridge, keep right along the broad and often-crowded walkway to Bear Lake. A thick subalpine forest encloses the trail along this stretch. You can identify the Engelmann spruce by its stiff, sharp needles, its smooth, cinnamon-brown trunk and its one- to three-inch-long cones hanging from the twigs. The subalpine fir has soft, dark-green needles, gray bark and dark-purple cones, which stand upright on the topmost branches.

In 1900, careless campers started a fire near Bear Lake, which destroyed many of the old-growth trees in the area. The spruce-fir forest that you see here somehow managed to survive the burn. One very tall Engelmann spruce near the tarn's outlet is more than 400 years old.

Veer right, enjoying the reflection of precipitous Hallett Peak in the glassy waters of Bear Lake. This is one of the best places to spot many of the creatures that inhabit the park. Look for gray and Steller's jays, Clark's nutcrackers, mountain chickadees, dark-eyed juncos, red squirrels, chipmunks and golden-mantled ground squirrels. Mallard ducks float on the lake and greenback

The trail ascends through the subalpine fir and Engelmann spruce

cutthroat trout glide beneath its surface.

Please do not feed the birds and animals despite their urgent begging. Giving tidbits to wildlife violates park regulations as it results in over-population during the summer and winter starvation. This area was once home to black bears. Today, with a total population of only 30 in the park, you are unlikely to encounter a bear at Bear Lake.

A sign directs you uphill to the right for Flattop Mountain. Rising steadily across a boulder-strewn slope above Bear Lake, the path leaves the conifers to pass through an attractive aspen grove. In the fall, the delicate rounded leaves trembling atop narrow, whitish trunks turn brilliant shades of yellow-gold.

After 0.4 mile, you reach an intersection with the trail to Bierstadt Lake.

Bierstadt Lake Junction to Emerald Lake Viewpoint

Take a sharp left and ascend to a promontory overlooking Bear Lake and Longs Peak. Traverse to the other side of the ridge to reach a second trail junction. Odessa and Fern lakes are straight ahead. Again, hook left for Flattop Mountain.

The trail switchbacks steeply through stands of spruce and fir. Reflections in Bear Lake glimmer through periodic gaps in the trees to the left.

After the breath-stealing slog uphill, you deserve a rest, and Dream Lake Viewpoint is the perfect place for it. Directly below, dark Dream Lake nestles in Tyndall Gorge amid a thick growth of conifers. Hallett Peak (to the left) and Flattop Mountain (to the right) loom over the valley, with Tyndall Glacier hugging the skyline between them. In the southeast, square-topped Longs Peak towers above Mills Lake, which reclines gracefully on a bench in Glacier Gorge.

You can see the work of the giant Bartholf Glacier. Thousands of years ago, it gouged its way down Glacier Gorge and the other hanging valleys of this drainage system, scattering tons of debris in Glacier Basin during its various retreats. Much of the landscape remains just as the ice mass left it with soaring ridges, broken cliffs, and polished and rounded lumps of schist, gneiss and granite devoid of vegetation. Less hostile areas sustain a dense growth of lodgepole pines, subalpine and Douglas firs and Engelmann spruce dotted with occasional aspens. Changing from green to gold in successive waves according to altitude, the aspens make for a colorful fall backdrop.

Due to its periodic increase in size following winters of high snowfall, Tyndall Glacier is one of six glaciers in the park that are considered still active.

Wild blueberry covers the ground as you switchback through the evergreens. Aspen daisies, mountain figwort and little clumps of goldenrod flourish alongside the trail.

The character of the vegetation changes as you approach the transition zone between subalpine forest and alpine tundra. Windswept "banner trees," with branches only on the east side of the trunk, cling to the steep mountainside. Their lopsided appearance reveals the fierce intensity of the prevailing westerly winds.

At tree line, only embattled islands of dwarf *krummholz* (a German word meaning "crooked wood") manage to survive in this severe climate. Wind-tortured and twisted to the contour of the slope, these slow-growing, stunted conifers bear little resemblance to those thriving 500 feet below.

Past timberline, you are well rewarded for your tortuous climb by the fantastic panoramas at every zigzag of the trail. Photographers will delight in the uninterrupted views of the summit of Longs Peak, with the magnificent cliff known as The Diamond to the east, the ridge of Storm Peak to the north, and the west-facing flank joined to pyramid-shaped Pagoda Peak by the jagged spires of the Keyboard of the Winds.

The excellent construction of the trail makes for easy progress through the boulders recklessly strewn over the hillside. Large cairns mark the switchbacks. In some places, piled rocks form a wall alongside the path.

Patches of grassy tundra among the rocks sustain a scattering of hardy mountain harebells, alpine cinquefoil and tiny Fendler sandwort.

Three miles into the hike, the trail reaches an overlook above Emerald Lake. Thirteen hundred feet below, the green water shimmers in the breeze within the bleak, glacier-carved basin at the foot of Hallett Peak. Notice that the rocky buttress commonly identified as Hallett Peak is actually the lower section of an escarpment that rises 700 feet to the real summit, now visible.

Emerald Lake Viewpoint to Flattop Mountain

The trail curves around the northern flank of Flattop Mountain across open tundra carpeted with ruby-red patches of fern-like alpine aven leaves. White tufts of cotton grass dance in the wind. Arctic gentians, western yellow paintbrush and American bistort succeed in bloom-

Yellow-bellied Marmot

The yellow-bellied marmot is an easily observed inhabitant of subalpine and alpine regions. You will often see it lazing on a boulder enjoying the sunshine. Usually, one member of the colony will act as a lookout. As you approach, it will emit a high-pitched whistle to warn other marmots of impending danger.

These chunky-bodied, yellowish-brown rodents are usually a couple of feet in length including a six-inch bushy tail.

They have short legs and a whitish patch between the eyes.

As marmots hibernate during the severe winter, they spend the short summer eating green plants and building up large reserves of body fat.

Often, a dominant male in the colony will have a harem of several females. Marmots give birth to one litter of three to six in April or May. Maturing quickly, the young are adult-sized by the end of August.

"Flag" or "banner" trees, with branches only on the leeward side, reveal the forces of the prevailing winds near tree line

ing despite the short growing season, howling winter winds and severe temperatures.

Green and gray patches of lichen decorate the many boulders dotting the slope. In some spots, squat high-altitude-loving willow shrubs have found a precarious footing. Because of the late onset of spring, furry catkins hang from the twigs even into late July. Reddish berries covering occasional wild gooseberry bushes, although unpalatable to humans, provide food for the animals inhabiting the tundra.

Listen for the high-pitched whistle of the yellow-bellied marmot. This plump rodent can frequently be seen sunbathing on a rock near its den.

Intent only on gaining sufficient weight to withstand the long hibernation ahead, it expends as little energy as possible during the summer.

The industrious pika, on the other hand, needs to amass enough food to see it through the winter months, when it remains awake beneath the snow. Toward the end of August, its activity grows ever more frantic as it builds piles of drying vegetation. By snowfall, each pika may have three or four bushel-sized haystacks stored near its burrow.

You may be surprised by a family of ptarmigan on the trail. They are so confident in their mottled-brown camouflage that a hen and her chicks

often appear underfoot so suddenly that you almost tread on them.

Stupendous vistas extend to the north, east and west. Bierstadt and Sprague lakes sparkle like jewels in the sea of conifers far below, with Bear Lake Road snaking past the many lighter green depressions that indicate the various "parks" within the park. Deer Mountain, craggy Lumpy Ridge and the Y-shaped couloir of Ypsilon Mountain are easily discerned against the waves of ridges fading toward the plains. You can see the broad plateau of Trail Ridge rising behind deep Forest Canyon. Trail Ridge Road, the highest continuously paved highway in the United States, winds for 50 miles across this tableland, reaching an elevation of 12,183 feet at its highest point.

The trail switchbacks toward the crest of the Continental Divide and reaches the typical triangular hitchrack of the park at the base of the final stretch of Flattop Mountain. To the left is a short wall, constructed to provide shelter against the ferocious winds. From behind this, you get a good view of the true top of Hallett Peak, of Tyndall Glacier, and of the cliffs falling beneath the summit of Flattop.

A short ascent brings you to the broad, flat expanse of aptly named Flattop Mountain.

Flattop Mountain to Hallett Peak

At a junction on the peak's summit, a sign points off to the right for the North Inlet and Tonahutu Creek trails.

39

Both of these lead down to Grand Lake on the western side of the park, offering extended hiking options.

A notice near this intersection indicates the presence of an archeological site. Since prehistoric times, local Native Americans have used Flattop Mountain as a hunting ground for bighorn sheep and other large game as well as for crossing the Continental Divide. Today, the peak contains one of the most extensive complexes of game-drive walls, blinds and cairns in the Colorado high country. To the untrained eye, however, these are difficult to distinguish from the other boulders littering the summit. The Rocky Mountain National Park Museum contains a large collection of artifacts gathered from this area.

For many, Flattop Mountain will be the final destination, but those continuing to Hallett Peak should take the faint trail around the head of Tyndall Glacier and then follow the cairns up the steep but short scramble up the 400-foot talus slope to the top.

Enjoy the gargantuan 360-degree panorama as you linger over lunch. Not only can you pick out all the points of interest on the east side of Rocky Mountain National Park, but you can see as far west as the Gore Range, more than 50 miles away.

The Arapaho Indians, who summered in the nearby valleys, called this peak *banah ah-nitsieux*, or "Thunder Cloud Peak." The mountain was subsequently named after William L. Hallett, a mining engineer and rancher who climbed in the area in the late 1800s. His summer home, still standing near Marys Lake, is one of the oldest buildings in Estes Park.

William L. Hallett

William L. Hallett, a mining engineer from Springfield, Massachusetts, first visited Estes Park in the summer of 1878 to climb mountains.

The following year, he and his bride honeymooned in the area. Abner Sprague, a local hotel keeper and mountain guide, led them on a 30-day camping trip across the mountains from Estes Park to Grand Lake on horseback.

In 1879, Hallett and two partners started a ranch with 1,200 cattle in North Park. Expanding this business into Powder River Basin, Wyoming, he created one of the area's largest cattle ranches. Later, he moved the business to Loveland and grazed his cows at Estes Park in the summers.

Hallett, his wife, his two daughters and four sons finally settled at 1200 Vine Street in Denver, where he worked as a mining engineer, smelter manager and later for the Denver Water Board.

He built Edgemont near Marys Lake in Estes Park as a summer home in 1881. The Victorian-style frame house became known for the lavish parties he held, replete with fireworks, speeches and poetry readings. Hallett House, as it is now called, is still standing and is one of the oldest buildings in Estes Park.

Hallett was an avid mountain climber. In 1896, he and 18 other men from Denver founded the Rocky Mountain Club, the first mountaineering organization in the region. Hallett was vice president and chairman of exploration. The club considered him to be one of their best climbers as they chose him to make a first ascent of Mount St. Elias in Alaska with a group of Italian climbers. Unfortunately, at the last minute, the Italians decided not to include any Americans in the expedition.

Hallett often climbed with Frederick H. Chapin. Eventually, each man named a mountain after the other. Mount Chapin is one of the peaks in the Mummy Range to the north of the park.

Hallett died at the ripe old age of 90.

Glacier Gorge, above Black Lake, sprawls beneath the towering western face of Longs Peak

~ 4 ~ Black Lake

This moderate trail through verdant subalpine forests and flower-strewn meadows is a favorite with hikers of all ability levels. It leads up Glacier Gorge, a classic ice-carved valley sprawling directly below the sheer western flank of Longs Peak, the park's highest mountain. Several waterfalls, lakes and numerous viewpoints along the route provide excellent picnic spots or serve as goals in themselves.

The impressive Alberta Falls, lying only 0.6 miles from the trailhead, is one of the most popular destinations in the park. Mills Lake, 2.5 miles into the hike, possesses such a spectacular backdrop that it was named after the park's founding father, Enos Mills.

Trailhead

Head west on US Highway 36 for a quarter of a mile past the Beaver Meadows Entrance Station. Drive south for 8.5 miles along the Bear Lake Road to the parking area in the middle of a hairpin bend. The Glacier Gorge Junction Trailhead is across the road to the southwest.
This is the starting point for one of the two most popular trail systems in the park. Therefore, in summer and early fall, it is advisable to arrive early in the morning or to use the free and frequent bus from the shuttle bus parking area 5.0 miles south from the start of Bear Lake Road.

Route

Day hike or overnight; 4.7 miles one way; moderate

Route	Elevation (ft.)	Distance (mi.)
Glacier Gorge Jct. Trailhead	9,240	0
Alberta Falls	9,400	0.6
North Longs Peak Jct	9,740	1.4
Loch Vale-Glacier Gorge Jct	9,780	1.9
Mills Lake	9,940	2.5
Jewel Lake	9,950	3.0
Glacier Gorge Campsite	10,000	3.5
Black Lake	10,620	4.7

USGS Topographic map: McHenrys Peak, Colo.

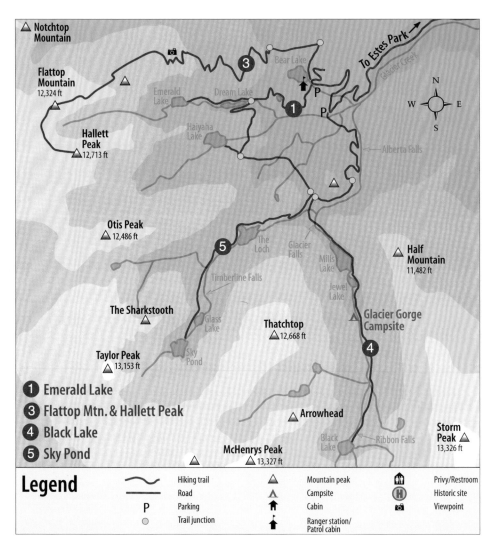

△ Notchtop Mountain

Flattop Mountain
12,324 ft △

Bear Lake

To Estes Park →

Glacier Creek

N
W ⊕ E
S

Emerald Lake
Dream Lake

P
P

Haiyaha Lake

Alberta Falls ←

Hallett Peak
△ 12,713 ft

1

△ Otis Peak
12,486 ft

5

The Loch

Glacier Falls

Mills Lake

△ Half Mountain
11,482 ft

Timberline Falls

Jewel Lake

The Sharkstooth △

Glass Lake

Thatchtop
△ 12,668 ft

△ Glacier Gorge Campsite

4

Taylor Peak
△ 13,153 ft

Sky Pond

1 Emerald Lake

3 Flattop Mtn. & Hallett Peak

△ Arrowhead

4 Black Lake

Black Lake

Ribbon Falls

Storm Peak △
13,326 ft

5 Sky Pond

McHenrys Peak
△   △ 13,327 ft

Legend

∼ Hiking trail	△ Mountain peak	🏠 Privy/Restroom
∼ Road	⋀ Campsite	Ⓗ Historic site
P Parking	⬆ Cabin	📷 Viewpoint
○ Trail junction	⬆ Ranger station/ Patrol cabin	

Trailhead to Alberta Falls

The hike begins at an intersection; veer left for Alberta Falls. After we cross the bridge over Chaos Creek, (a lively brook which descends from lofty Lake Haiyaha), the trail from Glacier Basin Campground merges from the left. Proceed straight on for Alberta Falls.

The broad, popular pathway traverses a rocky slope through the spruce and lodgepole pines, gaining little altitude for the first quarter mile. In autumn, the abundant aspens alongside the trail light up the hillside with a brilliant gold. Unfortunately, most of the greenish-white trunks growing within arm's reach have fallen prey to the knives of vandals.

Watch for golden-mantled ground squirrels scampering alongside the trail. With markings similar to their smaller cousin, the chipmunk, these mammals lack the chipmunk's facial stripes. An incessant chattering high in a conifer betrays the presence of a red squirrel. These creatures are widespread throughout subalpine woodlands in the park.

In 1900, careless campers started a forest fire in this area that raged out of control for days. On many sections of the rocky hillside, nature is slow to make a comeback.

Views are excellent but there is little shade.

The trail crosses another couple of bridges and then ascends more steeply, zigzagging and looping back and forth. The northernmost of the two Glacier Knobs juts out to the right. Shortly before Alberta Falls, the trail skirts the deep gorge of Glacier Creek.

After 0.6 mile, you reach rambunctious Alberta Falls. Water rushes madly over a 25 foot drop, crashes into a boulder-filled catch pool and then thunders over a series of cascades through a deep ravine that it has gouged for itself from the solid bedrock. Numerous stone slabs provide perfect seats for spectators. However, don't expect to have this place to yourself. People come here if they only have a couple of hours in the park and you may find all the prime picnic rocks occupied.

Alberta Falls to North Longs Peak Junction

The trail rises in broad switchbacks, briskly gaining altitude beneath the cliffs below the Glacier Knob.

Morning light best illuminates the ever-increasing views to the north, east and west. The peaks of the Mummy Range, with Ypsilon Mountain's distinctive Y-shaped couloir, define the park's northern boundary. Across Glacier Basin and Estes

Enos Mills

Enos Mills (1870-1922), the nationally recognized naturalist, conservationist, lecturer, photographer, explorer, nature guide and writer of 16 books and numerous articles, is considered to be the founding father of Rocky Mountain National Park.

Mills was a Kansas farm boy of 14 when he first came to Colorado. In 1885, he made his first ascent of Longs Peak and began to explore the mountains seriously. The same year, he built a small cabin in the Tahosa Valley. He spent his summers working for his cousin, the Reverend Elkanah Lamb, on a ranch near Fort Collins. In the winter, he earned his keep at the Anaconda Copper Co. mines at Butte, Montana, where he eventually became a stationary engineer. He encountered his first national park when he helped to survey the roads in Yellowstone.

Although he only had an eighth-grade education, Mills was an avid reader. He was relentless in his quest for knowledge about the area that later became Rocky Mountain National Park. He kept a journal of his careful observations of plants and animals and their methods of adapting to the high-altitude environment.

When he was 21, he accidentally met the well-known naturalist and conservationist, John Muir, who became his mentor. Through his friendship with Muir, Mills became a dedicated naturalist.

Mills bought Longs Peak House resort, and began guiding groups up Longs Peak and conducting local nature trips. When the hotel burned down, he constructed rustic Longs Peak Inn.

In 1909, Mills proposed that the region become the country's tenth national park in order to preserve its natural environment. With the full endorsement of the Colorado Mountain Club and the Estes Park Protective and Improvement Association, he used his inexhaustible energy to lecture all over the country and lobby Congress to create the new park. His dream came true on January 26, 1915, when, under President Woodrow Wilson, Rocky Mountain National Park was established.

Mills married Esther Burnell, an artist, poet and interior decorator. The next year, their daughter Enda was born. Tragically, Mills died in September, 1922, after surgery for an abscessed tooth.

The Enos Mills Cabin, Mills' first home, is now a museum and nature center run by his descendants. Located nine miles south of Estes Park on Colorado Highway 7, the museum is open to visitors during the summer.

Park rise the granite crags of Lumpy Ridge, offering rock climbers some of Colorado's best vertical challenges. In the west, the plateau of Trail Ridge rises behind Forest Canyon. Trail Ridge Road, the country's highest continuously paved highway, winds for 50 miles across this tableland. Eleven of these miles are through the harsh windswept alpine tundra zone.

Frequent boulders provide perfect rest benches and at least one stand of aspens displays red autumn hues, unlike the yellow-gold of neighboring clones.

The trail swerves around the northernmost Glacier Knob and forks 1.4 miles into the hike with the North Longs Peak Trail, which angles off to the left. Continue straight for Mills Lake.

North Longs Peak Junction to Loch Vale-Glacier Gorge Junction

Span a rocky promontory dotted with limber pines. These resilient trees are capable of withstanding an inordinate amount of adversity, thriving on ridges exposed to the full force of the elements. Limber pines are easy to recognize, being the only conifer in Rocky Mountain National Park with needles in bundles of five.

The trail traverses a talus slope beneath the northernmost Glacier Knob. Glacier Creek gurgles 50 feet below and massive cliffs loom to the left. Ahead, you can see the ice-carved hanging valleys of Glacier Gorge and Loch Vale, which empty into this defile. Young aspens struggle to survive in the poor soil along the trail.

Drop briefly through the Engelmann spruce and subalpine firs to a Y-junction with the trails to Loch Vale and Lake Haiyaha heading right. Stay left for Mills and Black lakes.

Trembling Aspen

The aspen is the most widespread tree in North America and the only common deciduous tree growing in the Colorado Rockies away from riparian environments. Look for aspens at the margins of meadows, in valleys and on hillsides up to an elevation of 10,000 feet.

In September, the leaves turn brilliant shades of yellow-gold. As many of the trails in this book begin through aspen groves, early autumn is a great time of year to enjoy nature's wonders in Colorado.

The scientific name, *Populus tremuloides*, refers to the small rounded leaves, which tremble in the lightest breeze on their flattened leafstalks.

Aspens reproduce by root suckering. They send vertical shoots from roots paralleling the surface of the ground. This results in groups of genetically identical trees or clones, which share a common root system. New trees can continue to sprout from this giant network for hundreds of years. The clones look similar and behave the same, producing leaves at the same time in spring and changing leaf color together in fall.

Aspens are one of the first species to colonize a slope that has been stripped of conifers by logging, fire, avalanche or other disturbance. The sun's warmth on the bare earth stimulates growth of a dormant root system. Eventually, shade-loving spruce and fir will again crowd out the aspens in forest succession.

The copious understory of aspen forests attracts a wealth of wildlife. Swallows, house wrens and bluebirds nest in cavities that woodpeckers have hollowed in the soft tree trunks.

Chipmunks, golden-mantled ground squirrels, cottontail rabbits and other small mammals make their homes in the brush, attracting predators such as coyotes, red foxes and hawks. Mule deer and elk seek rest, cover and food, and cow elk hide their young among the aspens while foraging. In autumn, bull elk rub the velvet from their antlers on the tree trunks and during winter, they often gnaw on the bark.

Sadly, many of the aspens growing within arm's reach of the most popular trails have been vandalized by irresponsible and insensitive hikers. It's hard to understand why some people feel the need to carve their initials and infatuations in the bark of a tree. This not only endangers the health of the tree but it spoils the landscape for other visitors.

The trail between Jewel Lake and Black Lake gains altitude by way of stone steps

Loch Vale-Glacier Gorge Junction to Mills Lake

The path tunnels through the evergreens, bends left to cross Icy Brook (descending from Loch Vale), and then degenerates to cairns, necessitating a bit of a scramble up a smooth outcrop.

Cross the bridge over Glacier Creek, make a sharp right and head through an aspen grove. Steps help upward progress until the trail disappears again, leaving cairns to direct the way along an exposed seam of bedrock.

Upon entering Glacier Gorge, views reveal the square-topped summit of Longs Peak, with Storm Peak to its left and the jagged series of spires known as the Keyboard of the Winds to the right. This musical name comes from the mournful tune played by the ferocious wind as it howls through the pinnacles. Triangular Pagoda Peak and Chiefs Head Mountain block the southern reaches of the valley. The gray, scree-covered flanks of this barren landscape are decorated with streaks of snow and residual icefields.

Continue to follow the cairns and, at 2.5 miles into the hike, arrive at Mills Lake. Many people consider this to be the most magnificent of all the tarns in the park. Sprawling just below tree line, Mills is the perfectly shaped glacial lake. Huge erratics, boulders deposited by the receding tongue of ice, and slabs of bedrock around its shore provide picnic spots where you can rest and savor the majesty of this pristine wilderness.

In the early mornings, before the daytime breezes start to riffle its royal blue waters, Mills Lake reflects Longs Peak and the mighty summits of the Continental Divide.

Mills Lake is named for Enos Mills, nationally recognized naturalist, writer and lecturer. His tireless lobbying led to the establishment of Rocky Mountain National Park on January 26, 1915.

Mills Lake to Jewel Lake

Forsaking bedrock for marsh, the trail skirts to the left of Mills Lake through subalpine firs, Engelmann spruce, dwarf junipers and occasional contorted limber pines.

Neither as large nor as spectacular as Mills Lake, Jewel Lake lies a few hundred yards to the south. In sharp contrast to its neighbor's rocky outline, Jewel reclines in a wide-open space amid luxurious bog grasses.

Jewel Lake to Glacier Gorge Campsite

The trail continues to the left of Jewel Lake. Strategically placed boardwalks across the boggy areas help avoid trampling the profusion of marsh marigolds, globeflowers and other moisture-loving plants.

Once past the lake, the trail meanders close to Glacier Creek, alternately crossing outcroppings of bedrock and stretches of marsh. Flora enthusiasts will delight in the colorful carpet of wildflowers, which change with the summer months.

After hiking for 3.5 miles, you come to a wooden bridge leading across the stream to Glacier Gorge backcountry campsite. This makes a wonderful base from which to explore. Be sure to purchase permits from the Backcountry Office at (970) 586-1242.

Glacier Gorge Campsite to Black Lake

The trail rises briskly to the left of Glacier Creek, at one point aided by a beautifully constructed stone staircase.

On leaving the forest, traverse a grassy area with a few willows clinging alongside the stream, and then climb beneath the talus slope to the left of the valley. Ribbon Falls, Glacier Creek's first cascade after leaving Black Lake, tumbles over smooth bedrock into the emerald meadow overgrown with arnica, yarrow, bistort, chimingbells, aspen daisies and ragwort.

As the trail zigzags up the rocky slab by the falls, you are well rewarded for your climb by the extensive panoramas back over Glacier Gorge and north as far as the Mummy Range.

Almost immediately upon cresting the moraine, you

Impressive Alberta Falls is one of the park's highlights

reach the outlet from Black Lake, where the trail momentarily disappears. Hopping over the boulders reunites you with the path around the left shore.

Black Lake snuggles in a tight embrace of sheer black cliffs. McHenrys Peak soars above a glacial shelf to the west and a jagged buttress known as the Spearhead juts up abruptly to the south.

Rocks around the shore provide good picnic spots and a little copse of trees in the middle of a grassy area by the inlet offers some shade.

This is where the official Park Service trail terminates. A sort of track continues up the talus slope by the inlet stream to the east of the lake, offering the opportunity to explore the most remote regions of Glacier Gorge.

Shimmering golden aspens light up the trail during the fall

~ 5 ~ Sky Pond

This hike past a series of serene alpine lakes and tumbling waterfalls is one of the park's most heavily used. It offers a spectacular close-up view of a glacier-carved valley and great opportunities to see and photograph fall foliage. Each of the cascades and lakes along the route makes an excellent destination in itself, providing options for hikers of all ability levels.

Trailhead to Alberta Falls

At Glacier Gorge Junction, ignore the right-hand path ascending to Bear Lake. Take the left fork for Alberta Falls, Mills Lake and Loch Vale.

Trailhead

Head west on US Highway 36 for a quarter of a mile past the Beaver Meadows Entrance Station. Drive south for 8.5 miles along the Bear Lake Road to the parking area in the middle of a hairpin bend. The Glacier Gorge Junction Trailhead is across the road to the southwest.
This is the starting point for one of the two most popular trail systems in the park. Therefore, in summer and early fall, it is advisable to arrive early in the morning or to use the free and frequent bus from the shuttle bus parking area 5.0 miles south from the start of Bear Lake Road.

Route

Day hike; 4.6 miles one way; moderate

Route	Elevation (ft.)	Distance (mi.)
Glacier Gorge Jct Trailhead	9,240	0
Alberta Falls	9,400	0.6
North Longs Peak Jct	9,740	1.4
Loch Vale-Glacier Gorge Jct	9,780	1.9
The Loch	10,180	2.7
Andrews Tarn Jct	10,380	3.6
Timberline Falls	10,500	4.0
Lake of Glass	10,820	4.2
Sky Pond	10,900	4.6

USGS Topographic map: McHenrys Peak, Colo.

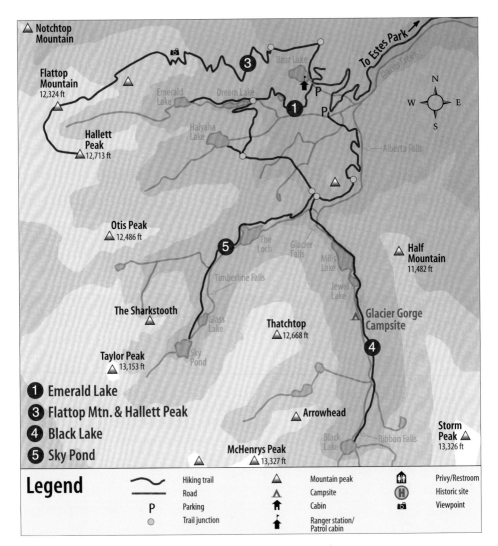

△ Notchtop Mountain

Flattop Mountain
12,324 ft

Hallett Peak
△ 12,713 ft

Otis Peak
△ 12,486 ft

The Sharkstooth
△

Taylor Peak
△ 13,153 ft

Bear Lake

Emerald Lake

Dream Lake

Haiyaha Lake

P

P

Alberta Falls

The Loch

Glacier Falls

Mills Lake

Half Mountain
11,482 ft

Timberline Falls

Jewel Lake

Glass Lake

Thatchtop
△ 12,668 ft

Sky Pond

Glacier Gorge Campsite
△

① Emerald Lake

③ Flattop Mtn. & Hallett Peak

④ Black Lake

⑤ Sky Pond

△ Arrowhead

Storm Peak △
13,326 ft

Black Lake

Ribbon Falls

McHenrys Peak
△ 13,327 ft

N
W — E
S

To Estes Park →

Legend					
～	Hiking trail	△	Mountain peak	🚻	Privy/Restroom
	Road	▲	Campsite	Ⓗ	Historic site
P	Parking	⌂	Cabin	📷	Viewpoint
○	Trail junction	▮	Ranger station/ Patrol cabin		

The trail bridges lively Chaos Creek and immediately sends a branch down to the left toward Glacier Basin Campground. Continue straight ahead. It traverses a fairly level section, crosses another stream and then climbs in earnest up a boulder-strewn moraine deposited during the retreat of the massive Bartholf Glacier, which carved this valley thousands of years ago.

Numerous strands of as-pens streak the lodgepole pines alongside the trail. In the fall, photographers will find it hard to resist capturing the delicate golden leaves trembling atop the whitish trunks with the cobalt Colorado sky as a backdrop.

You will often see red squirrels chattering in the pines and golden-mantled ground squirrels sitting up on their hind legs, begging for a handout. Remember, it is illegal to feed animals and birds in the park because it impedes their ability to survive as wild creatures.

After 0.4 mile, the sound of rushing water betrays your proximity to Glacier Creek and the trail skirts the rim of a ravine, where you can look down on the vivacious stream.

The path ascends in a series of broad zigzags to Alberta Falls, one of the most breathtaking cascades in the park. A magnificent sheet of white foam plunges 25 feet between outcroppings of bedrock and hurtles around the boulders that block its path at the base of the chute.

Plenty of comfortable rock slabs provide rest spots overlooking this dramatic spectacle, but, unless you arrive at the crack of dawn, you will have lots of company.

Alberta Falls to North Longs Peak Junction

The trail snakes upward through an area still recovering from the devastating burn of 1900, which started when campers lost control of a campfire.

Aspens quake in the breeze, enhancing the expansive views opening across the eastern side of the park. To the north soar the peaks of the Mummy Range, with Mount Ypsilon easily identified by its distinctive Y-shaped snowfield. Look for the irregular domes of Lumpy Ridge behind Estes Park. To the west, you can see Flattop Mountain and Hallett Peak, two summits of the Continental Divide, and the plateau of Trail Ridge rising behind Forest Canyon. Many boulders invite you to sit for a while to take in this wonderful panorama.

Directly to the south looms the most northerly of the two Glacier Knobs. This huge mass of glacially polished bedrock somehow withstood complete destruction by the cruel gouging of ice age glaciers.

After 1.4 miles, the trail reaches an intersection. The North Longs Peak Trail heads left toward the distant summit of Longs Peak. Keep right for Loch Vale and Glacier Gorge.

North Longs Peak Junction to Loch Vale-Glacier Gorge Junction

The trail crosses a rocky shoulder beneath the Glacier Knob. Limber pines, the only conifers in the park with needles in bundles of five, grow from cracks in the the rock. These hardy pines survive in conditions too inhospitable for other tree species. At tree line and on exposed ridges, high winds often contort the limbs into photogenic shapes.

You now enter the defile created by the union of the Glacier Gorge and Loch Vale glaciers, tributaries of the giant Bartholf Glacier. Ahead, the two U-shaped drainages gouged by these tongues of ice can be seen hanging high above the level of the valley. To the left is Glacier Gorge, to the right, Loch Vale.

Wispy aspens sprout alongside the trail as it traverses a boulder field beneath the Glacier Knob. Swerve to the right and descend into a forest of tall subalpine firs

Clark's Nutcracker

The cacophonous "*kra-a-a*" of the Clark's nutcracker is a familiar sound in many of the most popular picnic areas in Rocky Mountain National Park. The least reticent of all the park's creatures, this crow-like bird will blatantly scavenge anything and everything it can grab with its long bill.

Light gray with black and white wing and tail feathers, the nutcracker is characterized by its undulating and rather heavy flight pattern. On the ground, it progresses by means of strong, bounding hops.

Primarily a nut eater, it can hold several nuts in a cheek pouch under its tongue as well as those it carries in its bill. Outstanding examples of birds that store food, nutcrackers spend much of their time during late summer and early fall finding, carrying and storing nuts in the ground. They remember the exact position of the store and will accurately locate them even through snow.

Nutcrackers nest early in the season in conifers. The female incubates from two to six green, spotted eggs while being fed by the male from his throat pouch.

49

and Engelmann spruce that somehow escaped the 1900 conflagration.

After hiking a total of 1.9 miles, come to a three-way trail junction with branches to Mills Lake, Loch Vale and Lake Haiyaha. Follow the signs for Loch Vale and Sky Pond along the middle fork.

Loch Vale-Glacier Gorge Junction to The Loch

Rising briskly, the trail enters a ravine carved by Icy Brook in its hasty descent from Loch Vale. You gain altitude in a series of switchbacks, with periodic views of the stream cascading beneath the sheer cliffs enclosing the gorge.

After a breath-robbing 400-foot ascent in only 0.8 mile, you cross the lip of the valley and come abruptly to the northeastern end of The Loch.

A rocky promontory extending to the left of the trail provides excellent picnic spots with vistas up the lake. Gnarled limber pines frame photographs of the peaks that loom all around.

Taylor and Powell peaks, high points along the Continental Divide, define the distant

end of the valley. Taylor Glacier hangs between these two summits, easily distinguished by its swallow-tail-shaped avalanche tracks dropping from the skyline. Cathedral Wall, the broken, rocky rampart thrusting to the west of The Loch, presents rock climbers with a formidable challenge. At the foot of this escarpment, Timberline Falls threads its way down a moraine blocking the valley. To the right of Cathedral Wall, you can glimpse Andrews Glacier behind the wooded slopes of Otis Peak.

The Loch to Lake of Glass

The trail continues to the right of The Loch, skirting a grassy patch dotted with Indian paintbrush, yarrow, ragwort, thistles and goldenrod. Conifers offer shade along the shoreline without obstructing the views of the sheer cliffs of Thatchtop Mountain to the south.

Ascend gently from the southwest corner of The Loch through a forest of tall Engelmann spruce and subalpine firs. Icy Brook babbles to

your left, sometimes bordered by thickets of willows and alders.

Cross Andrews Creek by a bridge of two rough-hewn logs and come to an intersection. The path to Andrews Tarn, at the base of Andrews Glacier, shoots steeply uphill to the right. Keep straight on for Lake of Glass and Sky Pond.

The trail emerges from the forest onto a broad, open area at the base of a 350-foot-high rocky moraine. The aptly named Timberline Falls dances down this wall in a series of cascades, splitting and mingling as it skips over ledges and around crevices, and splashes off polished stone surfaces. Plank boardwalks aid progress across marshy spots near the catch basin. Strategically placed rocks provide rest benches for those who prefer to end their hike here and forgo the tiresome and often slippery scramble up the steep headwall.

The faint trail zigzags up the talus slope to the right of the falls. Snowbanks lingering into early summer can make the route-finding difficult and the going treacherous. If the trail is obliterated, aim for the gully formed by the branch of the falls farthest to the right Listen for the peep of the tiny

Colorful aspens alongside the trail

pika as you pick your way through the scree. At your approach, these guinea pig-like rodents utter a high-pitched call to warn other pikas of impending danger.

Clamber up the slick bedrock of the chute. About halfway up, an overlook to the left offers an excellent view of the main channel of Timberline Falls as it plunges majestically over a rocky slab. Panoramas extend northeastward down Loch Vale and over the park.

Despite the plentiful handholds, the next 20-foot scramble up a sheer rock face to the right of the falls can be daunting for some. Take great care as the rock is frequently wet and slippery. Upon reaching less-vertical ground, burrow through a thicket of krummholz. Immediately, the Lake of Glass sprawls in front of you. (USGS Topographical maps identify this as Glass Lake. It is commonly referred to as the more melodious Lake of Glass.)

Lake of Glass nestles in a cirque carved out of granite and schist by the Loch Vale glacier and backed by towering Taylor and Powell peaks. Despite its name, Lake of Glass can be anything but glass-like. Shelter from the fierce winds can be found on and around the big slabs of bedrock to the right of the tarn.

Lake of Glass to Sky Pond

To proceed to Sky Pond 0.4 mile onward, stay to the right of the Lake of Glass, follow the cairns up the rocks and then drop back down to the lake's edge. Tunnel through the thickets of dwarf conifers along the shoreline, scrambling now and again up and over the outcroppings that obstruct your progress.

After leaving the Lake of Glass, follow the cairns across a boulder field and traverse a meadow decorated with masses of marsh marigolds. Clamber up by a tiny waterfall, veer to the left

Why Aspen Change Color in the Autumn

The Rocky Mountains are at their most spectacular during autumn when the aspens turn a brilliant yellow-gold. Fall foliage viewing in Colorado starts in early September at the high elevations and progresses gradually downhill throughout the month.

For a long time, people have sought an explanation for this strange and wondrous phenomenon. Indian legend has it that when the Great Bear smelled the hunter's fire in autumn, the resulting fight splashed yellow cooking grease and red blood on the aspen leaves.

Today, scientists know that these colorful effects are caused by a chemical change triggered by variations in temperature, light and moisture.

Chlorophyll is the green pigment in leaves. During the summer, chlorophyll carries on photosynthesis, transforming sunshine into food and energy for the tree. As this happens, the green coloring in the leaves predominates.

Shorter days and lower temperatures, indicating the approach of winter, produce the breakdown of the chlorophyll, revealing the hitherto hidden reds, yellows and oranges in the leaves.

Aspens grow in "clones," a number of individuals sprouting from the same root system. Autumn makes clones conspicuous, as groups of trees change in unison to exactly the same shade of red or gold.

Septembers with the right combination of sunny days and cool nights produce the best spectrum of colors.

51

Lake of Glass nestles in a cirque carved out of granite and schist by the Loch Vale Glacier

of the thickets of krummholz and arrive at Sky Pond—twice the size of Lake of Glass and infinitely more majestic.

Barren and austere, Sky Pond snuggles into an amphitheater of naked rock. The dark gray cliffs and talus slopes of Powell Peak (to the left) and Taylor Peak dominate the lake, divided by the contrasting whiteness of Taylor Glacier, one of the few active glaciers in the park. Taylor Peak is Colorado's northernmost Thirteener on the Continental Divide. Both peak and glacier were named after Albert Reynolds Taylor, a Kansas schoolteacher who visited the area in 1895.

To the right, Cathedral Wall thrusts skyward in a series of jagged spires culminating in the Sharkstooth (to the left), a freestanding pinnacle only accessible to technical climbers.

Red Squirrel

One of the most familiar sounds in the forests of the Rocky Mountains of Colorado is the chatter of the red squirrel or chickaree. The anxious complaint of this little grouch continues until you leave its territory.

Colorado red squirrels, which tend to be more grayish brown than red, prefer to eat pine seeds but also feed on nuts, berries, fungi and eggs. You will often see one with a mouthful of pine cone scurrying up a tree to its favorite branch for a leisurely feast.

As you hike, watch for squirrel middens along the trail. These piles of cone cores and scales can be a number of yards across and several feet deep.

Red squirrels do not hibernate, but cache food for the winter. They build nests of twigs, bark and leaves in a hollow tree or the fork of a branch. A lively nuptial chase precedes mating, and two litters of three to five young are born during spring and summer.

Longs Peak as seen from Twin Sisters Peaks

~ 6 ~ Longs Peak

Rising to a lofty 14,255 feet, Longs Peak is the monarch of Rocky Mountain National Park. The only "Fourteener" in the park, it is the 15th highest

mountain in Colorado. Despite an elevation gain of almost 5,000 feet and round-trip distance of 15 miles, the ascent of this majestic peak presents an irresistible challenge to both local "peak baggers" and visitors to the state. During the short, non-technical climbing season, thousands reach the summit. You are, therefore, unlikely to find solitude along this well-used trail.

Trailhead

Drive south from Estes Park on Colorado Highway 7 for 8.9 miles, passing the Lily Lake Visitor Center. Turn right (west) at the Longs Peak area sign and follow the road uphill for 1.0 mile to the large parking area at the Longs Peak Ranger Station. An early start will ensure a place in the lot for this popular trailhead. The trail starts to the left of the ranger station.

Longs Peak Ranger Station to Goblins Forest Campsite

As the wide trail ascends briskly through the subalpine forest, the tall, straight-trunked

Route

Day hike or overnight; 8 miles one way; strenuous

Route	Elevation (ft.)	Distance (mi.)
Longs Peak Trailhead	9,400	0
Storm Pass Trail Jct	9,700	0.5
Goblins Forest Campsite	10,120	1.2
Battle Mtn Group Campsite Jct	10,960	2.5
Chasm Jct	11,600	3.7
Granite Pass	12,080	4.2
Boulderfield Campground	12,760	6.0
The Keyhole	13,160	6.3
Longs Peak Summit	14,255	7.5

USGS Topographic map: Longs Peak, Colo.

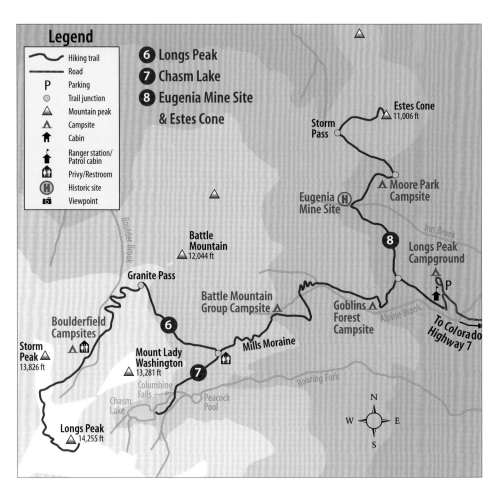

Legend

∿	Hiking trail
—	Road
P	Parking
○	Trail junction
△	Mountain peak
⚠	Campsite
♠	Cabin
⛪	Ranger station/Patrol cabin
🚻	Privy/Restroom
Ⓗ	Historic site
📷	Viewpoint

6 Longs Peak
7 Chasm Lake
8 Eugenia Mine Site & Estes Cone

Estes Cone 11,006 ft
Storm Pass
Moore Park Campsite
Eugenia Ⓗ Mine Site
Inn Brook
8 Longs Peak Campground
Battle Mountain 12,044 ft
Granite Pass
Battle Mountain Group Campsite
Goblins Forest Campsite
Alpine Brook
To Colorado Highway 7
Boulderfield Campsites
6
Storm Peak 13,826 ft
Mount Lady Washington 13,281 ft
7
Mills Moraine
Columbine Falls
Chasm Lake
Peacock Pool
Roaring Fork
Longs Peak 14,255 ft
N W E S
Boulder Brook

lodgepole pines soon make room for Engelmann spruce and subalpine fir.

Stay left at an intersection half a mile into the hike, where the path from Storm Pass and Estes Cone joins from the right. The trail to Longs Peak traverses the forested slope of Pine Ridge until it meets Alpine Brook and then ascends in a series of long switchbacks.

After 1.2 miles, you pass Goblins Forest backcountry campsite. Above to the left, the sheer east face of Longs Peak juts over the ridge of Mills Moraine. Mills Moraine

and Mills Glacier, which sprawl above Chasm Lake,

were named after the park's founder, Enos Mills. They look

Suggestions for Hiking Longs Peak

A hike to the top of Longs Peak should not be taken lightly. It's best reserved for experienced hikers only. However well prepared you are, it can expose you to many hazards, including altitude sickness, dehydration, sunburn, lightning storms and rapid weather changes. It is very important to turn back if conditions deteriorate or if you begin to experience nausea and severe headaches.

Start from the trailhead before 3 a.m. in order to reach the summit by noon. Dangerous storms often brew during the afternoon. Alternatively, camp at the Boulderfield and allow two days to make the ascent. Reserve one of the nine tent sites in advance at the park's Backcountry Office. Call 970-586-1242.

All hikers should sign in at the trail register located by the Ranger Station.

The Allure of Longs Peak

Sunrise on the summit of Longs Peak with the cliff known as "The Diamond" to the left

Longs Peak has attracted climbers for hundreds of years. Rising to a lofty 14,255 feet, it is the highest mountain in Rocky Mountain National Park and the northernmost "Fourteener" in the Colorado Rockies.

As with all dominant mountains, adventurers have searched and found new ways to reach the summit. Longs Peak bears an impressive roster of "firsts."

The Arapaho called it and neighboring Mount Meeker *Nestotaieux*, the Two Guides. They used these prominent peaks as a compass point during their travels on the plains. It is likely that the Arapaho were the first to scale Longs Peak, climbing it in order to trap eagles.

In 1820, Stephen Harriman Long, a young army officer, led 22 men on horseback southward along the Front Range of the Rocky Mountains. He made the first recorded sighting of the peak, which was subsequently named in his honor.

The first recorded climb was made on August 23, 1868, by Major John Wesley Powell, a geology professor from Illinois, with a party of seven of his geology students and William Byers,

founder of Denver's *Rocky Mountain News*. Powell later became famous for his exploration of the Grand Canyon.

The Reverend Elkanah J. Lamb, a minister for the United Brethren Church, came to Estes Park in August, 1871, expressly to climb Longs Peak. He gained the distinction of being the first to descend by the sheer east face, surviving a near-fatal fall down an icefield that became known as "Lamb's Slide." He later settled in the Tahosa Valley, running the Longs Peak House resort and becoming a pioneer guide on the mountain. He and his son, Carlyle, led parties of visitors to the top of Longs Peak for $5 a trip, contributing immensely to the popularity of the climb. In 1902, he constructed the first official trail to the Boulderfield.

In 1873, Addie Alexander became the first woman to scale the peak, or so a newspaper of the time reported.

In September, 1922, Professor James. W. Alexander made the first solo ascent of the east face in one day using ropes and pitons.

Agnes Vaille succeeded in becoming the first woman to

climb the peak in winter on January 12, 1925, but fell and froze to death during her descent.

During the 1930s, Walter Kiener, the Swiss mountaineer and botanist, studied the alpine tundra of the mountain and pioneered a route up the east face, which is now named after him.

David Rearick and Bob Kamps from California were the first to climb straight up the Diamond, the 1,000-foot cliff on the east face. After two days of difficult rock and aid climbing, they arrived at the summit on August 3, 1960.

Wayne Goss and Jim Logan made the first free climb of the Diamond in July, 1975.

Today, Longs Peak is one of the most popular mountains in the western United States. Of the 15,000 people who attempt the climb each year, 10,000 attain the summit.

There are more than 100 different routes up Longs Peak, although most of these are technical rock climbs of the east face. The majority of climbers follow the East Longs Peak Trail, ascending via the Keyhole, Trough, Narrows and Homestretch.

down on the site of Mills' famous hotel, the Longs Peak Inn, from which he guided ascents of the mountain in the early 1900s.

Goblins Forest Campsite to Battle Mountain Group Campsite Junction

The trail follows the course of Alpine Brook, zigzagging to

gain altitude, and then crosses a bridge over the lively stream. The trees become more and more stunted as you snake up Mills Moraine. "Banner" or "flag" trees, with branches growing only on the

Camping in Rocky Mountain National Park

Campground	Tent/RV Sites	Cost	Open / Day Limitation	Reservations
Aspenglen	54	$16/night	Open May 14-Sept.. 20; 7 day max. stay*	First-come, first served
Glacier Basin	150	$16/night	Open June 4 to Labor Day; 7 day max. stay	Required June to September; 800-365-2267
Longs Peak	26 tent sites; no RVs	$16/night	Open year-round; 3 day max. stay*	First-come, first served
Moraine Park	247	$16 non-reserved $16 reserved $12 during winter	Open year-round; 7 day max. stay*	Reservation required Memorial Day to September; 800-365-2267
Sprague Lake Handicamp Backcountry	tenting for 12 people	$15 permit fee	Open Summer and Fall; 3 day max. stay	Reservation required; 970-586-1242
Timber Creek	100	$16/night	Open year-round; 7 day max. stay*	First-come, first served

* Parkwide camping is limited to seven nights from Memorial Day to Labor Day. An additional 14 nights parkwide is permitted after Labor Day to before Memorial Day. At Longs Peak Campground, a three-day limit applies between May 22 to Sept. 30.

Longs Peak as seen from Bear Lake Road

east side of the trunk, attest to the ferocity of the winter winds and blowing snow.

Above, the east face of Longs Peak is flanked by Mount Lady Washington on the right and Mount Meeker to the left. It gradually gains in stature as you ascend the ridge. Behind the knobby summits of Twin Sisters Peaks to the east of the Tahosa Valley, the plains seem to stretch to infinity. If it is still dark, you may even spot the distant twinkling lights of Denver.

At tree line, isolated islands of *krummholz* decorate the barren, windswept slope. These dwarf conifers survive in the battle zone between the upper limits of tree growth and a climate too harsh for the existence of any but the most minute of plants. Gnarled and twisted into strange configurations, they develop very slowly due to the intense cold, fierce winter winds and brief, two-month growing season.

Above the domain of the subalpine forest stretches the alpine tundra, a rich mosaic of tiny grasses, sedges and mosses. More than 100 species of plants thrive in this high-altitude environment on Longs Peak. Both diminutive versions of subalpine species, such as fireweed, cinquefoil and mountain harebell, and flowers unique to this region, such as alpine avens, kings crown and koeniga, bloom on the rich green carpet.

Listen for the metallic squeak of the elusive little pika. Difficult to spot among the boulders littering the slope, this round-eared relative of the rabbit frantically stockpiles large stores of vegetation to eat during the long winter.

Watch for the yellow-bellied marmot lazing on top of a sunny rock. Unlike the hardworking pika, the only job of this plump rodent is to gain a sufficient quantity of body fat to see it through its winter hibernation.

The ptarmigan is another tundra inhabitant. Changing its camouflage with the seasons, it turns a pure white in winter to blend with the snow, and in summer, its mottled-brown coloring makes it almost invisible between the rocks along the trail.

After 2.5 miles, you pass the junction with the track ascending for 0.3 mile to Battle Mountain group campsite.

Battle Mountain Group Campsite Junction to Chasm Junction

The trail hastens up the increasingly barren moraine with the help of high steps.

Jims Grove, a copse of hardy conifers on the slope to the right, is where mountain man Jim Nugent camped with Englishwoman Isabella Bird during their ascent of Longs Peak in 1873. You can read about this climb in Bird's book, *A Lady's Life in the Rocky Mountains*.

As you crest the ridge of Mills Moraine, you are confronted by one of the most majestic scenes in the park: Ahead towers the massive east face of Longs Peak in all its glory. Rising a total of 2,500 feet from Chasm Lake, this forbidding gray wall is considered by many to be the most impressive cliff in the country. The top 1,000-foot section is known as the "Dia-mond," a choice playground for technical climbers. The emerald tarn huddled below in the valley of the Roaring Fork is Peacock Pool, into which Columbine Falls cascades down a headwall below Chasm Lake.

Mills Glacier arches gracefully across the slope beneath the east face. This is all that remains of the ancient tongue of ice that carved this impressive cirque between the northern flank of Mount Meeker, the east face of Longs Peak, and the south side of Mount Lady Washington. The debris from the glacier's destructive sculpting was deposited as the ridge of Mills Moraine.

The trail reaches an intersection with Chasm Lake straight on, an outhouse off to the left and Longs Peak summit to the right. Go right at this intersection.

Plenty of boulders provide perfect seats for a snack and a rest.

Chasm Junction to Granite Pass

A gradual traverse along a talus slope falling from Mount Lady Washington brings you to Granite Pass, a depression to the left of an irregular rocky outcropping. At this point you leave the upper reaches of the Tahosa Valley and progress into the Estes Valley. This can be a windy spot as it is the path taken by air currents shooting north

Agnes Vaille

Colorado Mountain Club member Agnes Vaille wanted to be the first woman to scale the massive east face of Longs Peak in winter.

After failing in three attempts, she set off on Sunday, January 11, 1925, from the Longs Peak Inn with Walter Kiener, an experienced Swiss mountaineer. Despite sub-zero temperatures and fierce gusts of wind, they fought their way up the formidable cliff, climbing all day and continuing in the darkness of night.

At 4 a.m. the following morning, Vaille and Kiener stood on the top, victorious, but were unable to sign in at the summit register because of frozen fingers.

As they were so cold, they decided to descend by the quickest way possible, the north route down to the Boulderfield. All went well until they reached the section where the incline changes from granite cliff to talus slope. Vaille slipped on sheet ice and fell about 150 feet. When Kiener reached her she insisted she was unhurt. Obviously in the first stages of hypothermia, she said she was so sleepy that she was going to take a rest. Kiener attempted to carry her but was so tired himself that he made little progress. At her request, he left her to go for help. When he returned with a search party of local men they found Agnes Vaille frozen to death.

During this climb, Kiener lost his fingers, most of his toes and part of one foot to frostbite. Herbert Sortland, caretaker at the Longs Peak Inn and a volunteer member of the rescue team, became disoriented in the blizzard while descending to the hotel. His body was found only 300 yards from the building a month later.

The Keyhole's unusual shape is striking when silhouetted against the sky

rows, greet hikers passing to or from the summit. This is often how valuable information is transmitted between climbers about conditions high up on the peak. Permits must be obtained in advance from the Backcountry Office (970) 586-1242.

Boulder Brook trickles through the campground, appearing and disappearing among the rocks. If you are using this as a source of drinking water, be sure to boil or otherwise treat the water as it is likely to be contaminated by *giardia* .

If you are ascending the peak in one day, this is a good spot to eat, drink and give the muscles a break. You have covered 6 miles and only have 1.5 to go. Also, you have climbed about 70 percent of the 5,000-foot elevation gain from the ranger station to the summit.

around Longs Peak.

Granite Pass to the Boulderfield

Immediately after Granite Pass the trail climbing from Boulder Brook Campsite and Bear Lake merges from the right; continue straight ahead.

Watch for bighorn sheep leaping among the boulders along the next stretch. The most outstanding feature of this, the Colorado state animal, is the large curled horns of the rams. These can be 40 inches long and weigh up to 35 pounds.

The trail skirts the north side of Mount Lady Washington and ascends toward the northern flank of Longs Peak in long, sweeping switchbacks. Boulder Brook, squeezed from the snowfield above the Boulderfield, sometimes flows along the route of the path. Ahead, you can see the Keyhole gaping ominously between Longs and Storm peaks.

Vistas extend north over

the park to the peaks of the Mummy Range, with Mount Ypsilon (easily recognized by its Y-shaped couloir), and northwest to Hallett Peak, Flattop Mountain and the other summits of the Continental Divide.

The grade lessens as you approach the Boulderfield, an area littered with massive chunks of granite. The trail disintegrates, leaving only cairns to guide the way through the sea of rocks.

Shortly, tents among the boulders and two outhouses indicate that you have arrived at the Boulderfield Campground. A night spent here enhances one's understanding of this elevated environment and provides a pleasant, more leisurely approach to the summit. There are spots for nine tents. Rock walls encircling flattened, tent-sized areas offer protection from the wind. Campers, who seem to resemble prairie dogs as they poke out of their bur-

The Boulderfield to the Keyhole

The trail peters out after the campground. Despite the fact that there are occasional cairns on the huge rocks, chances are good that you will be following a meandering line of other people, so route finding should not be difficult. Gradually, as you head toward the Keyhole, the slope steepens. This oval notch, open at the top, looks like a defiant crab when silhouetted against the sky.

A stone shelter to the left of the Keyhole commemorates

Agnes Vaille, who made the first successful winter climb of the east face of Longs Peak on January 12, 1925. Unfortunately, she fell as she was descending the icy slabs just above the Boulderfield and died of exposure before rescuers could reach her.

As you scramble toward the lip of the Keyhole, you can hear the wind howling through the gap. Brace yourself as you step over the narrow rim and get your first glimpse of the spectacular view westward. Glacier Gorge sprawls 3,000 feet below with tiny tarns glistening like gems amid the barren rocks and patches of tundra. Pagoda Mountain, Chiefs Head Peak and McHenrys Peak define the southwestern reaches of the glacier-gouged trough, their rugged flanks speckled with ragged snowfields.

The Keyhole to the Summit

From here to the summit, red and yellow splashes of paint blaze the route.

Be extra careful as you traverse the talus-strewn northern flank of Longs Peak. For many, the half-mile stretch to the Trough will seem extremely exposed. The sections of trodden earth are few and far between and, below the trail, the slope plunges into the valley.

Wind your way up the Trough, a 600-foot-high, 35-degree gully that gradually tapers upward. As you ascend, the nearby peaks shrink until you are higher than every single one of them.

A 20-foot vertical scramble brings you to the saddle at the top of the Trough. Ahead, along the south side of the peak, stretches the Narrows—a skinny ledge above a sheer drop. This is the most exposed part of the hike and requires considerable caution. Despite the fact that the shelf is generally about the width of a sidewalk, there are several spots where the going can get rather tricky when hikers are traveling in both directions.

From the end of the Narrows, an ungainly shuffle on all fours takes you up the vertical fractures of the Homestretch, a slabby couloir leading directly to the summit.

The flat, football-field-sized summit plateau of Longs Peak affords a breathtaking 360-degree panorama. This reward makes the laborious climb well worthwhile. Pikes Peak rises 100 miles to the south. To the north, you can pick out the mountains of the Medicine Bow Range in Wyoming. To the west, the Continental Divide snakes its way across the state. You can look down the 2,500-foot east face to Chasm Lake and Peacock Pool. Behind Twin Sisters Peaks and the waves of ridges forming the foothills of the Rockies, the plains disappear into the distance. On a clear day, the horizon that you are looking at may be 150 to 200 miles away.

Pika

As you hike through boulder-covered slopes above timberline, you will often hear the shrill squeak of the pika warning its neighbors of approaching danger. As the call echoes back and forth across the hillside from one member of the colony to another, it is difficult to spot its source. If you get too near, the pika disappears within a rocky crevice.

Pikas (also known as conies or rock rabbits) live on boulder fields in the subalpine and alpine tundra zones of Colorado. Tiny gray-brown mammals with small rounded ears and no visible tail, they average about eight inches in length. Unlike yellow-bellied marmots, they do not hibernate.

Pikas feed on a variety of vegetation including grasses, sagebrush, pine needles, fireweed and thistles. Toward the end of summer, they create bushel-sized haystacks of foodstuff to cure in the sun. When the hay is sufficiently dry, they stockpile it in their rocky burrows. During the long, harsh alpine winter, the pika remains active beneath the deep snow, surviving on its store of hay.

A litter of three or four is born between late May and August. Naked and blind at birth, the young can walk in a week and are mature in six weeks.

The hike up to Chasm Lake crosses the alpine tundra

~ 7 ~ Chasm Lake

Longs Peak and Mount Meeker, the two highest summits in Rocky Mountain National Park, combine to create the most majestic mountain cirque in Colorado. Snug in the embrace of this natural amphitheater lies Chasm Lake.

For the first 3.7 miles, this strenuous hike follows the route taken by climbers heading for the summit of Longs Peak. One of the most popular trails in the park, it ascends through subalpine forest to open tundra, offering spectacular views and opportunities for spotting the park's abundant wildlife. Because of the high elevation, the trail can be snowbound until late June.

Trailhead

Drive south from Estes Park on Colorado Highway 7 for 8.9 miles, passing the Lily Lake Visitor Center. Turn right (west) at the Longs Peak area sign and follow the road uphill for 1.0 mile to the large parking area at the Longs Peak Ranger Station. An early start will ensure a place in the lot for this popular trailhead. The trail starts to the left of the ranger station.

Route

Day hike or overnight; 4.2 miles one way; moderate

Route	Elevation (ft.)	Distance (mi.)
Longs Peak Trailhead	9,400	0
Longs Peak-Storm Pass Jct	9,700	0.5
Goblins Forest Campsite	10,120	1.2
Battle Mtn Group Camp Jct	10,960	2.5
Chasm Jct	11,600	3.7
Chasm Lake	11,800	4.2

USGS Topographic map: Longs Peak, Colo.

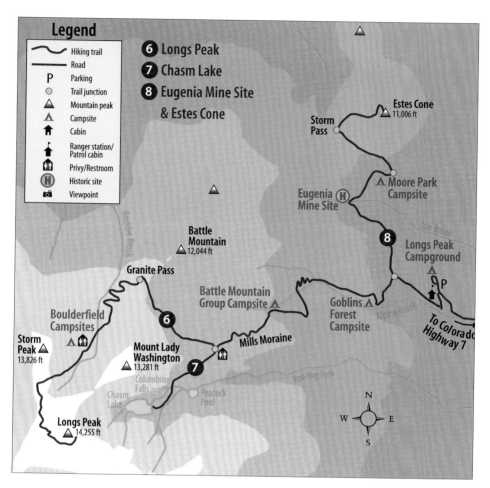

Legend

- 〰️ Hiking trail
- ─── Road
- P Parking
- ○ Trail junction
- △ Mountain peak
- ⚠ Campsite
- 🏠 Cabin
- 🏠 Ranger station/Patrol cabin
- 🚻 Privy/Restroom
- Ⓗ Historic site
- 📷 Viewpoint

6 Longs Peak
7 Chasm Lake
8 Eugenia Mine Site & Estes Cone

Estes Cone △ 11,006 ft

Storm Pass

Moore Park △ Campsite

Eugenia Ⓗ Mine Site

Iron Brook

8

Longs Peak Campground ⚠ P

Battle Mountain △ 12,044 ft

Boulder Brook

Granite Pass

Battle Mountain Group Campsite ⚠

Goblins △ Forest Campsite

Alpine Brook

To Colorado Highway 7

Boulderfield Campsites ⚠ 🏠

6

Mount Lady Washington △ 13,281 ft

Mills Moraine 🚻

7

Roaring Fork

Storm Peak △ 13,826 ft

Columbine Falls

Chasm Lake

Peacock Pool

N W E S

Longs Peak △ 14,255 ft

Longs Peak Ranger Station to Goblins Forest Campsite

The broad, well-constructed Longs Peak Trail hastens uphill from the start through a shady forest of Engelmann spruce and subalpine fir, interspersed with lodgepole pines and occasional aspens.

Stay left at a Y-junction 0.5 mile into the hike. The right branch leads to the Eugenia Mine site and Estes Cone. The trail swerves to the left and traverses the slope of Pine Ridge. A mile from the ranger station, Alpine Brook gurgles to the left, offering a pleasant spot for a snack.

The trail ascends in a series of long switchbacks with views of Twin Sisters Peaks framed by periodic openings in the subalpine conifers.

After 1.2 miles, pass Goblins Forest backcountry campsite. Such a short distance from the trailhead, this would make an excellent destination for young or inexperienced backpackers. To the left, you catch your first glimpse of the massive east face of Longs Peak towering above Mills Moraine, one of

the bulky mountain's eastern ridges. Mills Moraine and Mills Glacier, located just above Chasm Lake, were named for Enos Mills, nationally recognized naturalist, writer and nature guide who dedicated his life to the creation of Rocky Mountain National Park.

Goblins Forest Campsite to Battle Mountain Group Campsite Junction

The trail parallels Alpine Brook, traversing a patch of scree and crossing Larkspur

Chasm Lake from the summit of Longs Peak

Creek. It zigzags rapidly uphill and then crosses broad Alpine Brook, with chimingbells, ragwort and other moisture-loving flowers dotting the banks.

The trees become more scattered and stunted as you snake up Mills Moraine. As timberline approaches, one-sided "banner" or "flag" trees make an appearance. At this altitude, winter winds frequently blow with such force that branches only grow on the leeward side of the trunk.

The increasing patches of alpine tundra sustain miniature gardens speckled with tiny mountain harebells, yarrow, alpine cinquefoil and fireweed. High above, the forbidding east face of Longs Peak gradually looms larger as the trail climbs mercilessly. Mount Lady Washington, Longs Peak's northeastern satellite, towers to the right.

At tree line, the upper limit of the subalpine forest is char-acterized by disjointed islands of *krummholz* (a German word meaning "crooked wood"). These malformed conifers develop very slowly in the harsh climate at this lofty elevation, somehow managing to survive the intense cold, fierce winds and short growing season. Waist-high trees with trunks only a few inches thick may be hundreds of years old.

Watch for the yellow-bellied marmot as the slope becomes windswept, barren and increasingly dotted with gray boulders. A shrill peep is often the the first indication of this creature's presence. If you follow the sound, you will often see the plump rodent lazing on a sunny rock.

Uninterrupted vistas extend eastward over the Tahosa Valley to the knobby summits of Twin Sisters Peaks and the ranges of the foothills. Tiny lakes dotting the plains glisten like jewels in the distant haze.

Two and a half miles from the Longs Peak Ranger Station, the trail sends a branch off to the right over Alpine Brook toward Battle Mountain group campsite. Continue left for Chasm Lake.

Battle Mountain Group Campsite Junction to Chasm Junction

Jims Grove, a group of hardy conifers, decorates the otherwise barren ridge to the right as the trail hurries up Mills Moraine with the help of high steps. Jims Grove is named for Jim Nugent, mountain man and companion to Isabella Bird on her ascent of Longs Peak in 1873. This climb is immortalized in Bird's book, *A Lady's Life in the Rocky Mountains.*

Finally, you top the ridge of the moraine and are confronted with a view of the magnificent east face of Longs Peak. Off to the left drops the ravine cut by the infant Roaring Fork River. The dark green pond seen far below is not Chasm Lake but Peacock Pool.

A sign at an intersection points straight ahead for Chasm Lake, the destination of this hike. The trail to the summit of Longs Peak heads off to the right. Along the ridge to the left stands a privy. Plenty of boulders provide perfect seats for those who want to relax and take in the view. Do not feed the chipmunks scurrying among the boulders, despite their shameless begging. Offering

65

tidbits to the animals violates park regulations, because a creature that relies on human food ceases to be wild and loses the ability to forage for itself.

Chasm Junction to Chasm Lake

Continuing straight, traverse the steep southern slope of Mount Lady Washington. A slight climb is followed by a long, gradual descent above Peacock Pool and Columbine Falls to flower-strewn Chasm Meadows. Look for the delicate blue columbine, Colorado's state flower, blooming near the top of the cascades. Cross the stream and pass the stone park service rescue cabin. A final burst of energy is needed to scramble up the short, rocky headwall of the gorge. Chasm Lake appears as you crest the rim.

Snug in the steely embrace of Longs Peak and Mount Meeker, Chasm Lake lies in a cirque gouged out of sheer granite by glaciers thousands of years ago. The east face of Longs Peak, rising 2,500 feet above the tarn, is perhaps the most majestic cliff in the United States. The upper section, consisting of 20 vertical acres of granite soaring from 13,000 to 14,000 feet above sea level, is called the Diamond. This diamond-shaped wall was first climbed in 1960 by Dave Rearick and Bob Kamps. Today it still offers technical climbers some of Colorado's greatest challenges on rock.

Boulders and slabs of bedrock around the shoreline form an irresistible invitation to stay and enjoy the scene.

Subalpine Forest

Throughout the Colorado Rockies, Engelmann spruce and subalpine fir huddle together on ridges and mountain slopes to form a dense band of forest. This region, between about 9,000 and 11,500 feet above sea level, is known as the subalpine life zone.

In its lower reaches, aspen, ponderosa pine, lodgepole pine and Douglas fir intermingle with the spruce and fir. Limber pines, bent and twisted into grotesque shapes, often take over on rocky, exposed ridges where the conditions are too severe for other species.

Timberline, the limit of tree life, defines the upper periphery of the subalpine zone. Above this, temperatures dropping to minus 30 degrees Fahrenheit, winter winds that can exceed 150 miles an hour and the short, two-month growing season inhibit the development of all but tiny ground-hugging tundra plants.

Approaching tree line, the spruce and firs become shorter and more sparse. One-sided "flag" or "banner" trees make an appearance, with branches only growing on the leeward side of the trunks. At tree line, only islands of elfin *krummholz* (a German word meaning "crooked wood") succeed in surviving the harsh climate. Growth is slow. A waist-high tree may be hundreds of years old. In fact, one inch of trunk diameter can represent as much as a century of life.

The understory of the subalpine forest usually consists of blueberry or huckleberry ground cover. The delicate pink blossoms of fairy slipper orchids dot the ground in spring. In summer, yellow arnica, brilliant pink fireweed and blue Jacob's ladder abound.

This high, dense forest is the natural habitat of the long-tailed weasel, ermine, red squirrel, least chipmunk, mule deer, elk and the rarely seen black bear.

Estes Cone boasts the most elegant shape of all the peaks in Rocky Mountain National Park

~ 8 ~ Estes Cone

E stes Cone boasts the most elegant shape of all the peaks in Rocky Mountain National Park. This perfect cone rises just to the northeast of Longs Peak.

Its crown of castle-like crags offers the hiker stupendous views over the east side of the park, taking in the Continental Divide, the Mummy Range, Lumpy Ridge, Twin Sisters Peaks, Longs Peak and Estes Park. The scant remains of a turn-of-the-century mine add interest along the way and are the final destination for many hikers.

Trailhead

Drive south from Estes Park on Colorado Highway 7 for 8.9 miles, passing the Lily Lake Visitor Center. Turn right (west) at the Longs Peak area sign and follow the road uphill for 1.0 mile to the large parking area at the Longs Peak Ranger Station. An early start will ensure a place in the lot for this popular trailhead. The trail starts to the left of the ranger station.

Longs Peak Ranger Station to the Eugenia Mine Site

For the first 0.5 mile, the route to Estes Cone follows the broad, popular Longs Peak Trail through a shady coniferous forest. Just after this perfectly conical peak becomes visible

Route

Day hike; 1.4 miles one way to Eugenia Mine Site, 3.3 miles to Estes Cone; moderate

Route	Elevation (ft.)	Distance (mi.)
Longs Peak Trailhead	9,400	0
Longs Peak-Storm Pass Jct	9,700	0.5
Eugenia Mine Site	9,908	1.4
Moore Park Campsite	9,760	1.7
Storm Pass	10,260	2.5
Estes Cone	11,006	3.3

USGS Topographic map: Longs Peak, Colo.

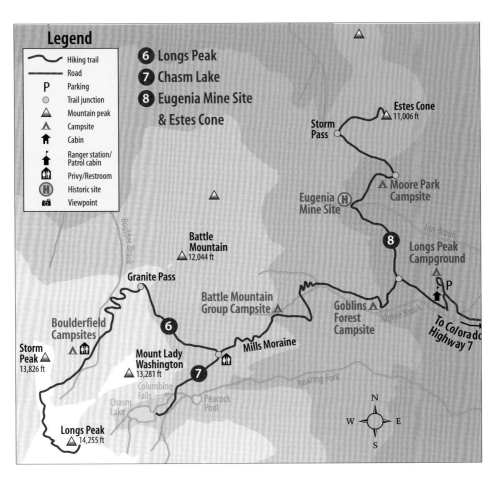

Legend

∿	Hiking trail
—	Road
P	Parking
○	Trail junction
△	Mountain peak
⬟	Campsite
♠	Cabin
♠	Ranger station/Patrol cabin
♿	Privy/Restroom
(H)	Historic site
📷	Viewpoint

6 Longs Peak

7 Chasm Lake

8 Eugenia Mine Site & Estes Cone

Estes Cone 11,006 ft

Storm Pass

Moore Park Campsite

Eugenia (H) Mine Site

Longs Peak Campground

Battle Mountain 12,044 ft

Granite Pass

Battle Mountain Group Campsite

Goblins Forest Campsite

Inn Brook

Alpine Brook

To Colorado Highway 7

Boulderfield Campsites

6

Mills Moraine

Storm Peak 13,826 ft

Mount Lady Washington 13,281 ft

7

Columbine Falls

Chasm Lake

Peacock Pool

Roaring Fork

N W E S

Longs Peak 14,255 ft

---

through the trees, turn right at the marker for Eugenia Mine and Estes Cone.

Bushy-tailed red squirrels are common along this stretch of trail, often to be heard complaining in the pines as you invade their territory.

After veering right, the trail passes through an attractive aspen grove.

In autumn, the golden leaves providing a colorful contrast to the dark green of the tall, thin lodgepole pines. These pines gained their name because early pioneers found them ideal for the construction of log cabins.

The trail traverses the side of Pine Ridge, wandering up and down as it journeys directly toward Estes Cone. The going becomes rougher as the trail is marred by tree roots and rocks. Keep straight on when a spur heads off to the right toward private property and the park boundary.

After 1.4 miles, the trail crosses Inn Brook by a wooden bridge and arrives at the remnants of the log cabin that once belonged to Carl P. Norwall, who worked the fruitless Eugenia Mine in the early 1900s. A scramble past the cabin along the right bank of the stream leads to the meager ruins of the actual mine—an unimpressive pile of tailings and a rusting boiler.

Although there is little to see at the Eugenia Mine site, its location by a pretty stream bordered with a wealth of mosses and wildflowers provides a pleasant spot to relax before returning to the trailhead or continuing to Estes Cone.

Eugenia Mine Site to Storm Pass

The trail meanders downhill from the Eugenia Mine site to Moore Park, a peaceful, flower-strewn meadow in the midst of forest, with Estes Cone rising as a backdrop. Elk or deer often linger here in the early morning, easily spooked by the chatter of hikers.

Moore Park Campsite is well situated at the edge of this idyllic setting, inviting you to pitch a tent and spend the night.

Two miles from Longs Peak Ranger Station, take a hard left turn to join the Storm Pass Trail, ignoring the right-hand branch descending to private property.

The rocky and root-covered trail zigzags upward along the sunny slope toward Storm Pass. A window in the lodgepole pines to the left frames the sheer east face of Longs Peak and its satellite, Mount Lady Washington. Estes Cone, directly ahead, looms ever larger. A few aspens survive among the old, gnarled pines. Large log steps aid in the brisk climb.

As altitude is gained, the trail becomes sandier and the trees shorter and more stunted.

A large cairn and hitching post mark Storm Pass, the saddle between Estes Cone and Battle Mountain. The path straight ahead leads down to Bear Lake Road 4.5 miles away. Follow the sign pointing right for Estes Cone.

Storm Pass to the Summit of Estes Cone

The trail climbs in a series of switchbacks, rapidly disappearing among the rocks that litter the rough terrain. Locating the next cairn—which may not be exactly where you expect it—before leaving the last rock pile enables you to stay on track.

Lodgepole pines now make way for a scattering of limber pines clinging to the scant soil of the dry south-facing slope. These tenacious trees, identified by their gnarled, squat appearance, their pinkish-gray, multiple trunks and needles growing in bundles of five, enjoy life on wind-exposed ridges shunned by other species. Tortured and misshapen ancients, bereft of bark or branches, often provide excellent foregrounds for photographs of the ever-improving views.

A breathless scramble over downed timber and lichen-covered boulders brings you to the summit crags. Infrequent cairns indicate the best route through a trough up the 30-foot wall. Lots of ledges and nicks in the rock make the going easier than it would appear at first. Take care on this section. Even though the exposure is minimal, it can be quite treacherous when wet.

Veer right upon reaching the tiny plateau at the top of the cliffs. The actual highest point is a little to the east.

Estes Cone offers a stupendous 360-degree panorama. To the southwest, you can see Longs Peak and Mount Meeker; to the east, the domes of Twin Sisters Peaks and the distant plains; to the northeast, Lake Estes and the town of Estes Park; to the northwest, the Mummy Range; and to the west, the Continental Divide and the tableland across which Trail Ridge Road, the highest continuously paved highway in the country, winds for 50 miles to Grand Lake.

Eugenia Mine

Only a **tumble-down** homestead, a rusting boiler and an unimpressive pile of tailings remain to tell the story of the Eugenia Mine.

On September 23, 1905, Carl P. Norwall, an affluent miner from California, and his partner, Edward A. Cudahy, discovered the Eugenia lode on the side of Battle Mountain. They recorded their claim in January, 1908, in the Larimer County office of Clerk and Recorder.

Norwall constructed a comfortable log cabin at the mine site, where he lived with his wife and two daughters. His sumptuous furnishings included a piano that was conveyed up the crude track by freight wagon and four horse team. Young mountain guides and visitors from Enos Mills' Longs Peak Inn enjoyed many musical evenings at the cabin.

Despite the fact that Norwall tunneled for more than 1,000 feet into the mountain, he extracted nothing of value. He filed his last claim in 1919, and shortly afterward, moved away from the site. The claim subsequently reverted to Rocky Mountain National Park. Nobody knows where the name "Eugenia" came from. It was most likely the name of Norwall's or Cudahy's wife.

Snow lingers around Ouzel Lake into early June

~ 9 ~ Bluebird Lake

W ild Basin, located in the southeastern corner of Rocky Mountain National Park, contains some of the most pristine countryside in the

park. The trail to Bluebird Lake leads through subalpine forests and across meadows often carpeted with wildflowers. Along the way, it passes tumbling cascades, an area devastated by the massive Ouzel fire of 1978 (the most extensive burn in the park's history) and pretty

Trailhead

From the east end of Estes Park, head south on Colorado Highway 7 for 12.7 miles, passing the Lily Lake Visitor Center and traveling through the community of Meeker Park. Turn right (west) at a large sign indicating Wild Basin Area. After 0.4 mile, take the first right, passing the Sandbeach Lake Trailhead on your right (north). Skirt Copeland Lake and follow this unpaved road for 2.2 miles to where it ends at the Wild Basin Ranger Station. The trailhead is at the southwest corner of the parking lot.

Route

Day hike or overnight; 6.3 miles one way; strenuous

Route	Elevation (ft.)	Distance (mi.)
Trailhead	8,500	0
Copeland Falls	8,515	0.3
Pine Ridge Campsite	8,880	1.4
Calypso Cascades	9,200	1.8
Ouzel Falls	9,450	2.7
Bluebird-Thunder Lake Jct	9,540	3.1
Bluebird-Ouzel Lake Jct	9,940	4.4
Ouzel Lake and Campsite	10,010	4.9
Upper Ouzel Creek Campsite	10,600	6.0
Bluebird Lake	10,978	6.3

USGS Topographic maps: Allens Park, Colo., Isolation Peak, Colo.

left: Ouzel Falls

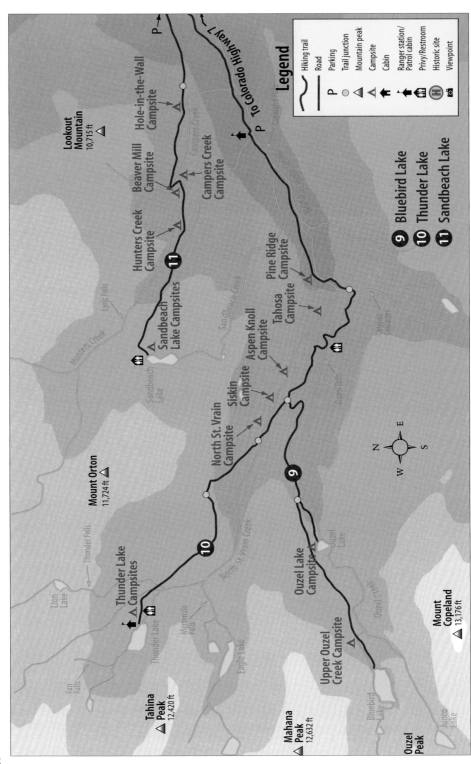

Legend

Hiking trail	
Road	
P	Parking
○	Trail junction
△	Mountain peak
◭	Campsite
◆	Cabin
◆	Ranger station/ Patrol cabin
🚻	Privy/Restroom
H	Historic site
📷	Viewpoint

9 Bluebird Lake
10 Thunder Lake
11 Sandbeach Lake

To Colorado Highway 7

Lookout Mountain 10,715 ft

Hole-in-the-Wall Campsite

Beaver Mill Campsite

Campers Creek Campsite

Hunters Creek Campsite

Sandbeach Lake Campsites

Pine Ridge Campsite

Tahosa Campsite

Aspen Knoll Campsite

Siskin Campsite

North St. Vrain Campsite

Mount Orton 11,724 ft

Thunder Lake Campsites

Ouzel Lake Campsite

Upper Ouzel Creek Campsite

Mount Copeland 13,176 ft

Tahina Peak 12,420 ft

Mahana Peak 12,632 ft

Ouzel Peak

Lyric Falls

Hunters Creek

Sandbeach Lake

Sandbeach Creek

Calypso Cascades

Ouzel Falls

Thunder Falls

Lion Lake

Fan Falls

Mertensia Falls

Eagle Lake

Thunder Lake

North St. Vrain Creek

Ouzel Lake

Ouzel Creek

Bluebird Lake

Junco Lake

Campers Creek

Copeland

N W E S

Ouzel Lake.

Each of the three waterfalls and Ouzel Lake make excellent hiking destinations. Because of the variety of distance options, this trail is not only popular with the avid hiker but with visiting relatives, families with young children, photographers, nature lovers and those interested in nothing more than a gentle stroll.

Trailhead to Copeland Falls

The initial part of the hike parallels North St. Vrain Creek through a sweetly scented montane forest. This level, well-trampled stretch of trail is especially spectacular when fall tints the aspens, maples, alders and thickets of shrubs gold, rust and orange.

The name of the creek comes from the French brothers Ceran and Marcellin St. Vrain who, in 1837, established a trading post on the South Platte River to the southwest of Greeley, which became known as Fort St. Vrain. There they did a lively trade in beaver pelts with trappers and Plains Indians. The St. Vrain Creek enters the river just above the fort.

In less than half a mile, the trail sends a branch off to the left for Upper and Lower Copeland Falls. Although modest compared to Calypso Cascades and Ouzel Falls, the silvery water bounces over a series of low cascades, offering a soothing backdrop while you take a break. A short side loop meanders along the water's edge past several perfect picnic rocks before reemerging a little farther up the trail. Be sure to stay on designated walkways and avoid areas closed for revegetation.

Copeland Falls to Calypso Cascades

After 1.4 miles you come to signs pointing right for Pine Ridge, Tahosa, Aspen Knoll and Siskin backcountry campsites; continue straight ahead.

Cross North St. Vrain Creek by a sturdy wooden bridge typical of those on the more popular trails in Rocky Mountain National Park.

The trail rises at an eager pace for 0.4 mile through the thick subalpine forest, leaving North St. Vrain Creek to follow its tributary, Cony Creek.

Just before you arrive at Calypso Cascades, 1.8 miles from the trailhead, the Allens Park Trail merges from the left. Bear right at this T-intersection.

Although lacking a single impressive drop, Calypso Cascades displays awe-inspiring grace and vigor as it hurtles down a 600-foot-long stretch of white water laced with massive boulders and tree-topped outcroppings. It is particularly spectacular in late spring and early summer, when the volume of snowmelt in the high country is at its greatest. Large outcroppings provide opportunities to rest and enjoy the superb river scenery.

The cascade derives its name from the exquisite pink Calypso orchid or fairy slipper, which blooms nearby in June.

Calypso Cascades to Ouzel Falls

The trail crosses three strands of Cony Creek by a series of footbridges and, almost immediately, emerges from the

---

Wild Basin

Wild Basin is the large fan-shaped valley in the southeastern corner of Rocky Mountain National Park. Carved by glaciers thousands of years ago, it is bordered on the west by the rugged summits of the Continental Divide and on the north by Longs Peak. Many consider it to be the most beautiful region in the park.

No one knows how Wild Basin got its name. Maybe Enos Mills, the park's founding father, was the first to call it "wild." The area still retains much of its unmarred character due to the wise decision of the Park Service fifty years ago to preserve it as wilderness.

Four major hiking trails lead past tumbling waterfalls, bubbling streams and breathtaking vistas to picturesque tarns nestled at the foot of soaring peaks.

Its flower-strewn meadows and subalpine forests are home to mule deer, elk, mountain lions, black bears, golden and bald eagles, several kinds of hawks and many of the park's smaller mammals and birds.

Prehistoric Native Americans traveled through Wild Basin in order to cross the Continental Divide. Remains of camps have been discovered near Thunder Lake at the base of Boulder-Grand Pass.

living trees onto an area deforested by the massive Ouzel fire of 1978. Charred lodgepole pines, stripped of branches and bark, march defiantly up the hillside. Blackened stumps decay into strange and photogenic configurations.

Anything but bleak and gloomy, this massive cemetery is filled with the wonders of nature's rebirth. Young spruce find room to breathe among the dead pines. Wildflowers dot the slope, including the wild rose and pervasive bright pink fireweed. Observant hikers may spot the regal Colorado blue columbine, the state's official floral symbol. Watch also for mule deer browsing on the new shrubs and the yellow-bellied marmot lazing its life away atop a sunny boulder. Views extend to the rocky summits of Longs Peak and Mount Meeker, which peek over the ridge to the north of Wild Basin.

The trail continues up the valley, with well-placed log steps and switchbacks making for easy altitude gain.

Aspens and the occasional Rocky Mountain maple turn shades of yellow and red in the autumn. Picnic spots abound, with extensive vistas over the burned area.

The roar of Ouzel Falls announces its presence before you see it. Magnificent at first sight, the foaming water tumbling 50 feet in a single sheet down a rock slab.

Scramble along a track to the left of Ouzel Creek and get close enough to feel its cooling spray.

Park founder, Enos Mills, named the falls, creek and

lake after the water ouzel or American dipper, which is often seen dancing on midstream rocks or diving into the rapids in this area.

Ouzel Falls to Bluebird-Thunder Lake Junction

Bridge Ouzel Creek in front of the falls and in 100 yards, veer left by a beautiful picnic rock with the best views so far down the valley and across to the burn.

Briefly switchback downhill and travel beneath a crag tinged with colorful patches

of lichen. Tufts of greenish-white alumroot sprout from fissures in the wall.

Just over three miles into the hike, you come to a junction. Thunder Lake is off to the right and Ouzel and Bluebird lakes are to the left.

Bluebird-Thunder Lake Junction to Ouzel Lake

Head left and ascend through spruce and fir trees for a short distance. The trail makes a sharp left turn and hastens up an old road bed toward the prow of a medial moraine

Wild Basin Reservoirs

A century ago, Joe Mills, brother of Enos Mills, sat on top of Longs Peak sketching Wild Basin. He referred to it as "Land of Many Waters," a suitable appellation for an area dotted with numerous lakes and crisscrossed by streams.

A local rancher called Emma Arbuckle was the first to utilize this valuable resource. In 1902, searching for water after a dry summer, she filed on five reservoirs in Wild Basin and began to construct dams at Bluebird and Pear lakes.

Two years later, the Arbuckle Reservoir Company purchased the water rights and built a third reservoir at Sandbeach Lake. Between 1912 and 1919, the company replaced a rubble dam at Bluebird Lake with a more substantial structure of steel-reinforced concrete. Because of the lack of sand at Bluebird Lake, the contractor used mules to pack in a rock crusher and an old automobile engine to power it.

When complete, the dam was 200 feet long and 56 feet high, forming a 22-acre reservoir.

In October, 1933, the company sold the rights to the Arbuckle Reservoirs to the City of Longmont. Later inspections proved the dams unsafe and, despite repairs, they were abandoned during the 1970s.

In 1987, Rocky Mountain National Park paid $1.9 million for Sandbeach, Pear and Bluebird reservoirs. In order to restore Bluebird Lake to its natural condition, work crews carefully broke the concrete dam apart with a hydraulic hammer and employed a helicopter to remove tons of debris from the site. A less serious undertaking, the smaller rock-fill dams at Sandbeach and Pear lakes were demolished and the detritus was buried on site.

Today, only the telltale "bathtub rings" around the lakes reveal their former reservoir status.

Ouzel Lake nestles within a thick growth of conifers, which survived the 1978 burn

Calypso Orchids

You can easily identify the exquisite fairy slipper or Calypso orchid by its inflated white, slipper-shaped lip crowned by thin, rose-pink petals. Purple stripes adorn the inside of the slipper and fluffy yellow hairs with purple spots decorate the top. One delicate flower hangs at the tip of a reddish stalk, two to six inches high, with a single, glossy leaf at the base.

The fairy slipper grows on decaying wood and moist, mossy ground in forests of lodgepole pine, Engelmann spruce and subalpine fir. It blooms soon after the snow melts in late May or early June.

The name Calypso orchid comes from the sea nymph "Calypso" of Homer's *Odyssey*, who entertained Homer on his way back from Troy.

It is against the law to pick flowers in Rocky Mountain National Park. Enjoy this lovely orchid, but take only photographs.

formed by the union of two branches of the Wild Basin Glacier thousands of years ago. Completely ravaged by the Ouzel fire, only a few pearly everlasting, pink clover, ragwort, fireweed and some short aspens decorate the slope.

As you crest the escarpment, the trail swerves right, striking west along the naked ridge top. Unbroken views extend in all directions. Longs Peak and Mount Meeker loom to the north of the glacier-gouged cleft of Wild Basin. In the east, you can trace the trough cut by North St. Vrain Creek through the foothills to the plains. Tamina Peak and Mount Alice, summits of the rugged Continental Divide in the west, are likely to be speckled with snow late into July. To your left, Mount Copeland towers above the shallow Ouzel Creek drainage.

Like ghosts on a battlefield, blackened lodgepole

pines either stand where they died or have toppled to decay, uprooted. Occasional spruce struggle to reclaim the land.

During the long, slow climb along the moraine, you see more and more of the 1,050 acres scorched in 1978, until the landscape appears unearthly.

The trail veers slightly left to follow the direction of Ouzel Creek into the hanging valley. To the right, a few wispy aspens add specks of fall color to the heavily ravaged eastern flank of Mahana Peak.

At 4.4 miles into the hike, take a turnoff to reach little Ouzel Lake. A half-mile of pleasant walking leads through arnica, aspen daisies, cow parsnips, fireweed, ragwort, and wild gooseberry and raspberry bushes to little Ouzel Lake. Ouzel Lake Campsite and an outhouse are off to the right within the thick growth of conifers surrounding the lake that somehow escaped the conflagration.

Above Ouzel Lake rise Mount Copeland to the south, Mahana Peak to the north and snow-dotted Ouzel Peak far to the west.

Ouzel Lake to Upper Ouzel Creek Campsite

For Bluebird Lake, retrace your steps to the intersection and go left. Traverse a talus slope above lily-covered Chickadee Pond, getting a brief glimpse of Ouzel Lake through the trees.

An erratic climb up the moraine above Ouzel Lake is punctuated by moderately level stretches through a se-

ries of meadows profuse with orange and pink Indian paintbrush, larkspur, arnica, elephant's head, bistort, ragwort, harebells, chimingbells and delicate yellow snow lilies.

Cross a boulder field with a good view of a waterfall dropping from Junco Lake, reenter the trees, and come to an outhouse and Upper Ouzel Creek Campsite.

Upper Ouzel Creek Campsite to Bluebird Lake

Planks aid progress across a flower-strewn marsh and then a rough-hewn bridge crosses Ouzel Creek.

Skirting a rocky promontory, you are surrounded by the ephemeral beauty of mountain wildflowers. Flora enthusiasts will rejoice in the addition of the blue gentian, Fremont geranium, Western yellow paintbrush and white bog orchid to the throng.

The trail snakes mercilessly upward next to the cliff, following cairns up a sloping stone slab. From an ideal picnic spot, you catch sight of Longs Peak peeping over the ridge to the north of Wild Basin and the plains stretching to infinity in the east.

When you reach the top of the outcrop, head left and pass through a dense thicket of krummholz. The trail continues to rise, following cairns over occasional patches of bedrock. A few final switchbacks up a narrow canyon deposit you on some rocks overlooking Bluebird Lake.

Desolate and magnificent, Bluebird Lake lies in a cirque gnawed out of sheer rock by ice age glaciers. Ouzel Peak

dominates the scene, its naked gray flanks rising abruptly from the dark water. A few ragged snowfields clinging to the weathered mountainside provide a contrast to the gray color of the rock.

Only a faint "bathtub ring" on the rumpled boulders and outcroppings around the tarn attests to its former use as a reservoir. In the late 1980s, Rocky Mountain National Park purchased the property from the City of Longmont and, with the use of helicopters, removed every sign of the dam confining the reservoir.

American Dipper

As you hike by fast-flowing creeks or waterfalls, you may see the entertaining American dipper or "water ouzel." This sooty gray, robin-sized bird displays a most unusual habit. It perches on midstream rocks and bobs up and down repeatedly as it watches for food. Upon spotting an aquatic insect, it dives into the rapids, running along the bottom with half-open wings and "swimming" underwater.

The dipper constructs a nest of moss and grass in a rocky crevice a few feet above the level of the stream. There, it incubates three to six white eggs.

The loud, bubbling song of the dipper carries over the roar of the water. During the winter, the dipper migrates from the mountains to a lowland riparian environment.

Thunder Lake lies within an amphitheater of gray peaks

~ 10 ~ Thunder Lake

Thunder Lake nestles in a natural amphitheater of rugged peaks deep within Wild Basin, in the southeastern corner of Rocky Mountain National Park. Despite its lengthy round-trip distance of 13.6 miles, the gentle elevation gain makes the hike considerably less difficult than the mileage would imply. Six backcountry campsites scattered along the route offer a variety of overnight options, including the possibility of combining this trip with one to Bluebird Lake or other hiking destinations in the valley.

Trailhead

From the east end of Estes Park, head south on Colorado Highway 7 for 12.7 miles, passing the Lily Lake Visitor Center and traveling through the community of Meeker Park. Turn right (west) at a large sign indicating Wild Basin Area. After 0.4 mile, take the first right, passing the Sandbeach Lake Trailhead on your right (north). Skirt Copeland Lake and follow this unpaved road for 2.2 miles to where it ends at the Wild Basin Ranger Station. The trailhead is at the southwest corner of the parking lot.

Trailhead to Copeland Falls

The first part of the hike to Thunder Lake is a level stroll to the right side of North St. Vrain

Route		
Day hike or overnight; 6.8 miles one way; strenuous		
Route	Elevation (ft.)	Distance (mi.)
Trailhead	8,500	0
Copeland Falls	8,515	0.3
Pine Ridge Campsite	8,880	1.4
Calypso Cascades	9,200	1.8
Ouzel Falls	9,450	2.7
Bluebird-Thunder Lake Jct	9,540	3.1
North St. Vrain Campsite	9,560	3.5
Thunder Lake and Campsite	10,574	6.8
USGS Topographic maps: Allens Park, Colo.; Isolation Peak, Colo.		

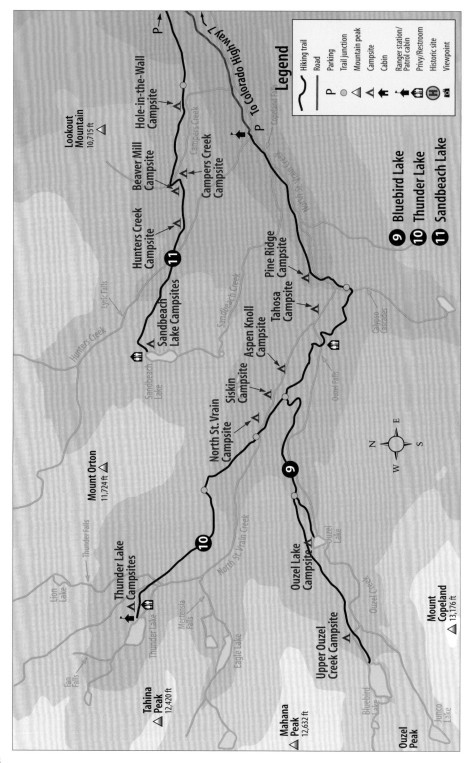

Lookout Mountain 10,715 ft

Beaver Mill Campsite

Hole-in-the-Wall Campsite

Campers Creek

Campers Creek Campsite

To Colorado Highway 7

Copeland Falls

North St. Vrain Creek

P →

P

Hunters Creek Campsite

11

Lyric Falls

Sandbeach Lake Campsites

Hunters Creek

Sandbeach Creek

Pine Ridge Campsite

Tahosa Campsite

Calypso Cascades

Sandbeach Lake

Aspen Knoll Campsite

Siskin Campsite

North St. Vrain Campsite

Ouzel Falls

Ouzel Lake

9

Mount Orton 11,724 ft

North St. Vrain Creek

Ouzel Lake Campsite

Thunder Falls

10

Lion Lake

Thunder Lake Campsites

Fan Falls

Thunder Lake

Mertensia Falls

Eagle Lake

Ouzel Creek

Upper Ouzel Creek Campsite

Mount Copeland 13,176 ft

Tahina Peak 12,420 ft

Mahana Peak 12,632 ft

Bluebird Lake

Ouzel Peak

Junco Lake

N
W — E
S

Legend

	Hiking trail
	Road
P	Parking
●	Trail junction
△	Mountain peak
◬	Campsite
♠	Cabin
♠♦	Ranger station/ Patrol cabin
🚻	Privy/Restroom
Ⓗ	Historic site
📷	Viewpoint

9 Bluebird Lake

10 Thunder Lake

11 Sandbeach Lake

Creek. Popular with the young and old alike, this broad section of trail can be crowded during sunny summer days. An early start will ensure peace and quiet and a parking space in the often-crowded lot.

A third of a mile from the trailhead, a rough track heads off to the left for Copeland Falls.

This was named after pioneer John B. Copeland who, in 1896, homesteaded 320 acres around present-day Copeland Lake. He built an earth-fill dam and diverted water from North St. Vrain Creek to enlarge the lake. He stocked it with trout and charged visiting fishermen to use his private reserve or "Copeland Park."

With only a ten-foot drop and several smaller riffles, Copeland Falls is less impressive than its more spectacular neighbors farther into the hike. Nevertheless, it is the only waterfall actually on North St. Vrain Creek, and numerous granite slabs along its shore provide excellent picnic spots.

Copeland Falls to Calypso Cascades

The wide and well-maintained path ascends gently through shady lodgepole pine and Engelmann spruce. In the fall, trembling aspens and Rocky Mountain maples light up the forest with crimson and gold. The sound of the river grows louder each time the trail approaches its banks and fades as it meanders away.

After 1.4 miles, a spur veers off to the right. This parallels North St. Vrain Creek to

Ouzel Fire

On August 9, 1978, lightning struck a tree near Ouzel Lake, sparking the largest forest fire in the history of Rocky Mountain National Park. In all, it burned 1,050 acres in the center of Wild Basin.

It started as a small burn and the Park Service, recognizing the ecological importance of natural fires, permitted it to smolder without human interference. A couple of weeks later, strong winds escalated the blaze. Due to public pressure, the park service immediately brought in fire fighters, who succeeded in controlling it with the help of rain and snow.

On September 15, westerly winds gusting at 30 mph aggravated the conflagration once again, causing it to rage eastward toward the town of Allenspark. As 350 terrified residents prepared to evacuate their homes, 500 fire fighters fought night and day, finally confining the blaze within the park boundary and extinguishing it by mid-October.

The Ouzel fire not only ravaged 1,050 acres of forest but threatened private property, seriously questioning the wisdom of the non-intervention policy.

Naturalists are well aware of the role fire plays in the maintenance of a balanced and healthy ecosystem. By ridding the forest of dead and downed trees, fires create clearings which provide a rich variety of habitats for wildlife and colonizing plants such as lodgepole pine, aspen and fireweed.

Whether or not natural fires should be suppressed is an ongoing dilemma. After the massive Yellowstone fire of 1988, each national park was required to develop a detailed fire management policy. Rocky Mountain National Park now allows naturally occurring fires to burn in certain prescribed zones only after taking into consideration such criteria as wind velocity, ground moisture, available equipment and personnel, and proximity to private land.

A log patrol cabin stands beside Thunder Lake

rejoin the trail farther up, bypassing Calypso Cascades and Ouzel Falls and providing access to Pine Ridge, Tahosa, Aspen Knoll and Siskin backcountry campsites.

The preferred route is straight on, crossing North St. Vrain Creek by an elaborate wooden bridge.

Gaining 300 feet in 0.4 mile with the help of carefully constructed log steps, the trail climbs through thick subalpine forest, with a rich sprinkling of blueberry ground cover—a rust-red carpet in the fall.

After passing the confluence with Cony Creek (named for the pika or cony),

North St. Vrain Creek is left behind to rumble in the valley base, a melody you will hear periodically throughout the remainder of the trip to Thunder Lake.

At 1.8 miles into the hike, you arrive at a T-junction, with the Allens Park Trail coming in from the left. Take a right and Calypso Cascades lies directly ahead.

In a 600-foot-long stretch of rapids, Cony Creek careens over a series of low falls, dividing and rebraiding itself as it tumbles around massive boulders. Flora enthusiasts will delight in the delicate pink Calypso orchid (or fairy slipper), from which the falls

derives its name. They adorn the banks in June.

Calypso Cascades to Ouzel Falls

After spanning Cony Creek on three sturdy footbridges, the trail traverses a slope devastated by the massive Ouzel fire of August 1978, the largest burn in the park's history. Skeleton lodgepole pines, blackened and denuded of bark or branches, dot the entire hillside. Some still stand erect while others recline in various stages of decay.

Indications of nature's regeneration are everywhere. Infant spruce thrive among the charred stumps. Fireweed, one of the first plants to recolonize an area, turns the summer slope into a sea of brilliant pink. Columbines, globeflowers, pearly everlasting and thistles bloom alongside the trail. Wild raspberry bushes hang with delicious red berries in the early fall.

Mule deer browse on the wealth of new shrubs. Listen for the shrill chirps of the yellow-bellied marmot sunning itself atop a nearby boulder. Views, once blocked by trees, now extend north over Wild Basin to Mount Meeker and Longs Peak.

The trail switchbacks up through sufficient aspens and Rocky Mountain maple to make this a colorful fall hike. Occasional rocky outcroppings afford excellent vistas back down the valley, allowing an appreciation of the extent of the destruction caused by the burn.

The thundering of water welcomes you to Ouzel Falls, a definite highlight of the trip and the final destination for many hikers. In one of the most dramatic cataracts in the park, Ouzel Creek slices through a narrow sluiceway and plummets 50 feet down a sheer rock wall into a boulder-packed catch basin. It then swirls madly as it foams over a series of lesser drops in its fervor to join North St. Vrain Creek.

Ouzel Falls gets its name from the American dipper or water ouzel, a sooty gray wren-shaped bird often seen bobbing up and down comically on midstream islets or diving into the whitewater in search of insects.

For the best view of the falls, clamber along a faint track up the left side of Ouzel Creek. Take care, the rocks can be wet and slippery.

An outhouse and hitchrack are located near the trail just before the falls.

Ouzel Falls to Bluebird-Thunder Lake Junction

The trail crosses a bridge—complete with handrails on both sides—over Ouzel Creek and curls past a stone slab, which presents breathtaking panoramas of precipitous Longs Peak and Mount Meeker towering over Wild Basin. In autumn, golden aspens on the ridge to the far side of the valley provide a stunning contrast to the dark turquoise of the evergreens.

The path descends in a couple of switchbacks around some boulders and traverses beneath an overhanging cliff face. Patches of orange lichen brighten the rock wall and small crevices nurture tufts of greenish-white alumroot.

After 0.4 mile from Ouzel Falls, you reach an intersection, with Bluebird Lake off to the left and Thunder Lake to the right; bear right.

Bluebird-Thunder Lake Junction to Thunder Lake

The trail meanders through a fairly flat area, then rises gently between stately Engelmann spruce and subalpine fir. At 3.5 miles into the hike, bridge North St. Vrain Creek and merge with the shortcut from down valley, continuing straight.

Switchbacking to the right of the broad drainage, the observant hiker will notice the inclusion of the hardy limber pine and the occasional dwarf juniper among the species of the subalpine forest.

Views southward through gaps in the trees improve with the steady climb. Now you can see almost the full length of the ridge, deforested by the 1978 Ouzel fire, with the rounded form of Mount Copeland protruding behind. Westward, glistening snow-

Bald eagles

fields speckle the gray, barren flanks and weather-beaten cliffs of the Continental Divide's wild summits. Far below, North St. Vrain Creek babbles its way toward the plains.

After 4.8 miles, the Lion Lake Trail splits off to the right. Zigzag again and continue high above the valley floor.

Green lichen splotches the many boulders and outcroppings alongside the wide and easily negotiated trail. Watch for the tiny stonecrop growing in the gravelly soil, its clusters of star-shaped yellow flowers framed by reddish rosettes of fleshy leaves.

An area of stunted trees allows you to discern rugged Isolation Peak and the raw angularity of the Eagles Beak guarding the head of Wild Basin. Directly ahead, Tanima Peak soars over unseen Thunder Lake.

Traverse a couple of side streams, their banks studded with aspen daisies, American bistort and arnica. On a somewhat level section, pass a clearing and pond to the left.

Finally, you reach a junction, with an outhouse off to the right, the group and individual campsites straight ahead, and Thunder Lake downhill to the left, past the stock campsite.

The trail emerges from the trees and crosses a lush meadow at the eastern end of the lake.

A scene of stark and desolate beauty confronts you. Breezes funneled over Boulder-Grand Pass animate the reflections of the amphitheater of gray peaks in the tarn's steely surface. At the tarn's

Copeland Falls is a favorite picnic spot for many people

western tip, a massive buttress, St. Pat's Cathedral, juts between Tanima Peak and Pilot Mountain.

An unmaintained track continues around the right shore of the lake and aids in the slow scramble past Lake of Many Winds to Boulder-Grand Pass. The remains of Native American camps discovered in this area indicate that this was most likely an ancient crossing of the Continental Divide.

The log patrol cabin at Thunder Lake is locked when not occupied by a park ranger.

Notice the profusion of blooming elephant's head on the meadow near the hut.

Each flower consists of a spike of numerous purplish-pink blossoms resembling minute elephant heads, complete with ears and long trunks.

For those who have obtained the necessary permit, a night spent at the Thunder Lake backcountry campsite holds the promise of solitude, further exploration and a real wilderness experience.

A stroll around the shore reveals views of the summit of Longs Peak beyond Mount Meeker

~ 11 ~ Sandbeach Lake

Snug beneath the rugged southern flanks of Longs Peak and Mount Meeker, Sandbeach Lake boasts a wide sandy beach as its main attraction. Only the

telltale high-water mark reveals the lake's former status as a reservoir for the City of Longmont.

The trail to Sandbeach Lake maintains a moderate grade through mixed woodland along the sunny south-facing slope to the north of Wild Basin. A wealth of aspens makes this an excellent fall hike. Clear when other trails in the area are still snowbound, this is also a good early-season trip. Five backcountry

campsites placed at regular intervals along the route offer an easy beginner backpack. Camping permits should be obtained in advance from the Backcountry Office at (970) 586-1242.

Trailhead

Drive two miles north from Allens Park or 12.7 miles south from the east end of Estes Park on Colorado Highway 7. Turn west at a large sign indicating the Wild Basin Area and travel for 0.4 miles, passing the Wild Basin Lodge on the left (south). Veer right with the sign for Rocky Mountain National Park Wild Basin. The parking lot for Sandbeach Lake Trailhead is immediately to the right (north).

Route

Day hike or overnight; 4.2 miles one way; moderate

Route	Elevation (ft.)	Distance (mi.)
Trailhead	8,320	0
Meeker Park Trail Jct	9,200	1.5
Hole-in-the-Wall Campsite	9,240	1.9
Campers Creek Campsite	9,600	2.3
Beaver Mill Campsite	9,640	3.0
Hunters Creek Campsite	9,760	3.3
Sandbeach Lake and Campsite	10,283	4.2

USGS Topographic map: Allens Park, Colo.

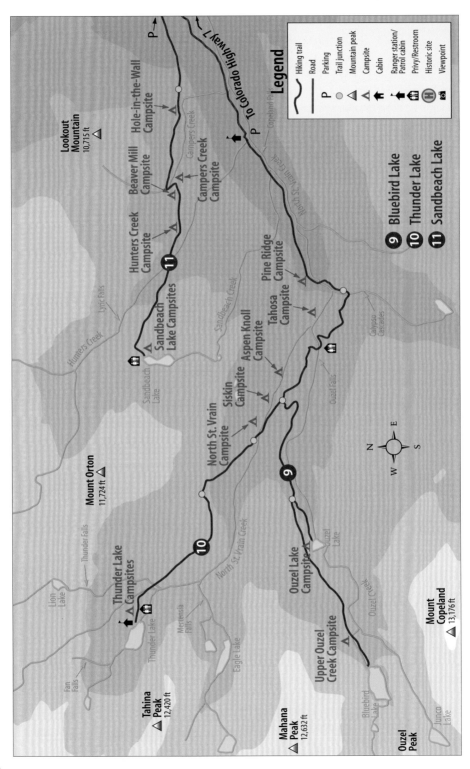

Sandbeach Lake boasts a wide, sandy beach as its main attraction

Trailhead to Meeker Park Trail Junction

The trail starts its journey with a brief, brisk climb along the sunny south-facing slope of Copeland Moraine.

This ridge was formed from debris deposited thousands of years ago during one of the retreats of the Wild Basin Glacier. Copeland Moraine, Copeland Mountain (rising to the south of the valley) and Copeland Lake (lying just below to your left) were named for pioneer, John B. Copeland, who stocked the lake with trout and charged visitors to fish there around the turn of the century.

After a couple of switchbacks, the trail moderates to the gentle grade it maintains for the majority of the remainder of the trip. Wooden steps packed with soil make for easy progress through an open montane forest of ponderosa pines and Douglas firs. Only a few goldenrod cling to the dry slope.

As you gain altitude, views extend over Wild Basin to the peaks flanking its southern and western margins. North St. Vrain Creek meanders through the valley, its journey obstructed by numerous beaver ponds.

The trail zigzags to the top of the moraine and, 1.5 miles into the hike, passes a spur heading off to the right to Meeker Park.

Meeker Park Trail Junction to Hunters Creek Campsite

Continue straight along the crest of the ridge and skirt a

Gray Jay

The gray jay is well known to anyone who has ever camped in the Rocky Mountains of Colorado. It is popularly called the "camp robber" because of its habit of hovering brazenly around campsites during mealtimes and snatching as much food as it can carry off.

Measuring about a foot in length, this fluffy bird has a long tail and a short bill. It has a dark gray back, a lighter belly, a whitish collar and forehead and a brown crown. Its whistled *pwee-ah* is considerably less harsh than the call of its relative, the Clark's nutcracker.

The gray jay nests very early in the season, laying three to five greenish-gray, spotted eggs and often incubates them with snow on its back.

craggy promontory on Lookout Mountain. Notice the bright orange lichen decorating the rocks to your right.

The soft, sandy trail passes through a shady tunnel of pines and spruce. In the autumn, trembling aspens enliven the dark green of the evergreens with a brilliant gold.

The cliffs of Lookout Mountain tower far above. Many hikers imagine that they see faces in the strange weathering of the rocks.

At 1.9 miles from the trailhead, a sign for Hole-in-the-Wall indicates the first of a string of backcountry campsites. This, or Campers Creek 0.4 mile later, make excellent base camps for the young or inexperienced backpacker.

The trail borders Campers Creek, then crosses it via a two-plank bridge. Swing left and traverse to the crest of another ridge. Veer right, ascending with the help of intermittent stone steps. A series of short ups and downs leads through ribbons of aspens and past tiny ponds in a low-lying clearing to the left.

Three miles into the hike, the trail passes Beaver Mill Campsite and, 0.3 mile farther on, Hunters Creek Campsite.

Hunters Creek Campsite to Sandbeach Lake

The trail climbs through lodgepole pines and Engelmann spruce, then crosses lively Hunters Creek.

This creek descends from Keplinger Lake, located high in a cirque beneath the summit of Pagoda Mountain. Hunters Creek was named in 1908 by Dean Babcock, who

Elk can often be seen grazing in this area

found a carving on a log that depicted a party of white hunters.

Steps cut in the bedrock aid in the final steep ascent to the lake.

It is immediately obvious why this body of water is called Sandbeach Lake. A broad stretch of fine, glacially ground rock sprawls around its shoreline. In 1987, Rocky Mountain National Park purchased this and two other reservoirs in Wild Basin from the City of Longmont for $1.9 million. With the dam removed, Sandbeach Lake is being allowed to return to its natural condition. Its southern orientation is an open invitation to the hiker to bask in the warm sunshine.

Across the outlet stream at the far end of the lake, a wonderful panorama extends over Wild Basin to the weather-beaten mountains of the Continental Divide.

A stroll around the left shore provides views north to Longs Peak and the gray slopes of Mount Meeker.

Paths between the trees lead to the individual and group campsites, an outhouse and the inlet creek—the campers' water supply. A profusion of white milkweed, goldenrod, aspen daisies and alpine avens grows on a little grassy patch near the inlet.

Steller's Jay

A frequently observed inhabitant of the Colorado Rockies is the Steller's jay, a handsome blue and black bird with white facial streaks and an impressive crest. Somewhat more bashful than its cousins, the Clark's nutcracker and the gray jay, it nevertheless will miss few opportunities to steal food from a picnic table or campsite.

You will often see a Steller's jay sitting quietly in a tree and then be surprised by its raucous *shaack shaack shaack* as it flies to a more advantageous spot from which to observe the goings on.

Tiny Gem Lake hides in a ridgetop pocket on Lumpy Ridge

~ 12 ~ Gem Lake

This short ascent leading through the surreal granite formations of Lumpy Ridge is perfect for hikers of all ability levels, including families with young children. It offers wonderful views and an intimate look at the diverse plants and animals of the montane ecosystem.

The low elevation and southern exposure make for a hot, thirsty climb during the summer, but render the route accessible when many of the other trails in the park are snowbound.

Trailhead

From Elkhorn Avenue in Estes Park, take Mac-Gregor Avenue north. Cross US Highway 34 Bypass (Wonderview Avenue) and proceed for 0.8 mile to the gate of MacGregor Ranch. Here the road makes a sharp right turn and becomes Devils Gulch Road. Go straight through the wooden entrance to MacGregor Ranch and stay on the paved road for 0.8 mile as it winds through the ranch property.

Parking spaces at the Twin Owls Trailhead are in high demand; arrive early. The Gem Lake Trail starts at the eastern end of the parking lot, near the outhouses.

The Devils Gulch Trailhead provides an alternative. It is located 0.7 mile past the entrance to MacGregor Ranch on the left side of Devils Gulch Road. This involves a 0.2-mile longer hike and a 180-foot greater elevation gain.

Route

Day hike; 1.8 miles one way; easy

Route	Elevation (ft.)	Distance (mi.)
Twin Owls Trailhead	7,920	0
Devils Gulch Jct	8,160	0.8
Gem Lake	8,830	1.8
Balanced Rock Option		
Balanced Rock	8,760	1.8 (From Gem Lake)

USGS Topographic map: Estes Park, Colo.

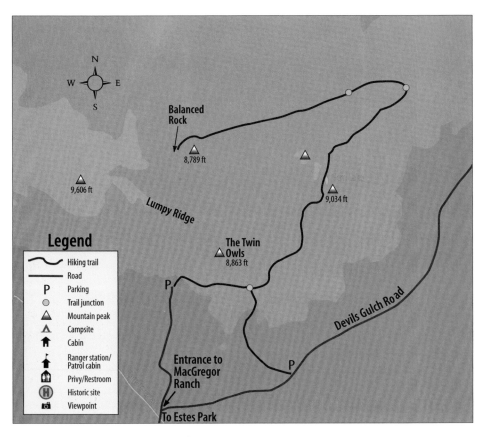

Trailhead to Devils Gulch Trail Junction

The Twin Owls Trailhead lies at the foot of the two giant monoliths that resemble these birds when viewed from the south.

The trail starts through aspens, which, because of the southerly aspect and low elevation, change colors later in the fall than most of the deciduous trees in the park.

Shortly, the first of several climbers' access tracks veers off to the left for Lower Twin Owls.

The trail to Gem Lake swerves to the right and begins its brisk ascent toward Gem Lake with the help of occasional switchbacks.

Massive granite crags, weathered into strange and fascinating shapes, tower high above, and smaller formations begin to appear alongside the trail.

The sweet fragrance of ponderosa pine fills the air. This is the dominant tree of the montane zone and has three- to six-inch-long needles in bundles of two or three.

The many dead or dying ponderosa visible during this hike are the work of the mountain pine beetle, a bark-boring insect that ravages pine forests periodically. Many of the standing dead were killed during a major epidemic in the late 1970s. Like natural fires, pine beetle infestations play an important role in thinning the forest. The dead pines make excellent homes for numerous species of insects and birds.

Douglas firs mix with the pines. Identify these by their cones, which have three-pointed bracts sticking out from under the scales.

Two kinds of juniper grow alongside the trail. Rocky Mountain juniper is a multi-branched evergreen with needles divided into tiny, scale-like segments that lie flattened against the twiglets. The dwarf juniper is a short shrub with sharp, prickly needles at the ends of the branches. Both plants bear bright blue berry-like cones.

Lumpy Ridge is composed of strange granite formations

Abert's Squirrel

The Abert's squirrel is one of the more unusual Colorado mammals. This ponderosa forest resident is easily identified by its conspicuous ear tassels, dark coloring and somewhat larger size than the more common red squirrel.

Unlike most tree squirrels, Abert's squirrels do not hoard food for the winter. Their diet changes with the seasons. During the summer, they feed almost exclusively on ponderosa pine cones. They turn to the sweet inner bark of small twigs for nourishment during winter, when pine cones are buried under layers of snowfall.

Watch for the tassel-eared Abert's squirrel. Darker and larger than the common red squirrel, this distinctive mammal lives exclusively in ponderosa forests.

Many kinds of birds frequent the montane region. Look for mountain chickadees, yellow-rumped warblers, mountain bluebirds, northern flickers and the ubiquitous Clark's nutcracker. Keep an eye open for hawks and other raptors patrolling from the air. Parts of Lumpy Ridge are designated raptor nesting sites and may be closed to the public during spring and early summer. These areas are clearly posted.

During the initial part of the hike, views extend through the widely spaced pines across the MacGregor Ranch to 14,255-foot-high Longs Peak, the king of the park.

After a few hundred yards, another climbers' access branches off to the left, mounting to Upper Twin Owls, Bowels of the Owls and Gollum's Arch; continue straight ahead.

The trail gradually swerves left to enter a gully between Lumpy Ridge and a small knoll to the south. After 0.8 mile, the trail climbing from Devils Gulch Parking Area merges from the right; keep straight on.

Devils Gulch Junction to Gem Lake

Meander through the Douglas firs, ponderosa pines and

junipers, and then ascend a shady ridge with gnarled granite formations to the right. A side track leads to an overlook on the rocks.

The trail sweeps round to the left toward the main bulk of Lumpy Ridge and climbs in broad switchbacks between huge chunks of bedrock.

As it straightens, the best view of this hike stretches to the south and east. You can easily spot Lake Estes, Lily Mountain, Twin Sisters Peaks, Estes Cone, Longs Peak, Flattop Mountain and Hallett Peak. Level slabs of granite provide excellent picnic benches, providing ample opportunity to take in the uninterrupted panorama.

Continue to work your way around the eastern side of the mountain, crossing a section between Lumpy Ridge and another knobby outcropping to the right.

The trail descends briefly and then carves through a shady ravine bordered on both sides by towering cliffs.

Wild raspberries ripen within arm's reach during August, thriving in the cool, moist atmosphere. Maples and aspens appear alongside a tiny stream, adding brilliant gold and red in the fall.

Switch back and forth up the wall at the head of the miniature canyon by rocks decorated with light green or orange splashes of lichen and patches of green moss.

Next to the trail stands one of the more unusual rock formations in this area of weird and wonderful examples of nature's handiwork. Resembling Paul Bunyan's boot, with its rounded hole in the sole, it provides an almost mandatory photo opportunity.

A series of zigzags makes for rapid altitude gain between the rock sculptures.

A solar-powered outhouse, balanced on the edge of a slope, announces your proximity to the ridgetop pocket that contains Gem Lake. Views extend to Twin Sisters Peaks and as far south as Longs Peak.

Unlike the typical alpine lake encountered on many of the hikes in Rocky Mountain National Park, Gem Lake is tiny. It barely covers 0.2 acre

Balanced Rock Sidetrip

This trail skirts to the left of Gem Lake, passes through a gap in the rock walls and begins its circuitous descent toward the valley of Cow Creek. Aspens, Douglas firs and ponderosa pines on this north-facing slope frame vistas across the deep drainage to the peaks of the Mummy Range. At first, the trail wanders in an easterly direction, finally traversing the shoulder of a ridge decorated by a chunk of granite punctured by a perfectly round hole.

The massive domes of Lumpy Ridge tower above as the trail loops left and hastens down the valley side. After crossing some more level terrain 0.9 mile from Gem Lake, you reach an intersection with the spur to Balanced Rock branching to the left.

This narrow track undulates in a southwesterly direction as it passes bizarre rock sculptures and becomes almost indistinct as it drops into dry gulches. Frequent stands of

aspens alongside the trail make this a spectacular fall hike.

Almost a mile from the trail junction, the pathway ends at Balanced Rock, a huge boulder perched above an outcrop, held there only by a narrow neck of granite. A crag to the left and several misplaced trees add to the challenge of photographing this formation.

Route

Route	Elevation (ft.)	Distance (mi.)
Gem Lake	8,830	0
Balanced Rock	8,760	1.8

USGS Topographic map: Estes Park, Colo.

Gem Lake sparkles like a jewel set within its backdrop of vertical slabs of granite

and is nowhere more than five feet deep. Nevertheless, Gem Lake sparkles like a jewel set within its backdrop of vertical granite slabs. A precipice, perhaps 50 feet high, rises directly from the right shore. Beneath the huge cliffs to the left, stone ledges and a small sandy beach offer wonderful spots to picnic and relax.

Gem Lake is different from most lakes in that it has no inlet or outlet stream. The water level is entirely sustained by rainfall and evaporation.

Observant hikers will notice another kind of tree growing around Gem Lake—the limber pine. This hardy conifer normally thrives near tree line in conditions too inhospitable for any other species. You can recognize the limber pine by its rounded or flat-topped appearance, its thick, often-misshapen multiple trunks, and its two- to three-inch-long needles in bundles of five.

Lumpy Ridge

Studded with granite crags and domes, Lumpy Ridge dominates the northern skyline of Estes Park. Its best-known formation, the Twin Owls, bears a startling resemblance to two of these birds perched side by side.

Lumpy Ridge was first named *"That-aa-ai-atah"* or "Mountain With Little Lumps" by the Arapaho Indians, who spent their summers in the nearby valleys. Over time, settlers and climbers condensed this to Lumpy Ridge.

The massive glaciers that shaped much of Rocky Mountain National Park never extended as far as Estes Park. Lumpy Ridge's exposed knobs are not the work of ice age glaciation, but are exfoliation domes that once lay deep beneath the earth's surface. As the overlying rock was eroded away, the granite expanded and split in concentric layers parallel to its surface. When the rock finally came in contact with the atmosphere, the alternate freezing and thawing of water within the cracks caused the curved slabs of granite to splinter away—very much like the peeling of a giant onion.

This collection of crags, pinnacles and buttresses is a Mecca for rock climbers, offering 31 routes of varying difficulty. A 1.8-mile trail gives hikers year-round access to tiny Gem Lake, set like a jewel in a rocky pocket high on the ridge's eastern flank. For those with more time, the trail continues to Balanced Rock.

MacGregor Ranch

Alexander Q. MacGregor

(1845-1896), an attorney from Wisconsin, first visited Estes Park on a camping trip in 1872. There, he met Clara Heeney, a student on a sketching tour. They fell in love and were married the following year.

Together with Clara's wealthy mother, they founded the Black Canyon cattle ranch, now known as the MacGregor Ranch. Estes Park's first post office was located in their home, with Clara serving as postmistress.

At the same time that the MacGregors were establishing their homestead, a Scotsman, Lord Dunraven, was implementing a bogus scheme to acquire property around Estes Park in order to establish a large private hunting preserve for himself. Alex MacGregor was one of the local landowners instrumental in bringing an end to Dunraven's illegal tactics.

With $10,000 from Clara's mother, MacGregor constructed a toll road from Lyons to Estes Park. Much of the road pioneered the route of the present US Highway 36. Unable to extract tolls from independent settlers, he sold the road in 1882. In 1896, he was killed by lightning while checking a mining claim on Fall River Pass.

Donald MacGregor, the only one of Alexander's three sons interested in farming, expanded the ranch through the first half of this century until it covered a total of 4,000 acres. When he died of asthma in 1950, his daughter, Muriel Lurilla MacGregor, the last remaining member of the clan, took over the ranch. She died in 1970 and her will specified that the ranch be maintained in its present condition for educational and charitable purposes.

Today it serves as a museum, working cattle ranch and youth education center, owned and operated by the private, non-profit Muriel L. MacGregor Charitable Trust.

The MacGregor Ranch, which is in the National Register of Historic Places, occupies 1,200 acres of land at the mouth of the Black Canyon, just north of Estes Park. The staff take care of about 70 head of Black Angus cattle, growing and bailing hay to feed them.

The ranch is open to the public in June, July and August, when skilled docents welcome visitors with a talk about its history and modern-day activities. During the rest of the year, it hosts several thousand school children who come for museum education, hiking, camping and wagon rides.

The MacGregor Museum, located in the building that served as Muriel's home, provides a well-preserved record of typical ranch life from the 1870s until the mid-twentieth century. Exhibits include historical photographs, paintings by western artists, personal belongings, family memorabilia and documentation of Alexander MacGregor's staunch stand against land-grabbing Lord Dunraven. The view of Longs Peak from Muriel's bedroom is among the best in Estes Park.

Near the museum is a collection of horse-drawn ranch equipment, still in use today, and the old blacksmith shop and forge.

Rock slabs around Ypsilon Lake provide relaxing picnic spots

~ 13 ~ Ypsilon Lake

T his trail offers spectacular vistas of the impressive Y-shaped snowfield on Ypsilon Mountain. It also rewards the hiker with a close-up look at the

damage caused when the Lawn Lake Dam collapsed in 1982.

The trail achieves its 2,180-foot elevation gain gently and steadily. A shady forest of ponderosa and lodgepole pines offers relief from the heat of the south-facing slope.

Trailhead to Lawn Lake Junction

A steep, 200-foot climb from the trailhead brings you to a T-junction. Head left for Ypsilon Lake on the often-sunny slope of Bighorn Mountain, a lateral moraine deposited during the retreat of the Fall River Glacier thousands

Trailhead

Head west of the Fall River Entrance Station on US Highway 34 for 2.1 miles. Turn west, following the sign for Fall River Road and Endovalley. The Lawn Lake Trailhead parking lot is to the north after 0.1 mile.

Route

Day hike or overnight; 4.5 miles one way; moderate

Route	Elevation (ft.)	Distance (mi.)
Lawn Lake Trailhead	8,540	0
Lawn Lake Jct	9,200	1.3
Chipmunk Lake	10,650	4.0
Upper Chipmunk Campsite	10,640	4.2
Ypsilon Lake	10,540	4.5

USGS Topographic maps: Estes Park, Colo; Trail Ridge, Colo.

95

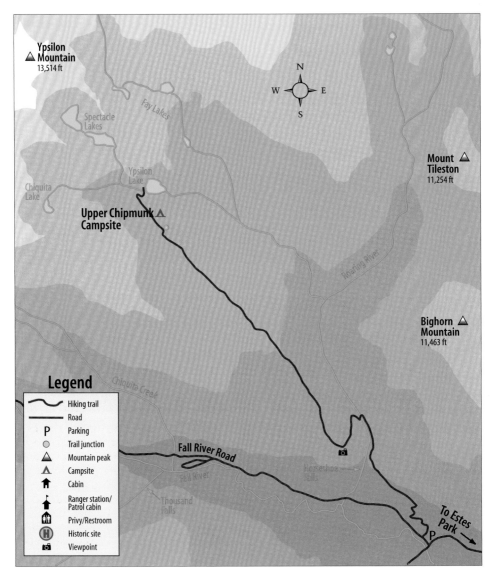

Legend

∼	Hiking trail
—	Road
P	Parking
○	Trail junction
△	Mountain peak
⌂	Campsite
♦	Cabin
♦	Ranger station/ Patrol cabin
🏠	Privy/Restroom
Ⓗ	Historic site
📷	Viewpoint

of years ago.

As you switchback to gain altitude, the ponderosa pines and Douglas firs frame views over Horseshoe Park and Fall River Road. Richardson geraniums, goldenrods, aspen daisies and small sunflowers flourish alongside the pathway.

After 0.5 mile, the trail skirts the rim of the deep ravine gouged when the Lawn Lake Dam failed on July 15, 1982. At exactly 5:30 in the morning, 674 acre-feet of stored water swept down the canyon, sometimes reaching depths of 30 feet. Everything in its path was ripped from the earth. Today, the naked banks and litter of massive rocks and uprooted trees attest to the ferocity of the flood.

The trail swings right and ambles gently up the hanging valley of the Roaring River, following the right bank of the V-shaped gash in the landscape.

Immediately with the change in orientation, the vegetation changes to lodgepole pines interspersed with aspens, Engelmann spruce and dwarf junipers.

Shortly you get your first view of Ypsilon Mountain. Its

Y-shaped couloir makes it easy to distinguish from its neighboring peaks in the Mummy Range.

Looking back, distant Longs Peak dominates the scene, clearly visible above the bare wound in the earth.

At an intersection 1.3 miles into the hike, the trail to Ypsilon Lake swings left, diverging from the Lawn Lake Trail. Bear left.

Lawn Lake Junction to Chipmunk Lake

Traverse a sandy area cleared through the rubble of rocks and splintered tree trunks and cross the creek by a substantial wooden bridge with a handrail.

Geology buffs will enjoy searching for small semicircular "chattermarks" on the granite, schist and gneiss boulders scattered over the flood zone. These are indications of rock crashing against rock.

The trail bends left and, with the help of log steps, makes a rapid ascent of the western flank of the valley, while backtracking along the route of the river. As the pathway sweeps to the right, high above the mouth of the ravine, a convenient rocky outcrop affords excellent views across Horseshoe Park.

Directly below, the barren alluvial fan deposited by the Lawn Lake flood has changed little with the passage of time. Sensitive to the interest of visitors, the park service has created a pathway through the debris to provide a close-up look at this scene of devastation. Past tiny Sheep Lakes, the Fall River meanders lazily through the meadow. It is obvious from its winding pattern why the region is called Horseshoe Park. The long lump of Deer Mountain rises to the southeast and, in the distance, you can spot Longs Peak, Estes Cone and the ridge of Twin Sisters Peaks.

Across the valley, Trail Ridge Road zigzags its way upward, beginning its 50-mile traverse of the plateau of Trail Ridge to the west side of the park. The highest continuously paved road in the United States, it reaches a lofty 12,183 feet above sea level, offering superlative vistas of glacier-gouged peaks and valleys, as well as a chance to view the alpine tundra ecosystem from behind the steering wheel of a car.

Old Fall River Road, which you can see crossing the alluvial fan, was the original high-

Ypsilon Mountain

Ypsilon Mountain, towering to a lofty 13,514 feet, is the fourth highest peak in Rocky Mountain National Park. It wears its name clearly on its southeastern face: A massive snowfield, settled into the sheer gray rock, distinctly forms a "Y"—and *ypsilon* is the Greek word for that letter.

One day in 1887, Frederick Chapin of Hartford, Connecticut, and his wife were fishing in nearby Wind River during an extended Appalachian Mountain Club climbing trip in the Rockies. Looking up, they saw a peak to the north with a perfect "Y" inscribed on its precipitous face. His wife instantly named it "Ypsilon Mountain," an appellation that was immediately accepted by local ranchers.

Subsequently, rancher William Hallett christened a neighboring peak in the Mummy Range "Mount Chapin" in honor of Chapin.

way over the Continental Divide. In use since 1920, it climbs with more than 15 switchbacks to join Trail Ridge Road at Fall River Pass.

Now the trail follows the prow of a ridge heading toward Ypsilon Mountain. Lodgepole pines and spruce provide welcome shade, but for much of the journey obscure views of the peak. The Roaring River can still be heard thundering far below to the right.

Occasionally, the pace slackens as the trail levels off for a distance before resuming its brisk ascent. From time to time, the hiker is rewarded with views of Ypsilon Mountain soaring above the trees.

After 4.0 miles, a brief downhill section deposits you alongside Chipmunk Lake. This minuscule pond does a wonderful job of reflecting 13,502-foot Fairchild Mountain and Ypsilon Mountain from the woods along its swampy eastern shore.

Few names in the park have political origins. Fairchild Mountain is one of the exceptions. Lucius Fairchild (1831-1896) was three times governor of Wisconsin, minister to Spain in 1880 under President Rutherford Hayes and a veteran of the Civil War. After riding the narrow gauge Georgetown

Tiny Chipmunk Lake reflects Ypsilon Mountain

Flood of 1982

Lawn Lake nestles at the foot of Mummy Mountain, the peak from which the range to the north of Rocky Mountain National Park takes its name.

In 1903, a 26-foot-high earthen dam was constructed, which more than doubled the size of the lake. This allowed for the storage of spring meltwater to be used for irrigation on the plains.

Poor maintenance by the irrigation company finally led to one of the greatest disasters in the history of the park. Water seeping through a failed outlet valve gradually eroded the embankment.

Suddenly, at 5:30 a.m. on July 15, 1982, the Lawn Lake Dam collapsed. More than 200 million gallons of stored water plunged down the valley of the Roaring River into Horseshoe Park and the Fall River drainage there. The 30-foot-high frothing deluge ripped trees, gravel and massive boulders from the earth, scouring a channel up to 50 feet deep.

Once the water hit the more level Horseshoe Park, it slowed and dropped an enormous amount of sediment, creating the giant alluvial fan visible today. The debris dammed the Fall River, causing the water to fill Horseshoe Park and then pour through Cascade Dam, through Aspenglen Campground and down the valley of the Fall River. The six-foot wall of water tore through the main street of Estes Park, finally stopped only by Olympus Dam on Lake Estes at 9:00 a.m.

Luckily, the quick reaction of a garbage collector working in Horseshoe Park enabled emergency personnel to close roads and evacuate people from the path of the flood. Also, it is fortunate that the disaster occurred in the early morning, before the park was chock-a-block with summer visitors.

Still, the failure of the Lawn Lake Dam killed three campers sleeping within the park—one in a backcountry campsite and two in Aspenglen Campground—and caused more than $31 million in property damage in the town of Estes Park.

Loop Railroad, he and his daughter were headlined in the Denver papers. As a result, some of his admirers, climbing in the region, named Fairchild Mountain after him.

Photographers, eager to capture the Y-shaped gully of Ypsilon Mountain, might use glassy Chipmunk Lake and its surrounding boulders as a foreground. Ypsilon Lake itself lies too close to the peak's precipitous southeastern flank for views of the snowfield.

Chipmunk Lake to Ypsilon Lake

The trail skirts the left side of the pool and continues its gentle descent to Upper Chipmunk campsite.

A short but steep climb past a typical triangular hitchrack brings you to the final 160-foot drop to Ypsilon Lake.

The inlet stream, immediately ahead as you approach the tarn, is enhanced by a delightful waterfall. To appreciate the splendor of this cascade, cross the footbridge and work your way upstream, past a riot of larkspur, aspen daisy and ragwort. Ypsilon Falls tumbles over a trench it has cut in the rock into a clear, deep pool.

A difficult 100-yard scramble up the rocks to the left of

Bighorn Sheep

The Rocky Mountain bighorn sheep, the Colorado state animal, is well adapted to the high altitude environment. A thick double-layered coat of hair protects it against the bitter cold, and specialized hooves aid in climbing near-vertical cliffs. A four-part stomach allows the sheep to consume large quantities of tough, dry vegetation rapidly and to chew the cud later.

Bighorns get their name from the massive curled horns of the rams. These weigh up to 35 pounds and measure more than 40 inches in length. Ewes sport smaller sickle-shaped horns.

Eight of the Best Viewing Areas in Colorado:
Big Thompson Canyon
Sheep may be observed here year-round, although peak viewing is early winter through late spring.
Horseshoe Park, Rocky Mountain National Park
A herd of about 200 sheep spend fall, winter and spring in and around Horseshoe Park.
Never Summer Range
Hikers and backpackers often spot sheep in the Never

Summer Wilderness Area during summer or early fall.
Mount Evans
Sheep can be seen on the tundra slopes of Mount Evans from late spring until early fall.
Waterton Canyon
Lying only 20 miles southwest of Denver, Waterton Canyon offers easily accessible, year-round viewing opportunities.
Georgetown
During fall and winter, numerous bighorn sheep can be seen along the north side of Interstate-70, just east of Georgetown. The best viewing is from the posted observation area along Georgetown Reservoir.
Pikes Peak
Sheep live on Pikes Peak year-round but viewing is generally limited to the summer and early fall when the cog railway and toll road are open.
Sangre de Cristo Mountains
About 550 sheep live throughout the Sangre de Cristo range. Observation is usually restricted to hikers or to those traveling by four-wheel-drive vehicle.

the falls brings you in sight of a second cascade.

The trail continues around the forested southeastern shore of Ypsilon Lake. Several short tracks lead down to the water's edge, where plenty of glacial erratics and rock slabs, some intruding into the lake, provide relaxing and fairly private picnic spots. Views are, however, limited as the tarn is tucked so snugly beneath the sheer flank of Ypsilon Mountain.

Scattered boulders display "chattermarks," evidence of rock crashing against rock during the flood

Trail Ridge Road

The 50-mile drive along Trail Ridge Road is one of the major attractions of Rocky Mountain National Park. Reaching an elevation of 12,183 feet above sea level, it is the highest continuously paved road in the United States and offers stupendous views at nearly every turn.

Completed in 1932 to facilitate travel across the Continental Divide, it was placed on the National Register of Historic Places in 1985 and named an "All-American Road" in 1996.

Trail Ridge Road, a stretch of Colorado Highway 34, starts at Deer Ridge Junction, just west of Estes Park. It ascends the plateau of Trail Ridge and winds for 11 miles above tree line through the alpine tundra—a world similar to that seen in the Arctic. After crossing the Continental Divide at Milner Pass, it drops into the Kawuneeche Valley and ends at the Grand Lake Entrance Station on the park's western slope.

Numerous pullouts, information signs and short trails allow visitors to experience the changing ecosystems along the route. The Alpine Visitor Center and a snack bar are located near the highest point on the road.

Depending on snow conditions, Trail Ridge Road is generally open from Memorial Day until mid-October.

The ruins of two tiny cabins, inhabited by miner Joe Shipler from 1876 until at least 1914, stand at the edge of a pretty meadow

~ 14 ~ Lulu City

During the late 1800s, adventurers flocked to Lulu City, lured by the tales of boundless deposits of gold and silver in the surrounding hills. For five

fleeting years, Lulu City was a mining boomtown. And then it went bust. Today, only a handful of dilapidated cabins and tailing-streaked slopes remain to tell the story of the once-vibrant community.

This easy, almost level stroll parallels the Colorado River as it meanders through the broad Kawuneeche Valley. Numerous wildflowers bloom alongside the trail, deer browse in the meadows and the workings of beavers dot the marshes.

Trailhead

The Colorado River Trailhead lies on the west side of the park, 9.5 miles north of the Grand Lake Entrance Station on Trail Ridge Road (Colorado Highway 34). The large parking area is indicative of the trail's popularity and an early start is advisable to avoid the crowds. The trailhead is at the north end of the lot.

Many excellent picnic spots line the river banks, especially during the first mile of the hike and around Lulu City. These provide relaxing destinations for hikers of all ability levels.

Route

Day hike; 3.7 miles one way; easy

Route	Elevation (ft.)	Distance (mi.)
Trailhead	9,010	0
Red Mountain Trail Jct	9,040	0.5
Shipler Mine	9,120	2.0
Shipler Cabin	9,160	2.4
Lulu City Trail Jct	9,590	3.5
Lulu City	9,360	3.7

Little Yellowstone Option

Little Yellowstone Canyon	10,031	5.1 (from Trailhead)

USGS Topographic map: Fall River Pass, Colo.

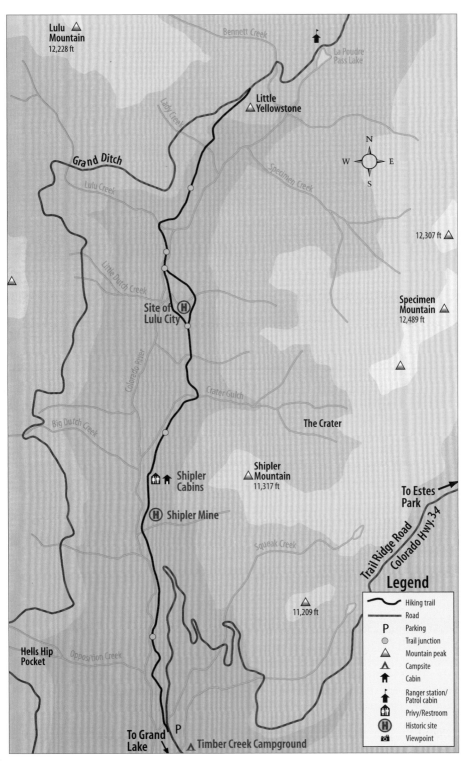

Lulu Mountain
12,228 ft

Bennett Creek

La Poudre Pass Lake

Little Yellowstone

Lady Creek

Grand Ditch

Lulu Creek

Specimen Creek

N
W   E
S

12,307 ft

Little Dutch Creek

Specimen Mountain
12,489 ft

Site of Lulu City

Colorado River

Crater Gulch

Big Dutch Creek

The Crater

Shipler Cabins

Shipler Mountain
11,317 ft

To Estes Park

Shipler Mine

Trail Ridge Road

Colorado Hwy. 34

Squeak Creek

11,209 ft

Legend

〰️	Hiking trail
─	Road
P	Parking
🔵	Trail junction
🔺	Mountain peak
🅰	Campsite
🏠	Cabin
🏠	Ranger station/Patrol cabin
🚻	Privy/Restroom
Ⓗ	Historic site
📷	Viewpoint

Hells Hip Pocket

Opposition Creek

To Grand Lake

P

Timber Creek Campground

Trailhead to Red Mountain Trail Junction

The wide, easy-to-follow trail heads north along the floodplain of the Colorado River.

La Poudre Pass, 7.4 miles to the north, marks the birthplace of this mighty waterway, which begins its epic 1,440-mile journey to the Gulf of California at this point.

Almost immediately upon leaving the trailhead, the pathway ascends a short but steep incline—the only real climb of the route. It then resumes its gentle course along the flat valley base, hugging the eastern bank of the river for much of the first half mile of the hike. Spruce, willows and alders flourish by the stream and an ever-changing display of wildflowers speckles the verge.

After 0.5 mile, the Red Mountain Trail makes a sharp left to begin its rapid 1,200-foot clamber to the Grand Ditch; continue forward. This ambitious project to collect water from the Never Summer Mountains and to carry it across the Continental Divide to Long Draw Reservoir. The Red Mountain trail provides access to several hikes in the Never Summer Wilderness.

Towering more than 3,500 feet above the floor of the Kawuneeche Valley, the ridge of the Never Summer Mountains was called *Ni-chebe-chii* by the Arapaho Indians who summered in the region. This translates to Never-No-Summer. The Colorado Geographic Board removed the double negative from the Anglicized name.

Stay right at the intersection for Lulu City.

Red Mountain Trail Junction to Shipler Park

The trail meanders through the spruce and aspens, sometimes winding across flower-strewn openings in the trees

Lulu City

During the 1870s, Joe Shipler and three companions made two silver claims in the Kawuneeche Valley. Word of the potential riches spread quickly. Miners William Baker and Benjamin Burnett also made claims in the valley and became the founders of Lulu City. The town was named after Burnett's daughter.

Prospectors immediately began to flock to the area. By June of 1880, the town layout was complete, with east to west streets numbered from 1 to 19 and north to south streets called Lead Mountain, Trout, Riverside and Howard.

"New discoveries are being found every day," exclaimed Georgetown's *The Colorado Miner*, as prospectors combed the surrounding hillsides.

In August, mail began to arrive over Thunder Pass by the Stewart Toll Road and September saw the opening of the stage road to Grand Lake.

Lulu City boomed during the following year. Lots were sold for $20 to $50 each. Stores offered clothing, hardware, liquor and groceries. A barber shop started business. Two sawmills produced timber for housing and mines. Twenty cows supplied milk and butter. A stage coach transported people from Fort Collins and Grand Lake. The Godsmark and Parker Hotel, replete with linen, silverware and elegant crystal, accommodated well-off visitors. And a brothel stood just to the north of town.

Lulu City became a vibrant community of miners and their families with plenty to occupy the townspeople. The descendent of one settler wrote that there were "horseshoes, dances, quilting bees ... and much good conversation and laughter around the cozy fireplaces."

At its height, the population in the Kawuneeche Valley reached 500 hardy souls, about 200 of whom lived in Lulu City.

In 1882, it began to be evident that the ore being produced was of poor quality. In fact, Grand County's output of precious metals was only $10,000—the lowest of any of Colorado's mining counties.

By fall of 1883, Lulu City was more or less deserted and mail had ceased delivery.

Today, little remains to tell the story of the boomtown in the valley of the Colorado River. All that can be seen is a handful of fallen-down wooden cabins, several piles of tailings, a few rusting pieces of equipment and indentations in the ground marking the route of the Stewart Toll Road.

or traversing along the eastern hillside a few feet above the level of the floodplain.

Beaver ponds, littering the low-lying land among the willows, reflect Mount Richthofen and the other peaks of the Never Summer Mountains.

Watch for mule deer browsing in the meadows and marmots sunning on the scree-covered slopes.

Two miles into the hike, yellowish tailings streak the hillside to the right and the trail sends a branch uphill to the remains of the unsuccessful Shipler Mine, dating from the 1880s and 1890s. Be particularly careful to keep children away from the shaft entrance and never enter an old mine unless it has officially been secured and declared safe. Return to the trail and continue on.

The ruins of two tiny cabins, inhabited by Joe Shipler from 1876 until at least 1914, stand at the edge of a pretty meadow 0.4 mile further on. A privy hides in the trees to the left of the trail just past the cabins.

Shipler Park to Lulu City

The trail now follows the route of a stage road that ran from Grand Lake through Lulu City and on over Thunder Pass to Walden. During the boomtown's heyday, three four-horse stagecoaches a week traveled this highway. On occasion, so many visitors and would-be prospectors converged in Lulu City that people were turned away for lack of accommodation.

The trail rises gently

through a shady forest of Engelmann spruce and lodgepole pines, forsaking the valley floor and leaving the Colorado River far off to the left.

3.5 miles into the hike, cross the bridge at Crater Gulch and come to a trail junction. A side loop drops down to the left, passing through the site of Lulu City and eventually rejoining the main trail before it continues on to Little Yellowstone and La Poudre Pass.

To visit Lulu City, take the left fork. After 0.2 mile, a few tumble-down wooden beams overgrown by forest are the first signs of the 19th-century mining town.

Another easily observed cabin lies a little farther along the trail, past the outhouse. The cabin is still clearly defined, although it is rapidly being overtaken by the spruce

trees growing up the middle.

The banks of the Colorado River and the wide, flowery meadow offer lots of choice picnic spots. The gentle babble of the water provides soothing background music as you relax in this immensely inviting setting amid the steep valley sides and soaring peaks—an apt reward for your 3.7-mile hike. Many will enjoy exploring the rich streamside environment or searching in the underbrush for rusting bits of machinery.

This is a good place to see chipmunks (striped backs and faces) and golden-mantled ground squirrels (a little bigger with no stripes on their faces). Remember, it is against park regulations to feed these creatures despite their persistent begging.

The Colorado River

Looking at the modest stream wandering though the Kawuneeche Valley, it is hard to believe that this is the beginning of one of the most significant rivers in the United States.

La Poudre Pass, to the north of Lulu City, is where the Colorado River is born and begins its 1,440-mile journey southwestward to the Gulf of California.

Along the way, numerous tributaries feed into the waterway. Among these are the Green, the San Juan, the Gunnison, the Escalante, the Dolores and the Little Colorado rivers. As the Colorado River passes through Colorado, Utah, Arizona, California and Mexico, its

drainage basin covers 244,000 square miles, including sections of seven Western states. For 17 miles it forms the international boundary between Arizona and Mexico before completing its trip by flowing for 80 miles through Mexico.

No other watercourse has cut so many deep trenches through the surface of the earth. The largest, the Grand Canyon, is one of the natural world's superlative wonders.

The Colorado River is the lifeblood of the arid Southwest. Today it is has many different uses including hydroelectric power, flood control, irrigation and recreation.

The trail to Lake Verna runs alongside East Inlet Creek

~ 15 ~ Lake Verna

Lush meadows, shady forests and sweeping vistas are all components of this ambitious hike to Lake Verna, a fjord-like tarn at the western foot of the Continental Divide. Reserving a spot at one of the many campsites (970-586-1242) dotted along the trail allows backpackers to linger and explore the area. Hardy hikers may venture farther up the valley to Spirit, Fourth and Fifth lakes or even continue over Boulder-Grand Pass into Wild Basin. The remains of Native American camps discovered around Thunder Lake to the east of the pass indicate that this was an ancient crossing of the Divide.

Trailhead

Drive 14 miles north of Granby on US Highway 40 and turn east onto US Highway 34 toward Grand Lake Village. Take the turn-off toward Grand Lake Village. After 0.4 mile, veer left, bypassing the town itself, onto West Portal Road. Continue for 2.0 miles around the northeastern shore of the lake to a large parking lot just above the West Portal of the Big Thompson Irrigation Tunnel. The East Inlet Trailhead is to the southeast of the parking area.

Route

Day hike or overnight; 6.9 miles one way; strenuous

Route	Elevation (ft.)	Distance (mi.)
Trailhead	8,391	0
Adams Falls	8,470	.0.3
East Meadow Campsite	8,550	1.5
Lower East Inlet Campsite	8,640	2.3
Cats Lair Campsite	9,200	4.0
Gray Jay Group Campsite	9,650	4.9
Lone Pine Lake	9,885	5.5
Slickrock Campsite	10,000	6.0
Solitaire Campsite	10,120	6.2
Upper East Inlet Campsite	10,200	6.6
Lake Verna	10,200	6.9
Lake Verna Campsite	10,280	6.9

USGS Topographic maps: Shadow Mountain, Colo.; Isolation Peak, Colo.

Trailhead to Adams Falls

Steps help in the initial ascent through a mixed forest of aspen, Douglas fir, lodgepole pine and Engelmann spruce.

The East Inlet Trail begins as a hikers' freeway. Unless you start your trip at the crack of dawn, it is likely to be choked with horse traffic and sneaker-clad families.

The crashing sound of Adams Falls announces its presence long before you actually see it. A third of a mile into the hike, a short branch to the right takes you to a dramatic viewpoint overlooking the cascade. From a rocky ledge, you can watch the powerful cataract as it rides its roller-coaster rush through a deep gash in the bedrock.

Jay E. Adams of San Antonio, Texas, constructed three houses on the shore of Grand Lake. In 1917, he held an elaborate picnic for the townspeople, and then asked them to help him name the waterfall, which had previously been known as Ouzel Falls. Everyone voted to call it Adams Falls in his honor.

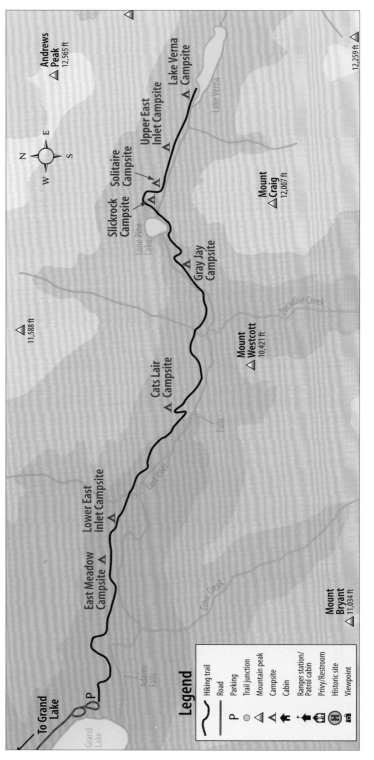

Andrews Peak 12,565 ft

Lake Verna Campsite

Upper East Inlet Campsite

Lake Verna

Solitaire Campsite

Slickrock Campsite

Mount Craig 12,007 ft

Lone Pine Lake

12,259 ft

Gray Jay Campsite

Paradise Creek

11,588 ft

Mount Westcott 10,421 ft

Cats Lair Campsite

Falls

East Inlet

Lower East Inlet Campsite

East Meadow Campsite

Mount Bryant 11,034 ft

Echo Creek

Adams Falls

To Grand Lake

Grand Lake

Legend

- Hiking trail
- Road
- **P** Parking
- Trail junction
- Mountain peak
- Campsite
- Cabin
- Ranger station/ Patrol cabin
- Privy/Restroom
- **H** Historic site
- Viewpoint

Morning mist hangs in the valley of East Inlet

Adams Falls to Cats Lair Campsite

The two-person-wide trail continues at a gentle grade through the forest to the left of East Inlet Creek. Shortly, it emerges alongside a series of broad, marshy meadows yielding views up the valley to Mount Craig. The lazy meanders of the stream promise trout fishers a taste of paradise.

If you are lucky, you may spot one of the park's reclusive moose standing among the trees or bedding down in the long grass. These hefty creatures are most easily identified by the massive antlers of the bulls, which are shaped like clawed scoops.

The East Inlet valley is also home to the beaver, one of the only animals besides man that adapts its environment to its needs. Signs of beaver ac-tivity along a river include large dams and cone-shaped lodges of sticks and logs.

After 1.5 miles, a sign points to East Meadow Back-country Campsite, the first in a string of well-placed spots to pitch a tent along the route.

The trail begins to ascend at a more eager pace, bridging a series of side streams and passing Lower East Inlet Campsite. Hugging the north-ern flank of the valley, it in-clines up a ledge—some of which has been blasted from sheer bedrock.

Orange lichen decorates the gnarled outcroppings. Greenish-yellow clusters of poker heuchera peek from shady crevices in the rock. Ominous black cliffs tower high above to the left.

Switchbacks make for rapid elevation gain, leaving the stream far below in the valley base.

Vistas extend northwest over Grand Lake to the conifer-clad hillsides beyond and eastward to the slopes of Andrews Peak and Mount Craig. Several balconies of rock to the right provide excellent picnic benches overlooking the deep gorge.

The trail weaves up and down through the evergreens, over slab outcrops and around enormous boulders. Finally, it meets East Inlet Creek above a steep section of rapids.

The path continues to the left of the stream, traversing a stretch of marsh dotted with ragwort and other moisture-loving flowers. It then re-sumes its hurried climb, zigzagging upward with the help of log steps.

Four miles into the hike, you come to Cats Lair Campsite.

Cats Lair Campsite to Lone Pine Lake

The trail switches back and forth up a ridge and then meanders through tall lodgepole pine, aspen and Engelmann spruce. Notice the yellowish marks where the bark has been stripped near the base of many of the pines. This is the work of porcupines. During the winter, when green vegetation is scarce, these spiny rodents feed on bark, often causing serious damage to the trees. You are unlikely to see a porcupine, as they are nocturnal animals.

The valley bends in an easterly direction and you catch a glimpse of the snowfields above tree line sparkling on the gray mountainsides.

After maintaining a level grade for some distance, the trail resumes its sinuous upward journey, aided in places by stone steps.

Cross the main stream by a sturdy wooden bridge with handrails on both sides. Now the trail snakes between the boulders on the south side of the narrowing drainage with East Inlet Creek cascading immediately to the left.

As the valley of Paradise Creek converges from the right, the trail hastens upward to continue in a more northeasterly direction around the rugged flank of Mount Craig.

After 4.9 miles, signs indicate Gray Jay Group Campsite off to the left and an outhouse to the right. Continue straight ahead. Swerve past an area littered with rocks and fallen timber.

Tiny conifers cling desperately to the barren hillside and pink fireweed, rag-wort and wild raspberry bushes grow in a bog alongside the path.

The trail traverses a terrace on the right-hand side of the drainage, with a beautifully constructed reinforcement rock retainer wall underneath. The trail crosses a plank over a little stream and, 5.5 miles from the trailhead, arrives at Lone Pine Lake.

Cradled in a pocket at the base of Andrews Peak and Mount Craig, this little body of water reflects the surrounding evergreens and chunks of bedrock in its glassy surface.

Originally, Lone Pine Lake was known as Verdant Lake. Later, a man called Fred McLaren said that the lake named itself for a single pine tree that stood on its only island. Nowadays, a number of

Porcupine

Equipped with a full set of built-in armor, the porcupine has little to fear from predators. It is covered with needle-sharp quills, which are concealed in a coat of long brown hair. Once embedded in the flesh of an enemy, the barbed points of these spines not only cannot be pulled out but work themselves in deeper.

When threatened, the porcupine hides its head between its forelegs and presents its rump toward the attacker. If touched, it will thrash out with its tail, planting hundreds of spines in the predator's nose.

Porcupines are nocturnal animals, so hikers rarely see them up and about. Occasionally, however, you may glimpse one snoozing in a treetop.

In summer, porcupines feed on a variety of green vegetation. In winter, they rely on tree bark for nourishment. Often, the only sign of their presence in an area is the damage they have done to the pines. This is in the form of bare patches, where the bark has been gnawed off the lower trunks.

Porcupines make their dens in a cave or hollow log. Their courtship is unusual in that the male sprays the female with urine before mating takes place. After a seven-month gestation, a single, well-developed kit is born in spring. It weighs about a pound, has its eyes open and is armed, just like its parents, with quills. It is a curious fact that the newly born porcupine is larger than a black bear cub, although the adult bear is considerably bigger than the full-grown porcupine.

young lodgepole pines, spruce and willows have supplanted the dead lone pine.

Lone Pine Lake to Lake Verna

The trail proceeds to the right of the lake and winds beneath a talus slope. It bridges East Inlet Creek, flowing through the boulders, and continues to climb through the conifers. Crossing several side streams, it winds up the hillside, past Slickrock Campsite to a rocky slab with a lovely view down to dark-emerald Lone Pine Lake. It then angles left to parallel East Inlet Creek for the final 0.7 mile and 150-foot elevation gain to Lake Verna.

The brook, choked with logs and tumbled rocks, makes its way through a series of shallow ponds. Pearly everlasting, tall alpine avens, rosy Indian paintbrush, thistles, harebells and cow parsnip thrive by the trail in this lush environment. Willows bow respectfully over the water.

Solitaire, Upper East Inlet and Lake Verna campsites, tucked away in the trees, provide wonderful base camps from which to explore the string of tarns above Lake Verna.

The trail rises briefly then descends to meet Lake Verna with dramatic suddenness at its northwestern tip. Long and skinny, this tarn resembles a fjord more than an alpine lake. Conifers cling to the talus slopes falling on either side. At the far end of the valley, the craggy ridge of the Continental Divide, streaked with snowfields, culminates in knobby Isolation Peak.

A few hundred yards further along the northern shore, rocky slabs provide a perfect picnic spot with a wonderful panorama up the lake.

The maintained trail ends after Lake Verna. A faint track continues up the valley to Spirit and Fourth lakes, more or less petering out before it reaches Fifth Lake about 1.5 miles further on. A tiresome scramble above Fourth Lake leads to Boulder-Grand Pass, believed to be an ancient route across the Continental Divide.

The five lakes along the East Inlet valley—Lone Pine, Lake Verna, Spirit, Fourth and Fifth lakes—are often called the "Paternoster Lakes," as they resemble the string of beads used for reciting a rosary.

Lake Verna was named for the sweetheart of a U.S. Geological Survey team member. History fails to record what survey or which member.

The Grand Ditch

The Grand Ditch is the long horizontal scar high on the eastern slopes of the Never Summer Mountains. This canal was constructed to collect and transport snowmelt water from the west side of the Continental Divide to Long Draw Reservoir to the east.

This project was started in 1890. Chinese and Swedish laborers toiled to cut the substantial channel, slowly inching south from La Poudre Pass. Finally, in 1932, it was completed to its present-day proportions.

Today, the 14-mile aqueduct begins in Baker Gulch and runs north to La Poudre Pass at a slant designed to keep the water flowing. It then flows down into Long Draw Reservoir. From there, it is used by farmers around Fort Collins to irrigate their crops in summer.

The ditch is owned and operated by the Water Supply and Storage Company, a non-profit farmers' cooperative with headquarters in Fort Collins.

A wide pathway runs alongside the Grand Ditch, making it pleasant for hiking and providing views to the east and south. A number of backcountry campsites are scattered along its route and several trails into the Never Summer Wilderness originate from here, allowing for base-camp explorations.

The Front Range

The three-day hike crosses meadows surrounded by strange rock formations

T he Front Range of the Colorado Rockies offers some of the most spectacular and popular hiking opportunities in the state. Immediately to the south of Rocky Mountain National Park, hikes 16 through 19 explore the Indian Peaks Wilderness, a region straddling

the Continental Divide.

The Indian Peaks are some of the most savage and inhospitable summits in the Front Range, and the surrounding scenery is characterized by stark and desolate beauty.

National Forest campgrounds are located at or near the trailheads. A permit is required to camp in the backcountry between June 1 and September 15. A good selection of restaurants and other services is available in the town of Nederland.

Farther south, Hike 20 ascends the Barr Trail. This is the classic hikers' route up Pikes Peak. Gaining 7,200 feet in 13 miles, it's a serious climb, requiring lots of stamina. Restaurants, motels and private campgrounds provide facilities around Manitou Springs.

Lost Creek Wilderness lies about 40 miles southwest of Denver in the Pike National Forest. Hike 21 follows a 24-mile circuit through an area dominated by giant granite

formations. There are a few National Forest campgrounds along the road to the trailhead and free sites abound in the wilderness. You should purchase food before heading to the area.

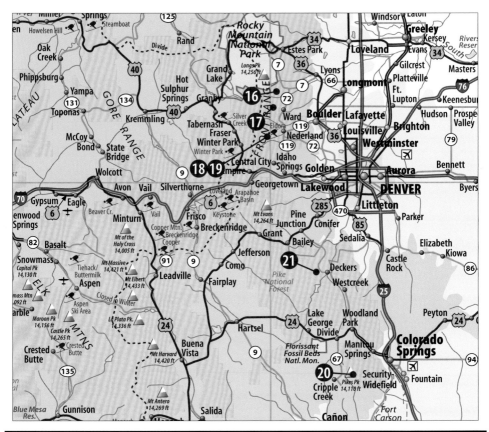

Additional Front Range Hikes

Lost Lake

Day hike, 2.0 miles one way
Elevation gain: 800 feet
Rating: Easy
USGS Topographic map: Nederland, Colo.

During the boom of the late 1800s, up to 200 people lived and mined around Lost Lake. Today, a hike to this easy destination in the Indian Peaks Wilderness not only provides a journey back into history but the opportunity to experience some of the breathtaking vistas and beautiful wildflowers seen in the wilderness area.

This trail begins just west of Nederland at the townsite of Hessie. It follows the route of an old mining road along the South Fork of Middle Boulder Creek. Tailings and the ruins of an old cabin decorate the slopes of Bryan Mountain rising above the lake.

Heart Lake

Day hike or overnight, 5.0 miles one way
Elevation Gain: 2,090 feet
Rating: Moderate
USGS Topographic map: East Portal, Colo.

The mountain chain comprising the Front Range contains some of the most pristine scenery and picturesque alpine tarns that are easily reached from Boulder and Denver.

Just to the south of the Indian Peaks Wilderness, a series of lakes lies tucked beneath the rugged summits of the Continental Divide.

Heart Lake, a popular destination for hikers, backpackers and fishermen, hides in a grassy basin above tree line near Rogers Pass. Using this as a base camp, you can make a number of side trips to other tarns in the area such as Iceberg Lakes and Rogers Pass Lake. Access to Heart Lake is from the East Portal of the Moffat Tunnel just to the southwest of Nederland.

The trail to Gibraltar Lake crosses a log jam by a little unnamed lake

~ 16 ~ Gibraltar Lake

At the upper end of the valley of Middle St. Vrain Creek lies some of the most remote and pristine scenery in the Indian Peaks Wilderness Area.

The St. Vrain Glaciers cling to the precipitous slopes flanking the Continental Divide, gloating over a landscape they carved with an icy grip thousands of years ago.

An overnight or multiday trip is necessary to experience this region of wild and savage beauty fully and to allow time to enjoy the peace and quiet.

Trailhead to Timberline Falls

To make the entire trip on foot, start along the Middle St. Vrain four wheel drive road. After 0.3 mile, follow the Buchanan Pass Trail #910 ,

Trailhead

Head 6.0 miles north of Ward on Colorado Highway 72 to Peaceful Valley. Turn left (west), passing through Peaceful Valley Campground and Camp Dick. It is about 1.5 miles to the trailhead parking lot from the highway.

If you have a rugged, high-clearance four-wheel-drive vehicle, you can cut this hike short by 4.0 miles. The extremely rough and rocky Middle St. Vrain 4WD Road follows the south bank of Middle St. Vrain Creek until it dead ends in a small parking area after 4.0 miles. At this point, the route bridges the stream to join the Buchanan Pass Trail.

Route

Day hike or overnight; 8.0 miles one way; strenuous

Route	Elevation (ft.)	Distance (mi.)
Trailhead	8,680	0
Timberline Falls	9,100	2.0
St. Vrain-Buchanan Pass Jct	9,583	4.0
Buchanan Pass/		
Red Deer Lake Jct	10,000	6.0
Gibraltar Lake	11,200	8.0

USGS Topographic maps: Allens Park, Colo.; Isolation Peak, Colo.

which branches off to the right to bridge Middle St. Vrain Creek; follow this trail.

The path meanders gently to the north of the stream, through shady forest and grassy openings. During the summer season, a multitude of wildflowers festoon the meadows.

Be alert for handsome specimens of the delicate fairy slipper adorning the banks of the creek and for Richardson geraniums and goldenrod studding the grass. In the fall, the aspens dotted among the Engelmann spruce grace the trail with yellow-gold.

Middle St. Vrain Creek babbles to your left. This soothing melody will accompany you throughout this hike as the trail rarely strays far from its banks.

After 2.0 miles, a balcony of rock to the left provides an overlook of spectacular Timberline Falls. Middle St. Vrain Creek, squeezed from the snowfields far above, thunders through a chasm it has carved in the bedrock. Slabs provide ample picnic spots for those preferring to end their hike here.

Timberline Falls to Buchanan Pass/Red Deer Lake Junction

The trail continues to rise gently, merging 4.0 miles into the hike with the path, which crosses the stream from the four-wheel-drive road.

Shortly, a sign announces your entry into the Indian Peaks Wilderness. Those planning to camp beyond this point are subject to the wilderness area regulations

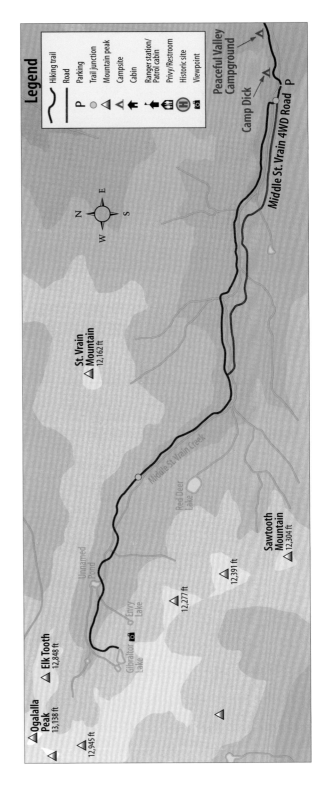

Legend

- ⌇ Hiking trail
- | Road
- P Parking
- ○ Trail junction
- ◁ Mountain peak
- ◀ Campsite
- ← Cabin
- ← Ranger station/ Patrol cabin
- 🛖 Privy/Restroom
- Ⓗ Historic site
- 📷 Viewpoint

Peaceful Valley Campground

Camp Dick

Middle St. Vrain 4WD Road   P

N E S W

St. Vrain Mountain
△ 12,162 ft

Middle St. Vrain Creek

Red Deer Lake

Sawtooth Mountain
△ 12,304 ft

△ 12,391 ft

△ 12,277 ft

Unnamed Pond

Envy Lake

Gibraltar Lake 📷

Elk Tooth
△ 12,848 ft

Ogalalla Peak
△ 13,138 ft

△ 12,945 ft

◁

Lovely flower gardens thrive on tiny islands in Middle St. Vrain Creek

blue columbine, proclaimed the state flower in 1899.

The distinctive Elk Tooth presides over the head of the valley and the scree-covered ridge to the right becomes progressively more rugged as you approach the Continental Divide.

Near the trail, the rusting remains of an old bedstead and stove serve as reminders of the miners who lived and prospected in the area during the 19th century.

At the end of the meadow, the trail to Buchanan Pass and Red Deer Lake splits off to the left, bridging Middle St. Vrain Creek. Miniature midstream islands nurture exquisite gardens of Parry primrose, brookcress and chimingbells. Continue straight on the St. Vrain Glacier Trail.

and need to be in possession of a permit between June 1 and September 15. Call (303) 444-6600 to obtain the permit.

Follow the route of an old mining road through subalpine forest interspersed with flower-strewn meadows.

Watch for mule deer among the conifers or feeding in the pastures. These yellowish-brown creatures are most often seen at dawn and dusk.

Ignore the St. Vrain Mountain Trail leading off to the right.

Cross a vast alpine meadow dotted with the stumps of old trees and studded with wildflowers. Look especially for the regal Colorado

Mule Deer

The mule deer is one of the most commonly observed big game animals in Colorado's Rocky Mountains. Yellow-brown in summer and grayish come winter, it has a white chin, throat and rump, large ears and a white tail with a black tip.

Adaptable and numerous, deer live in a wide range of Colorado's many habitats, including open shrub land, montane and subalpine forest and tundra grassland. In addition, the deer have adjusted so well to human encroachment on its environment that it is often seen in Estes Park itself and many suburban—and even urban—communities. This is particularly so during fall and winter, when heavy snowfall forces its migration down from the high country.

Dawn and dusk are the best times to spot small groups of does or solitary bucks browsing on sagebrush, grass or shrubs. If spooked, they will rapidly leap behind a hill or other obstacle.

The most outstanding feature of mule deer are the antlers of the bucks. These are multi-branched, the number of forks being influenced by the age and diet of the animal. The racks develop velvet, which the males remove by rubbing against a tree, and the antlers drop off each winter.

In fall, bucks compete for does with postural displays, threats and shoving matches. One or two young, weighing about eight pounds, are born six to seven months after mating takes place. Mothers quickly lick their newborn dry and encourage them up onto their wobbly legs. They then keep them concealed until they are strong enough to flee effectively from predators.

Buchanan Pass/Red Deer Lake Junction to Gibraltar Lake

The trail begins its serious ascent through a cornucopia of Indian paintbrush, little sunflowers and waist-high cow parsnip. Planks or stepping stones aid in traversing several marshy sections.

Narrowing, the trail arrives at the first of three river crossings. A sturdy stick will help your balance as you inch your way across the precarious, unsteady logs.

The trail continues to the south of the stream through forests of conifers and across waterlogged meadows.

Shortly, it recrosses the creek via a rickety tree trunk. Many hikers who are afraid of heights choose to remain to the south of the brook. This necessitates a short bushwhack upstream, sometimes following a faint deer track through bogs resplendent with marsh marigolds and globeflowers. The trail makes its final crossing of Middle St. Vrain Creek back to the left side by way of a logjam at the eastern end of a small unnamed pond.

Jump a large side stream issuing from Envy Lake, high in a cirque at the foot of one of the St. Vrain Glaciers. The frigid meltwater ripples beneath glistening snowbanks well into late July.

The trail traverses beneath the sheer slopes of a rocky promontory that separates the Gibraltar Lake drainage from that of Envy Lake.

A profusion of delicate glacier lilies creates splashes of gold on the saturated ground. Often, the impatient buds peek through the melting snow.

The trail creeps along rocky slabs, through thickets of low brush and among the jumbled boulders strewn alongside the stream.

Another unnamed lake, which could be called "Lower Gibraltar Lake," nestles at the end of the valley, embraced by the gray ridge of the Continental Divide and the rugged Elk Tooth. The St. Vrain Glaciers, remnants of the powerful St. Vrain Glacier that sculpted this valley thousands of years ago, cling to the naked wall above the tarn.

Both stream and trail curl abruptly to the left, climbing steeply southward up a slope dotted with rosy paintbrush and other tundra wildflowers. Suddenly, the trail fades out, leaving the braided creek to direct you to its origins in Gibraltar Lake. This steely body of water hides behind a lump of moraine, which juts in front of the southern flank of the valley.

Gibraltar Lake, which ac-

Aspen daisies

tually consists of two tarns separated by a rocky spit, huddles at the foot of two of the St. Vrain Glaciers. Beneath the lingering snowbanks scattering the landscape is an agglomeration of cleaved and quarried stones and glacial debris. Few scenes in Colorado compare to this for stark and desolate beauty.

Pick your way through the least-dense thickets of krummholz to the summit of the rocky promontory to the east for stunning views of Envy Lake, Gibraltar Lake, the St. Vrain Glaciers and the Elk Tooth.

Glacier Lily

Impatient to bloom at the first signs of spring in the Colorado high country, the delicate buds of the glacier or snow lily can often be seen poking through

melting snowbanks. As the snow recedes, the golden flowers carpet the soggy meadows.

The delicate blossoms, each with a halo of backward-curving petals, hang at the end of a six- to ten-inch-high stem.

The leaves, growing in pairs from the base of the plant, become yellowish after the flower has withered. These add splashes of color to marshes throughout the summer.

Mount Audubon rises behind Brainard Lake in the Indian Peaks Wilderness

~ 17 ~ Mount Audubon

Mount Audubon is one of the most easily accessible superlative viewpoints of the Front Range. Its summit offers vistas north to Longs Peak, south to Mount Evans, east across the plains and west as far as the distant Gore Range and Mount Zirkel. Because the trail starts at a lofty 10,480 feet, it rapidly leaves the subalpine forest for the alpine tundra, providing unobstructed panoramas almost right from the beginning.

Except for the last 623 feet, all of the 2,743-foot elevation gain for this hike is on a well-marked, heavily traveled trail. Therefore, this makes an excellent mountain ascent for beginners.

Be sure to start your climb early in the day so that you are off the exposed tundra before the afternoon thunderstorms, which often blow in.

Trailhead

Take Colorado Highway 72 (also known as the Peak to Peak Scenic and Historic Byway) to the turnoff just north of Ward's northern city limit sign. Head west for the Brainard Lake Recreation Area. Follow the paved road for 5.8 miles, passing an entrance pay station and Brainard Lake, to the Mitchell Lake Trailhead parking area. The Mount Audubon Trailhead is to the northwest of the lot.

Route

Day hike; 4.0 miles one way; moderate

Route	Elevation (ft.)	Distance (mi.)
Trailhead	10,480	0
Beaver Creek Jct	11,280	1.5
Saddle	12,600	3.0
Mount Audubon Summit	13,223	3.5

USGS Topographic map: Ward, Colo.

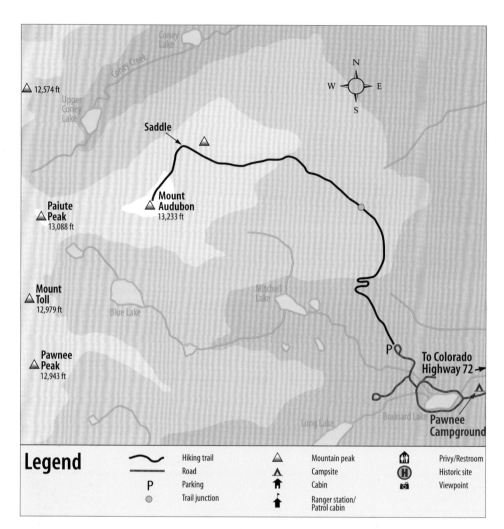

Legend

～	Hiking trail	△	Mountain peak	⌂	Privy/Restroom
──	Road	▲	Campsite	Ⓗ	Historic site
P	Parking	♠	Cabin	📷	Viewpoint
◉	Trail junction	♠	Ranger station/ Patrol cabin		

Trailhead to Beaver Creek Trail Junction

From the trailhead, take the Beaver Creek Trail #911, shortly passing the wooden sign for the Indian Peaks Wilderness Area. The broad pathway ascends gently through tall Engelmann spruce and subalpine fir for 0.6 mile, where its forward progress is halted by a steep talus slope beneath a rocky ridge.

Veering sharply to the right, it rises through a wide set of switchbacks, with views over Brainard Lake and nearby Pawnee Campground.

A multitude of wildflowers, including bistort, asters, fireweed, goldenrod and arnica speckle the verge.

As the trail makes a long, leisurely traverse of the east-facing side of the mountain, the spruce and firs diminish in stature, with branches only growing on the leeward side. Shortly, these "banner trees" shrink to gnarled, disjointed

islands of krummholz. Occurring at an altitude of between 11,000 and 11,500 feet in Colorado, these trees mark the transition point between the subalpine forest and the alpine tundra zones. These malformed and diminutive conifers struggle against the strong winds, severe cold and short growing season. A few dwarf willows and stunted raspberry bushes manage to survive along with the evergreens.

Vistas grow ever more

extensive as altitude is gained. You can see Mitchell Lake, cradled beneath the southern flank of Mount Audubon to the southwest, with the ragged summits of the Indian Peaks defining the Continental Divide. Beaver Reservoir huddles within the dark green tangle of forest to the northwest and, far out on the plains, tiny lakes and reservoirs glisten like jewels.

Above timberline, gray rocks blanket the slope. Considerable work must have gone into creating the smooth and easily followed pathway through the sea of boulders. Fendler sandwort and minute cinquefoil dot the occasional green patches of tundra.

After 1.5 miles, the Mount Audubon Trail splits off to the left. The Beaver Creek Trail descends into the valley of Middle St. Vrain Creek.

Beaver Creek Trail Junction to the Saddle

Veering left, the Mt. Audubon Trail heads up the wide open slope directly toward the rounded top of Mount Audubon. A precipice plunges to the south of the summit, with a snowfield in front. Above you, a long knobby ridge protrudes northeast from the peak.

When they are in season, the leaves of alpine avens paint large patches of the tundra a bright, rust red. A multitude of Lilliputian but vibrant wildflowers thrive in this high-altitude garden, including kings crown, western yellow paintbrush and delicate Arctic gentians.

Listen for the high-pitched peep of the elusive little pika, a guinea-pig-like relative of the rabbit. The ventriloquist quality of the mammal's call often obscures its location.

Watch closely for the difficult-to-spot white-tailed ptarmigan, a small grouse that lives on the alpine tundra year-round. Relying on camouflage for protection, it changes its plumage to match the seasons. In winter it is pure white but in summer it turns a mottled brown, making it almost impossible to identify from the surrounding rocks.

The broad trail gradually rises toward the saddle between the rocky summit dome and the northeastern ridge, with large cairns marking the way.

Finally, the trail ends abruptly at a vertical drop, which plunges to the north of the saddle.

Upper Coney and Coney lakes sparkle nearly 2,500 feet directly below, backed by the austere humps of the Indian Peaks.

The Saddle to the Summit

Massive cairns mark the final 623-foot scramble through the carelessly strewn boulders to the summit, where a number of waist-high rock shelters provide protection from the strong winds.

The stiff climb rewards hikers with a gargantuan view in every direction. Wedge-shaped Longs Peak thrusts mightily to the north over the deep, glacier-carved drainages of Wild Basin and Middle St. Vrain Creek. To the northwest, past the jagged summits of the Indian Peaks, sprawls Lake Granby. Beyond rise the Never Summer Mountains, marking the northwestern boundary of

Ptarmigan

The white-tailed ptarmigan is the only species of bird that inhabits the alpine tundra year-round. It is a small grouse with feathers growing on its legs and feet.

The ptarmigan relies on its excellent camouflage for protection from predators. In summer, it is mottled brown and black with a white underside and tail, making it practically invisible among the rocks. During winter, it turns pure white to blend perfectly with the snow.

Hikers are often startled when nearby "rocks" suddenly burst into flight or scurry off across the tundra. Ptarmigans lay six to eight buff-colored and faintly spotted eggs in a shallow hollow lined with grass, leaves and feathers. Shortly after hatching, the chicks are able to scamper after their mother.

Rocky Mountain National Park. The Gore Range and Mount Zirkel appear as light turquoise lumps far away on the western horizon.

In the south, the ragged and inhospitable Navajo, Shoshoni and Pawnee peaks brood over the valley of the South St. Vrain Creek. Long Lake rests calmly in the forest above Brainard Lake. In the distance juts the precipitous north-facing slope of 14,264-foot Mount Evans. To the east, past the waves of foothill ranges, the plains seem to stretch to infinity.

Mount Audubon was named in honor of the naturalist and painter, John J. Audubon (1780-1851), by botanist Dr. C.C. Parry and zoologist Dr. J.W. Velie, who, in 1864, made the first recorded ascent. Audubon was world famous for his portraits of birds and animals. Unfortunately, he never set foot in Colorado.

Alpine Tundra

Naturalist John Muir called the alpine tundra "...a land of desolation covered with beautiful light." At first glance this frigid, treeless region in the Rocky Mountains of Colorado may seem barren, but in fact, it supports more than 300 species of plants as well as numerous animals, birds and insects.

Tundra is a Russian word meaning "land of no trees." Arctic tundra exists north of the Arctic Circle. Alpine tundra is the name given to the life zone existing where the tops of peaks jut above the level of tree growth. In Colorado, this begins at an altitude of approximately 11,500 feet.

Above tree line, harsh physical conditions prevail for most of the year. Summer lasts for a brief 40 frost-free days with temperatures rarely exceeding 60 degrees Fahrenheit. In winter, the temperature often falls to minus 30 degrees, with winds gusting to more than 160 mph. Temperatures generally remain below freezing for at least five months a year. Precipitation, most of which falls as snow, is a meager 25 inches.

Few animals inhabit the tundra year-round. Marmots hibernate during the winter. Pikas store large supplies of food underground but remain awake beneath the snow. Ptarmigans change from a mottled brown to a pure white and grow feathers on the bases of their feet. Elk, bighorn sheep and mule deer are abundant during the warmer months.

Plants survive in this inhospitable environment by clinging to the ground. Many are miniature relations of those seen at lower elevations. The rich bed of mosses, lichens, sedges and grasses is studded with a profusion of vibrant wildflowers throughout the short summer. Yellow alpine avens, blue harebells, red kings crown and white Arctic gentians stand out like jewels in the bright sea of green.

Diamond Lake sprawls at the foot of unnamed peaks

~ 18 ~ Diamond Lake

Flora enthusiasts will delight in the multitude of summer wildflowers growing alongside this popular trail in the Indian Peaks Wilderness. With only

800 feet of elevation gain, this is a hike the whole family will enjoy.

Diamond Lake is well endowed with secluded campsites. Therefore, this makes a pleasant destination for beginners or youthful backpackers.

Trailhead

Near the south end of Nederland on Colorado Highway 72/119, turn west onto County Road 130. Drive west for 4.7 miles, going through the small community of Eldora. Take the right fork at a Y-junction. Another 5.0 miles along a bumpy dirt road brings you to the Buckingham Campground. The parking lot for the Fourth of July Trailhead is uphill to the right, past the outhouses.

Trailhead to Arapaho Pass Junction

The Arapaho Pass Trail rises briskly from the Fourth of July Trailhead, traversing along the south-facing flank of the valley that holds the North Fork of Middle Boulder Creek. Planks aid in several stream crossings, although keeping your feet dry is difficult during the peak of spring runoff.

Route

Day hike or overnight; 2.5 miles; easy

Route	Elevation (ft.)	Distance (mi.)
Trailhead	10,160	0
Arapaho Pass Jct	10,850	1.0
Diamond Lake	10,960	2.5

USGS Topographic maps: East Portal, Colo.; Monarch Lake, Colo.

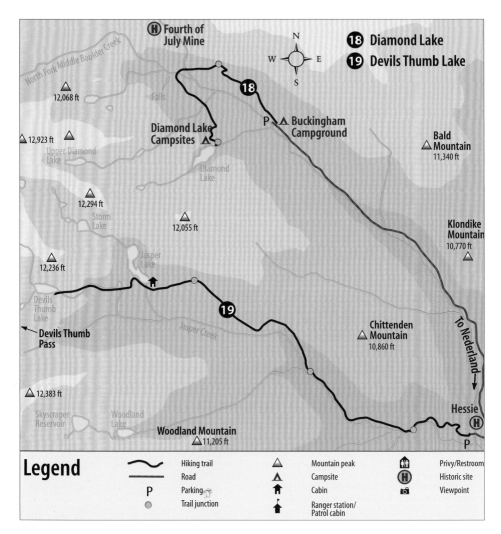

Legend

〰	Hiking trail	△	Mountain peak	⛺	Privy/Restroom
—	Road	⚲	Campsite	Ⓗ	Historic site
P	Parking	🛖	Cabin	📷	Viewpoint
○	Trail junction		Ranger station/ Patrol cabin		

A few wispy strands of aspen struggle to survive among the subalpine firs and Engelmann spruce at this lofty starting elevation. Shrubby willows and tall fireweed enjoy the frequent boggy terrain.

After about 0.5 mile, a sign indicates that you are entering the Indian Peaks Wilderness.

Shortly, the limber pine makes an appearance. This hardy conifer can be identified by its short needles growing in bundles of five.

As the trail climbs higher up the hillside, leaving the stream far below, views extend in all directions. Ahead, the weathered gray peaks of the Continental Divide, streaked here and there with glistening snowfields, rise in bold relief against the sky. The massive cascade straight across the valley emanates from Diamond Lake. Above the waterfall tower nameless summits cradling this tarn.

The trail switchbacks to gain altitude and then contin-

ues at a more leisurely gradient, crossing several creek beds and grassy openings. The lush growth of vegetation reflects the abundance of moisture and the rich environment it fosters.

This area is a jewel throughout the summer, sporting a wealth of elephant's head, clover, harebells, kings crown and waist-high cow parsnip. Particularly spectacular is the profusion of dainty blue columbines, the Colorado state flower.

Pick your way across the rocks over a large side stream and, 1.0 mile into the hike, reach an intersection. The Arapaho Pass Trail continues to the right. Take the left fork to follow the Diamond Lake Trail.

Arapaho Pass Junction to Diamond Lake

The trail meanders up and down for a while through the wildflowers and willows, crossing another creek via two logs and traversing a marshy area with the help of strategically placed planks.

It then swoops down to bridge North Fork of Middle Boulder Creek, rapidly losing 240 feet.

Just upstream from the bridge, a little waterfall tumbles over the rocks and several outcroppings offer excellent picnic spots. This is a fitting destination for those who prefer to avoid the final uphill slog to Diamond Lake.

After crossing the creek, the trail swerves to the left, contouring around the drainage. It then ascends seriously between magnificent examples of large, old-growth conifers.

Upon arriving at the lip of the hanging valley, which contains Diamond Lake, the trail emerges from the trees into an expansive flower-strewn meadow. In an effort to prevent erosion of the fragile ecosystem, the forest service has placed a series of planks to use in your traverse.

The Diamond Lake Trail branches to the left, heading south to join the Devils Thumb Trail. At this junction, continue straight on for a few hundred feet for Diamond Lake.

As you approach the tarn, a map shows the location of the 10 campsites hidden among the surrounding trees.

A meadow strewn with bistort and delicate Rocky Mountain gentians stretches in front of the lake. Inhospitable gray cliffs speckled with permanent icefields loom behind it.

The trail proceeds to the right of Diamond Lake, with paths splitting off to the campsites along the way. After an inlet creek, only a faint fishers' track continues to wind around the shoreline.

Beavers

The technical skills of the beaver to adapt its environment to its needs is, among mammals, only rivaled by humans. It fells trees, cuts the timber into small sections, eats the bark and uses the logs and twigs to dam streams and build lodges. It camouflages the underwater entrance to its nest chamber by keeping the water in the pond at a constant level.

After completing its initial construction work, the beaver continues to excavate channels and build additional dams. It also anchors harvested twigs to the bottom of its pond to eat during winter when the water is frozen.

Beavers are covered by a thick coat of brown, waterproof fur. During the 19th century, the fur was much in demand for hats and coats, and the creature was almost trapped to extinction. Today, it has reestablished itself in most of its former territory.

The largest rodents in North America, beavers can exceed 50 pounds in weight. A layer of subcutaneous fat keeps them warm in the water, and webbed hind feet make them excellent swimmers. They can hold their breath underwater for up to 15 minutes, during which time transparent eyelids allow for constant vision, and the ear and nose orifices can be kept closed.

A beaver, its mate, yearlings and this year's young occupy a lodge. An average of three kits are born in late spring, fully furred and with their eyes open. They remain with their parents for two years.

Diamond Lake sparkles in the evening light

Mountain Lion Etiquette

The mountain lion, which also goes by the name cougar, panther and puma, lives in the mountains and foothills throughout Colorado. A nocturnal animal, it is one of the few predators which presents a real threat to man.

While the possibility of encountering a mountain lion should not deter anyone from venturing into the Rockies, a certain lion etiquette should be observed.

First, jogging along mountain trails is inadvisable, as a fast-moving person is mimicking—to the lion's eyes—the behavior of a deer, which is the lion's preferred entrée. Children should always stay near their parents.

If you are ever threatened by a mountain lion, do whatever you can to appear as large as possible. Raise your arms above your head, speak firmly or shout at the animal, wave your arms and, always facing the animal, back away. Never run. Pick up small children, as their size and behavior makes them most vul-

nerable. A child seated on your shoulders makes you look much larger. If you are attacked, try to remain standing and fight back.

Warning signs are located at trailheads in areas where lions might be encountered.

In truth, it is unlikely that you will ever see a mountain lion except in the zoo.

Because the lion is so big, weighing on average 130 pounds, it is unmistakable. Tawny in color, it has a long, lithe body, short, muscular legs and a lengthy, black-tipped tail.

The mountain lion prefers to feed on large mammals—a deer or two per week forms an ideal diet. When deer are not available, the lion will eat rabbits, marmots, raccoons and other small mammals.

It relies on speed and strength to strike down its prey and then uses its powerful feline teeth to kill instantaneously with a bone-snapping bite at the base of the skull.

Lions are strongly territorial, living almost entirely within their home ranges. Generally loners, only breeding pairs and females with kittens spend time together. Females have no set breeding season and may come into heat at any time of year. In the Colorado Rockies, mating usually takes place in winter or early spring. One to six furry but blind kittens are born about 12 weeks later. The young develop quickly, are weaned after three months and stay with their mothers for a couple of years while they learn necessary survival skills.

Jasper Lake reflects the unnamed peak to its west

~ 19 ~ Devils Thumb Lake

Starting from the ghost town of Hessie, this pleasant trail leads to a lake-speckled basin at the foot of the massive rock buttress known as the Devils Thumb. Most of the hike is through open terrain, entertaining the hiker with vistas at every step.

Trailhead to Devils Thumb Trail Junction

An old mining road runs west for 4.5 miles from Hessie to Jasper Lake. Sometimes the trail coincides with the road; at other times, it deviates to one side or another.

From the Hessie Trailhead, follow the road through a shady forest of aspens and Engelmann spruce. Shortly, the trail begins to ascend along the right flank of the valley, using broad, sweeping switchbacks to gain altitude quickly.

From June until late September, the landscape is an ever-changing kaleidoscope of

Trailhead

To get to Hessie Trailhead, take Colorado Highway 72/119 to the south end of Nederland and turn west onto County Road 130. Drive for 4.7 miles, passing through the small community of Eldora. At a Y-junction, drop down to the left, following the sign for Hessie Townsite. The rough dirt road dead-ends 1.0 mile later in a small parking area. If the road past the intersection is inundated, park along the preceding verge and follow the footpath around the stream.

The trail starts across a wooden bridge over North Fork of Middle Boulder Creek.

Route

Day hike; 5.5 miles one way; moderate

Route	Elevation (ft.)	Distance (mi.)
Trailhead	9,010	0
Devils Thumb Trail Jct	9,430	0.8
Jasper Lake	10,814	4.5
Devils Thumb Lake	11,150	5.5

USGS Topographic maps: Nederland, Colo.; East Portal, Colo.

125

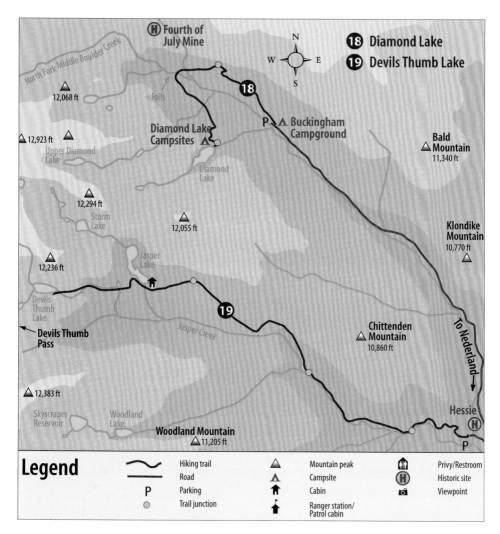

Legend

~~ Hiking trail	△ Mountain peak	🏚 Privy/Restroom
Road	⛺ Campsite	Ⓗ Historic site
P Parking	🏠 Cabin	📷 Viewpoint
⊙ Trail junction	🏠 Ranger station/Patrol cabin	

color. In summer, the hillside by the trail explodes with wild-flowers. Orange and brown butterflies flit from blossom to blossom, pausing to sample the nectar through taste buds in their feet. During early fall, aspens shimmer with gold, each group of trees connected by a common root system changing color in unison.

Forest rapidly gives way to wide-open views extending in all directions. A little cabin near the base of the valley and tailings streaking the opposite slope are signs of mining activity during the 1890s.

To the left, South Fork of Middle Boulder Creek roars its way over a cascade. This spirited waterway forms the main drainage channel for a large basin to the east of the Continental Divide. A little way upstream, it is joined by Jasper Creek emanating from Jasper and Devils Thumb Lakes, as well as a number of other high alpine tarns.

After 0.8 mile, the old road veers left to cross South Fork of Middle Boulder Creek. Stay to the north of the stream on the Devils Thumb Bypass Trail.

Devils Thumb Trail Junction to Jasper Lake

Climb steeply through spruce and aspen, and emerge onto a series of broad meadows dotted with Western yellow paintbrush, bushy cinquefoil and gaillardia.

The sheer, snow-streaked slopes of the Continental Di-

The ruins of a cabin stand near Jasper Lake

your attention. Chittenden Mountain towers to the right and Jasper Creek babbles to the left.

About 0.5 mile past the Indian Peaks Wilderness boundary board, the trail meets the old road returning from the south side of the creek. Turn right for Jasper and Devils Thumb lakes, ignoring the confusing sign indicating that the "Devils Thumb Trail" heads in both directions.

For the next 2.0 miles, the trail winds back and forth across the road, its route often indicated by cairns. Sometimes, the road is overgrown and impassable. On occasion, it is a drier and more direct alternative to the trail.

Pass places where the road has been blasted into the hillside or where the original logs used to construct its surface are still visible.

Ignore the Diamond Lake Trail diverging to the right. This circles around the unnamed mountain separating Jasper Lake from Diamond Lake.

Numerous wildflowers thrive along the verge or in periodic patches of marsh, including larkspur, scarlet paintbrush, Richardson geraniums, goldenrod and fireweed. Greenish-white clusters of poker heuchera adorn crevices in rocky outcrops. Several little ponds sparkle in depressions to the right of the pathway.

vide dominate the western skyline, while an impressive but nameless peak in front of unseen Devils Thumb catches

Hessie, Colorado

After locating silver during the winter of 1891-1892, Captain J. H. Davis built a cabin near the junction of the north and south forks of Middle Boulder Creek, six miles west of Nederland. Word of the riches spread quickly and prospectors flocked to the area.

By December of 1892, a small community had developed, with a school, sawmill, boarding house, two stores and 12 cabins. Davis' wife Hessie joined him and immediately opened a post office. The miners were so delighted that they named the settlement in her honor .

The majority of the mines

that supported the town were around Lost Lake and along Jasper Creek to the west. The largest was the Fourth of July Mine, near Arapaho Pass.

By 1900, most of the silver veins had ceased to produce.

In 1914, only 12 people remained in Hessie. Among them was a 50-year-old bachelor named Champ Smith who worked the Caledonia Tunnel on Bryan Mountain. One day, mailman G. W. Orear discovered Smith's mutilated body in the tunnel.

The coroner and investigators from the Sheriff's office

found that someone had intentionally placed Smith's body over a dynamite charge. During the subsequent inquest, it was discovered that Smith had been a fervent fish and game warden in a community where few people bothered to purchase licenses. He had been shot and his body blown apart for taking his job seriously.

Finally, Wilson Davis and the Smally brothers were apprehended, but they were soon released for lack of evidence. Even today, Hessie's most notorious murder remains unsolved.

Swing left upon approaching the ruins of a cabin and ascend the few feet to pretty Jasper Lake. The sparkling blue waters do an excellent job of reflecting the nameless peak immediately to the west.

Jasper Lake to Devils Thumb Lake

The trail crosses Jasper Lake's outlet stream by a log-jam just above an attractive waterfall and flowery meadow. It borders the southwestern tip of the lake and heads back into the conifers. Now it climbs and moderates, passing through forest and meadow, and completes the final 336-foot elevation gain to Devils Thumb Lake in another 1.0 mile.

Hop over the stepping stones in the outlet. Take a sharp right turn and make your way through the tangle of bushes surrounding Devils Thumb Lake to get the best available view of the Devils Thumb. This abrupt pinnacle presiding over the steel-gray water appears as if it is in the process of falling away from its adjoining mountain.

Talus slopes topped by sheer cliffs fall directly to the northern shore of the tarn. Thickets of dwarf conifers hug the south bank. In the west, scree slopes rise directly to Devils Thumb Pass on the Continental Divide.

The trail climbs to the left of the lake, crossing a vast meadow adorned with a multitude of vibrant wildflowers. Look especially for bright pink elephant's head. A closer examination of this fascinating

The trail passes several reflecting ponds along its route

blossom reveals that it mimics a totem pole of tiny elephant heads, each sporting an up-turned trunk.

While this hike officially ends at Devils Thumb Lake, the 600-foot scramble to the pass is worthwhile for wonderful views north to the Never Summer Wilderness Area, west to the Gore Range and east across the foothills to the plains.

Moose

The moose, with its bulky dark-brown body, overhanging muzzle, short neck and long legs, is most easily distinguished by the bulls' gigantic scoop-shaped antlers.

The word "moose" comes from the Algonquin word *mong-soa,* meaning "twig eater." Adult moose eat up to 60 pounds of willow and aspen saplings a day. They also feed on aquatic plants with their heads completely submerged underwater.

Their rut takes place in September and October. The cows give birth to one or two calves weighing about 25 pounds after an eight-month gestation. Feeding on their mother's milk, the young may gain 150 pounds by the time they are five months old.

You can sometimes see moose in the low-lying valleys on the west side of Rocky Mountain National Park. While they are normally bashful and reclusive, cows with calves and rutting bulls can be unpredictable and dangerous. Keep your distance at all times.

The trail up Pikes Peak provides extensive views

~ 20 ~ Pikes Peak

Pikes Peak is unquestionably the monarch of the southern Front Range and one of the most celebrated peaks in the United States. Nevertheless, it is a gigantic mountain from the hiker's perspective and a climb to its summit should be considered a very serious venture. Although no technical skills are required, it is a long arduous trip, requiring plenty of stamina. The Barr Trail, the classic hikers' route, climbs 7,200 feet in 13.0 miles. This is not for the unconditioned or inexperienced.

With a pre-dawn start, a hardy hiker can complete the 26-mile round trip in a minimum of 16 hours. Many choose to camp along the way or to lodge at Barr Camp, the halfway point. An alternative to walking down is to drop off a car at the summit and to consider this as a shuttle hike, or to have friends meet

Trailhead

From Colorado Springs, go west on US Highway 24 for about 6.0 miles. Take the first exit for Manitou Springs and head through town in a westerly direction. Look for signs for the Pikes Peak Cog Railway. Turn left (south) onto Ruxton Avenue and drive for about 0.7 mile to the railway depot. Continue past the station and turn right up a steep hill following the sign for Barr Trail Parking. Bathrooms, a drinking fountain, picnic tables and a board giving information about flowers, etc. are to the left of the trailhead in the large gravel parking area.

Route

Grueling day hike or two-day hike; 13.0 miles one way; strenuous

Route	Elevation (ft.)	Distance (mi.)
Trailhead	6,600	0
Barr Camp	10,200	7.0
Timberline Shelter	11,500	10.0
Summit	14,110	13.0

USGS Topographic maps: Manitou Springs, Colo.; Pikes Peak, Colo.

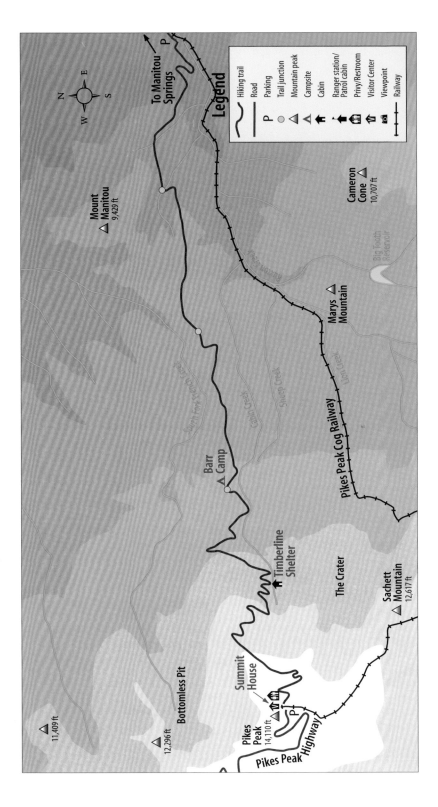

Legend

- ⌇ Hiking trail
- — Road
- P Parking
- ● Trail junction
- △ Mountain peak
- ◁ Campsite
- ◀ Cabin
- ᐤ Ranger station/Patrol cabin
- 🚻 Privy/Restroom
- 🏠 Visitor Center
- 🔭 Viewpoint
- ┼ Railway

N W E S

To Manitou Springs P

Mount Manitou △ 9,429 ft

Cameron Cone △ 10,707 ft

Big Tooth Reservoir

Ruxton Creek

Marys Mountain △

South French Creek

Cabin Creek

Sheep Creek

Lion Creek

Pikes Peak Cog Railway

Barr Camp △

⛺ Timberline Shelter

The Crater

Sachett Mountain △ 12,617 ft

Bottomless Pit

△ 11,409 ft

△ 12,296 ft

Summit House

Pikes Peak △ 14,110 ft

Pikes Peak Highway

you there. Some climbers attempt to ride the train down, but this is only possible on a space-available basis.

The Barr Trail is in Pike National Forest. Forest Service regulations apply to its use.

Trailhead to Barr Camp

Right from the start, the trail shoots steeply upward, using tight zigzags to gain altitude along the northern flank of Englemann Canyon.

Prickly pear, yucca, pinon pine, mountain mahogany and gambel oak dot the open hillside, allowing for unobstructed views.

To the north, across US Highway 24 and the parking lot for the Cave of the Winds, the red rock formations of the Garden of the Gods tower impressively. To the east, the Great Plains stretch behind the sprawling urban development of Manitou Springs. In the base of Englemann Canyon, Ruxton Creek parallels the route of the Manitou and Pikes Peak Cog Railway.

The first part of the trail is a work of art. Reconstructed by the Pikes Peak Young Adult Conservation Corp from 1978-1981, it utilizes wooden railings to prevent hikers from shortcutting the switchbacks.

Gradually, the gambel oak makes room for Douglas fir and ponderosa pine as the trail completes its relentless ascent out of the canyon.

The trail contours around the 9,250-foot peak called Rocky Mountain, rising to the west of Manitou Springs, with the stream flowing far below.

Head left at an unsigned junction and again switchback up the prow of a ridge. As the trail moderates, it yields the first distant vista of the summit of Pikes Peak.

Continue at a more gentle grade along the ridge, heading straight for the bulk of the mountain. Massive granite outcroppings decorate the landscape, offering a respite from the conifers blanketing the foothills.

Pikes Peak is made up of billion-year-old Pikes Peak granite, a mass of once-molten rock that cooled inside the earth. The distinctive pink color of the granite is caused by iron oxide in the rock.

Occasionally, the trail swerves to dodge a gigantic boulder or interrupts its upward progress with a brief descent. More and more aspen offer the potential for excellent fall foliage viewing.

Barr Camp

The Barr Camp makes an ideal base for a two-day climb to the summit of Pikes Peak. It is located at an altitude of 10,200 feet, about halfway along the Barr Trail, the standard route up the mountain.

Fred Barr, the creator of the Barr Trail, built this camp between 1921 and 1924 to use as a rest stop for the burro trips which he led to the top of the peak. Hikers have used it ever since for overnight accommodations (for a small fee) and a place to rest. Maintained by a non-profit organization, it operates year-round.

The rustic, main cabin is the central gathering place in the camp. Warmed by a wood-burning stove, it provides bunk-house accommodations for up to 20 hikers. A second cabin, sleeping 10, is perfect for private youth or church groups. There are also three lean-to shelters which sleep from two to four, an outhouse and places to erect a tent.

The Barr Camp supplies propane cooking stoves, cooking and eating utensils, mattresses, filtered drinking water, picnic tables and emergency first aid. Hikers can purchase snacks during the summer. Call (719) 636-1602 for reservations.

Finally, after 7.0 relentless miles, the trail staggers into Barr Camp.

Barr Camp to Timberline Shelter

Lying at an altitude of 10,200 feet, Barr Camp is a popular place to stop for a well-deserved rest and something to eat. Water is available and, in summer, snacks are sold. You can pitch a tent here free of charge. Those who have reserved a spot in advance (at 719-636-1602) may spend the night in the bunk house for a small fee. Be sure to sign the trail register.

Just past Barr Camp, the trail reaches an intersection. The path to Elk Park, Cascade and Oil Creek Tunnel veers off to the right. Stay left for Pikes Peak.

The trail wanders back and forth, sometimes edging close enough to Cabin Creek to hear the sound of rushing water. A thick subalpine forest of Engelmann spruce and subalpine fir alternates with extensive groves of aspens. The higher the elevation, the earlier the deciduous leaves attain their characteristic fall gold.

At the end of a long northerly traverse, a side trail splits off for Bottomless Pit. Take a sharp left following the sign that reads: Pikes Peak Summit: 4.8 miles.

Notice a large area of dead conifers. These were transformed into lifeless sticks during the mid-1980s by an infestation of spruce bud worm.

As the trail snakes upward, bristlecone pine make an appearance. This species can be identified by its bottle-

The trail heads toward the summit of Pikes Peak

brush-like branches, with needles grouped in distinct bundles of five.

After hiking a total of 10.0 miles, you pass the turnoff to the Timberline Shelter.

Timberline Shelter to the Summit

A short detour to the left takes you across Cabin Creek to a tiny A-frame hut. Open at the front, it offers little more than a covered area to lay a sleeping bag. A sign indicates that it is maintained by the Pikes Peak group of the Colorado Mountain Club and is for emergency use only.

The flower-strewn area alongside the stream is a good place to take a short break while contemplating the steep slopes of Pikes Peak still looming high above you.

Ignore the begging chipmunks and Clark's nutcrackers. It is against forest service regulations to feed them. A creature that relies on humans for food ceases to be wild and becomes unable to forage for itself.

As the trail continues its sinuous upward journey, the conifers get visibly shorter. The strong winds create "banner trees," with branches only growing on the eastern side of the trunks. Then, with the approach of timberline, the evergreens become sparse and stunted, until only occasional tree islands of *krummholz* are able to survive the harsh conditions at this elevation.

Trees on the slope of Pikes Peak have been killed by a beetle infestation

Past the domain of the subalpine forest, the stiff climb rewards you with uninterrupted panoramas. To the east, Pikes Peak swoops downward to the low foothill ranges, slashed by deep canyons, which dwindle to the north and south. Tiny reservoirs sparkle like diamonds amid the dark turquoise sea of conifers.

The Manitou and Pikes Peak Cog Railway

The Manitou and Pikes Peak Cog Railway enables passengers to experience the sensational panorama from atop 14,110-foot Pikes Peak in the comfort of a train.

A man named Zalmon Simmons from Wisconsin first had the notion of building a railroad up Pikes Peak, after a painful ascent on a mule called Balaam. His objective, states historian Marshall Sprague, was "to alleviate the suffering of the soft-bottomed human race."

The first train on the Manitou and Pikes Peak Cog Railway reached the top of the mountain in June, 1890, at a cost of $1,250,000. It has operated every summer since then.

At the time of construction, the railroad was the highest in the world. Today, it is the highest standard-gauge line in the world. A cog system between the tracks provides the pull mechanism for the cars.

Swiss-built diesel trains have superseded the old steam engines. The railway travels 8.9 miles from the Manitou Springs depot to the summit on a 25% grade. Round-trip journey time is about three hours, including a 30 minute break on top. The railway operates from April through October, depending on weather conditions.

Pikes Peak is perhaps the most famous mountain in the United States. It dominates the surrounding landscape, presiding like a sentinel over the town of Colorado Springs and the Great Plains.

The superlative panorama from its 14,110-foot summit inspired Katharine Lee Bates to compose the words to the classic American anthem *America the Beautiful*.

Captain Zebulon Pike first saw the peak that would later bear his name in November, 1806 as he was leading an expedition up the Arkansas River. Together with a small party of men, Pike made a valiant effort to scale the mountain. He stated in his journal how his ill-equipped party fought snow and wind and only succeeded in reaching an intermediate summit. He concluded, "I believe no human being could have ascended to its pinnacle."

Although unsuccessful, Pike made history with the first recorded attempt to climb any mountain in Colorado.

On July 13, 1820, botanist Dr. Edwin James and two others from Major Stephen Long's expedition to Colorado set out to conquer the peak. The first evening, they camped below timberline. On the afternoon of July 14, James and his companions stood on the summit. Again, history was made with the first successful recorded ascent of a United States Fourteener.

Unfortunately, the party returned to their base camp only to discover that their smoldering campfire had spread to the surrounding forest. Unable to fight the conflagration, they left it to

burn itself out.

Major Long rewarded James by calling the mountain "James Peak." However, as Pike had been the first person to write about the peak, it generally became known among mountain men as "Pikes Peak." That name became official in 1843 when John Fremont used it on one of his maps.

During the 1850s, the first trail to the summit was built. On July 6, 1858, Julia Holmes scaled the peak, becoming the first woman to climb a North American Fourteener.

With the founding of Colorado Springs in 1871 and the development of Manitou Springs as a health center, the area began to draw tourists like a magnet. The ascent of Pikes Peak became popular, especially after

the construction of an improved trail. For a while it was even considered fashionable to ride to the top on a donkey.

In 1889, a carriage road to the summit was completed, and the following year saw the opening of the Manitou and Pikes Peak Cog Railway. Twenty-five years later, the carriage road was converted into the automobile highway now used by more than 250,000 motorists per year.

The Barr Trail was finished in 1920, and remains the most popular hiking route up the mountain.

Today, hundreds of thousands of people reach the summit of Pikes Peak by train, car or on foot. Few would deny that it is one of the most outstanding experiences this country has to offer.

Ponderosa pine cones

Behind the foothills sprawls Colorado Springs and a little to the north rise the minuscule undulations of the Black Forest. The gray-brown plains stretch eastward as far as the eye can see.

The trail now switchbacks through the alpine tundra ecosystem, a region with conditions similar to those found in northern Canada and Siberia.

Despite the rigorous climate, more than 300 species of plants thrive on the Colorado tundra. Watch closely for miniature gardens supporting Arctic gentians, Western yellow paintbrush, kings crown and sky pilots. In the early fall, this landscape explodes in a fantastic display of rust-red alpine aven leaves.

Look and listen for the animals and birds that inhabit this region during the short summer. The bighorn sheep, the Colorado state animal, is so sure-footed that even a three-day-old lamb can leap safely from one narrow rock ledge to another. The yellow-bellied marmot often betrays its location by a high-pitched whistle, intended to warn neighboring marmots of impending danger. The elusive and industrious pika is much more difficult to spot. This tiny guinea-pig-like creature spends the summer storing grass in miniature haystacks. By first snowfall, the pika may have 50 pounds of hay to eat during the long winter. The ptarmigan is the only bird to call the tundra its year-round home. Relying on camouflage for protection from predators, it is almost impossible to identify from the surrounding rocks in summer.

Granite outcroppings, the size of buses and trucks, dominate the landscape. Erosion has left its mark with vertical fractures towering to domes and turrets and curious rock sculptures. Here, the imagination can work overtime. From the right angle, rock sculptures look like faces, animals or cartoon characters.

A respite from the grueling climb comes with a lengthy contour to the south along the eastern flank of the mountain. This terminates at the edge of a cirque, 1,500 feet deep and over half a mile wide, chiseled from the core of the peak by ice age glaciers. If the wind is not too fierce, you may hear the cog train as it struggles up the opposite ridge. With only 800 feet left to gain and one mile to go, you can begin to

Pikes Peak Highway

Each year, about a quarter of a million visitors drive to the summit of Pikes Peak on this toll road, experiencing some of the United States' most breathtaking scenery from the comfort of a car.

As the Pikes Peak Highway climbs from an elevation of 7,400 to 14,110 feet in 19 miles, it passes through forests of pine, spruce and aspen and eventually enters the alpine tundra, a life zone similar to that existing north of the Arctic Circle.

For a long time, people had been intrigued by the possibility of driving up Pikes Peak. The first carriage road was opened in 1889 and in 1900 a well-known Coloradan named John Brisben Walker attempted to reach the top by automobile. Despite the fact that he only got to an altitude of 11,000 feet, the *Rocky Mountain News* boasted that it was the highest point ever reached by an auto in the world.

The following year, W. B. Felker and C. A. Yont attained the summit in a Locomobile Steamer.

Cripple Creek mining magnate Spencer Penrose converted the old carriage road into an automobile highway in 1915. To help pay the then-staggering cost of $350,000, he started the first Pikes Peak Hill Climb. Twenty drivers raced to the summit. Rea Lentz won in an eight-cylinder Romano.

Today, the second oldest race in the United States (the Indianapolis 500 is older) is an annual event, hosting premier race car drivers from around the country.

The terrain grows more rocky as the trail approaches the summit

feel the sense of accomplishment in a laborious job almost complete.

Again, the trail zigzags upward at breakneck speed. Boulders blanket the slope, stifling even the most tenacious of plants. A plaque on one granite outcrop honors Fred Barr, who constructed the trail between 1914 and 1918.

All of a sudden you arrive at the summit—the top of the world. Before you spreads the magnificent panorama that inspired Katharine Lee Bates to write *America the Beautiful* in 1893.

"Oh beautiful for spacious skies, for amber waves of grain, for purple mountain majesties above the fruited plain…"

The Pikes Peak Summit House, next to the railway depot, has a snack bar, gift shop and restrooms. If a train has just arrived, you may have to wait in line to enjoy these facilities.

Before you start your descent, take the time to examine the boards identifying the

Sangre de Cristos, Collegiate Peaks and numerous other distant mountain ranges.

Fred Barr and Barr Trail

The Barr Trail is the classic hikers' route up Pikes Peak. Gaining 7,200 feet in 13 miles, it offers the greatest base-to-summit climb on any mountain in Colorado.

Fred Barr (1882-1940) first had the idea of constructing a trail to the top of the famous mountain. A road and cog railway had both been completed in the late 1800s, so people were familiar with the sensational panorama from the lofty 14,110-foot-high summit.

Barr's business was providing burro sightseeing tours around Manitou Springs for tourists. He thought that burro

trips to the summit of the region's highest peak would become a popular alternative to ascending by car or train.

Between 1914 and 1918 he constructed the Barr Trail and, in 1924, he opened the Barr Camp for use as an overnight rest station. His unusual outing delighted visitors for many years.

Today, numerous hikers enjoy the trail. Each summer, the Pikes Peak Ascent and Marathon attract thousands of runners from all over the United States.

The trail passes by fascinating rock formations

~ 21 ~ Lost Creek Wilderness Loop

The Lost Creek area was a favorite retreat of Denver and Colorado Springs residents long before it achieved wilderness status. Giant rock formations tower above the landscape, creating an individuality and wild grandeur rarely found so

Trailhead

Take US Highway 285 to Pine Junction and turn south onto County Road 126. Drive for 21.8 miles, passing through Pine and Buffalo Creek. Just south of the Wigwam Campground, take a right **(west)** on Forest Road #211, following the signs for Cheesman Lake and Goose Creek Campground. After 2.0 miles, turn right for Lost Valley Ranch and Goose Creek Campground. Go west for 1.1 miles, stay left at a fork in the road and continue for another 5.2 miles. At a junction past Molly Gulch Campground, turn right for Goose Creek Campground. Drive for 4.7 miles, bearing left when Forest Road #541 descends to the right-Cross Goose Creek and pass Goose Creek Campground. Head right onto the Goose Creek Trailhead access road and drive for 1.3 miles to the large parking area. The trailhead is to the left. The Goose Creek Trail is extremely popular.

Route

Three-day backpack; 24-mile circuit; moderate

Route	Elevation (ft.)	Distance (mi.)
Trailhead	8,200	0
Hankins Pass Trail Jct	8,000	0.2
Historic Buildings Jct	8,620	3.9
McCurdy Park Trail Jct	9,430	6.5
Brookside-McCurdy Trail Jct	10,900	14.0 (Approx.)
Lake Park Trail Jct	10,740	15.0 (Approx.)
Highest point of the hike	11,600	17.5 (Approx.)
Hankins Pass	10,000	19.6
Hankins Pass Trail Jct	8,000	23.8
Trailhead	8,200	24.0

USGS Topographic map: McCurdy Mountain, Colo.

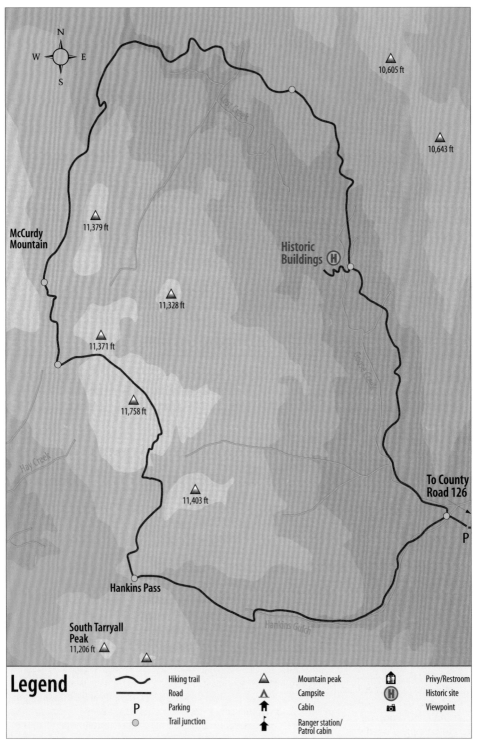

N
W · E
S

10,605 ft

10,643 ft

Hay Creek

11,379 ft

McCurdy
Mountain

Historic
Buildings Ⓗ

11,328 ft

11,371 ft

Goose Creek

11,758 ft

Hay Creek

11,403 ft

To County
Road 126

P

Hankins Pass

Hankins Gulch

South Tarryall
Peak
11,206 ft

Legend

〜 Hiking trail
— Road
P Parking
○ Trail junction

△ Mountain peak
⚑ Campsite
♠ Cabin
⬆ Ranger station/
Patrol cabin

🏛 Privy/Restroom
Ⓗ Historic site
📷 Viewpoint

In places, rocks aid in maintaining the route of the trail

Lost Creek vanishes and reappears many times in Lost Creek Wilderness

close to large centers of population.

During the first half of the circuit, the trail undulates along the eastern flank of the vast canyon carved by Goose Creek (which becomes Lost Creek further up its drainage), climbing and dropping around deeply eroded side valleys. The second half of the route consists of a long climb to a spectacular viewpoint, followed by a lengthy descent.

As no organized facilities exist along the trail, backpackers must bring all food and other necessities for the three-day hike.

Trailhead to Historic Buildings Junction

The trail falls steeply from the trailhead, through a montane forest of ponderosa pine and Douglas fir. After 0.2 mile it bridges Hankins Gulch and reaches a junction. The Hankins Pass Trail #630 heads to the left. The Goose Creek Trail #612 veers right. To hike the loop in a counter-clockwise direction as described here, start by going to the right. You will end your journey at this point after descending from Hankins Pass.

Shortly, the trail encounters Goose Creek and turns left to parallel the spirited stream through a narrow canyon. Willows and a host of other water-loving bushes thrive in this lush environment. Richardson geraniums, goldenrods and black-eyed Susans dot the trail's edge.

After 0.6 miles, cross Goose Creek by a metal footbridge and continue along its right bank.

The unusual granite formations that characterize this region loom above the ridges enclosing the valley or recline alongside the trail. As Goose Creek meanders around huge boulders, deep pools promise a fisherman's paradise.

A number of flat grassy stretches, both near the trail and on the other side of the stream, are suitable for camping.

Soon, the trail emerges from the thin defile and starts to ascend the eastern flank of a broad valley.

A mountain ridge towers

to the west, sculpted by nature into a dramatic geological masterpiece. Weather-beaten turrets, cathedral-like spires and rounded domes soar above sheer cliffs. A distinct thumb-like pinnacle juts to the northwest, with a natural arch and massive dome nearby.

The trail now rises and falls, rounding side valleys and surmounting ridges, and rewarding hikers with periodic views of the formidable canyon. As with much of this circuit, the wealth of quaking aspens decorating the gullies lights up the landscape with brilliant yellow in early fall.

After 3.9 miles, a sign indicates "Historic Buildings" downhill to the left.

Historic Site

A couple of log cabins stand a few hundred yards to the left of the trail next to the ruins of two other buildings.

Between 1891 and 1913,

The Colorado Trail

The Colorado Trail is a continuous, non-motorized recreational pathway that wanders through the Colorado Rockies. It starts at Waterton Canyon, just southwest of Denver, and runs for 500 miles to Durango. Along the way, it traverses five major river systems, six designated wilderness areas, seven national forests and eight mountain ranges.

The trail was designed to link some of the most stunning scenic areas and fascinating historical regions in the state. During the trail's long journey, hikers have the opportunity to experience the popular resorts of Breckenridge and Copper Mountain, the historic mining towns of Leadville and Creede, the unusual rock formations of Lost Creek Wilderness and the remote splendor of the San Juans.

The Colorado Trail exists today largely thanks to 15 years of hard work by Colorado Mountain Club Member, Gudy Gaskill. Gaskill, who is now in her 70s, was born in Oslo, Norway, and came to the United States as an infant. Involved with the trail's development since 1973, she became the driving force behind the organization, recruitment and motivation of volunteer construction crews.

In an opening ceremony at

the Waterton Canyon Trailhead on Sunday, July 24, 1988, Gaskill modestly stated, "…for the thought that this is my doing…I've had a lot of dreams about it, but I can't believe it's actually succeeded."

Both novice and experienced hikers can enjoy the Colorado Trail. While some are content to do day hikes, others plan to do the entire 500-mile trip. As this takes from six to eight weeks, most choose to backpack different segments each summer. You do not need to be a hiker to enjoy the spectacular scenery and serenity of this long-distance pathway. Some people prefer to travel on horseback, by llama trekking, running or by bicycle. However, as bikes are not permitted in designated wildernesses, cyclists must find alternate routes around these areas.

In order to travel along the Colorado Trail, it is advisable to purchase *The Colorado Trail: The Official Guidebook* by Randy Jacobs, which is published by the Colorado Trail Foundation. Breaking the trail into 28 segments, this book provides invaluable details on points of access, campsites, distances and mountain bike detours, together with information on the history of the trail and the geology, flora and fauna

observed along the route.

The Colorado Trail is administered and maintained by the Colorado Trail Foundation in cooperation with the U.S. Forest Service. The Colorado Trail Foundation is a nonprofit educational organization run mostly by volunteers and funded primarily by Friends of the Colorado Trail. It recruits and trains volunteers for trail construction, organizes an Adopt-a-Trail maintenance program and distributes trail-related literature.

For those who would like to hike the Colorado Trail in the company of a group of like-minded adventurers, the Colorado Trail Foundation offers eight, week-long treks from late June through mid-August each year. These treks allow you to hike 10 to 20 miles each day with a knowledgeable guide, while carrying only a day pack. Support staff transport personal gear from campsite to campsite, erect a base camp each night complete with kitchen tent, "john" tent and shower tent, and cook all meals. In order to participate on a Colorado Trail Trek, you must be a Friend of the Colorado Trail.

For more information about the Colorado Trail, call the Colorado Trail Foundation at (303) 384-3729, Extension 113.

the Antero and Lost Park Reservoir Company made a futile attempt to construct a subterranean dam on Goose Creek. The aim was to create a reservoir to supply water to Denver. The huts, still visible, served as housing for employees involved in the project.

Next to the cabins is the mysterious grave of a prospector who may have died while searching for the Lost Jackman Mine—once believed to be richly supplied with gold deposits.

The trail leading to the right of the standing cabins drops into a skinny ravine and, after about 0.7 mile, arrives at the shafthouse, marked by a rusting steam engine. From this spot, a shaft was sunk down to the river as it flowed through an underground passage. If the dam had been successful, water would have inundated Reservoir Gulch, the magnificent valley to the north.

Historic Buildings Junction to McCurdy Park Trail Junction

The Goose Creek Trail climbs steeply, descends into Watkins Gulch, crawls upward again and drops into Reservoir Gulch.

This is the pattern for the first half of the circuit. The trail slogs uphill only to dive back down into the many deep-cut valleys etched into the perimeter of the canyon. Hard-earned elevation gain is quickly lost, to be re-attained with even greater effort.

Off to the west, Lost Creek now appears and disappears, losing itself beneath the jumble of castle-sized outcroppings littering the scene.

Sometimes the trail approaches Lost Creek. This allows you to explore giant boulder caves, box canyons and possibly one of the large tunnels created by the stream as it worms its way through the granite.

The bounty of creeks along this stretch provides ample opportunities to refill your water bottles. Be sure, however, to filter the water to remove the *giardia lamblia* cysts present in most Rocky Mountain streams.

Unless you decide to stop early for the night, the prime camp spots may already be occupied. Remember to pitch your tent more than 100 feet away

from all waterways, in keeping with wilderness regulations. Fire rings and charred logs, signs of past campsites, can be an eyesore in the landscape. Cause the minimum impact to the environment by removing all traces of your overnight stay.

Keep a lookout for the numerous creatures inhabiting this wild canyon. Most commonly spotted are mule deer, elk or the Rocky Mountain bighorn sheep, Colorado's state animal. Less often seen are the raccoon and nocturnal bobcat.

The trail switchbacks upward to attain its highest point so far in the hike. An excellent panorama extends back down the canyon, offering an overview of the terrain that you have hiked and providing another opportunity for you to observe the fascinating rock sculptures.

McCurdy Park Trail Junction to Brookside-McCurdy Trail Junction

Six and a half miles into the hike, at an altitude of 9,420 feet, you reach a junction with the McCurdy Park Trail #628. The Goose Creek Trail continues straight on. Take the left fork and zigzag down through the ponderosa pine, Douglas fir and aspen into another arm of the Lost Creek canyon.

Wilder and even more

left: **Amanita muscaria**, *a common mushroom*

141

Interesting granite formations characterize the scenery in Lost Creek Wilderness

spectacular, the landscape is a jumble of rounded domes, precariously perched monoliths, smooth cliffs and fallen chunks of granite. A careless giant could not have wreaked more havoc.

Entering Refrigerator Gulch, the trail tunnels through a deliciously cool aspen grove before it crosses a creek via two logs. Several good camp spots are dotted along the floor of the ravine.

The trail continues to alternate between clambering upward and dipping into side gulches as it progresses westward through the agglomeration of tumbled boulders.

Once again the pathway drops to meet Lost Creek, just where the water emerges from an underground passage to flow through a won-

derland of fantastic rock sculptures. Trout hide beneath its banks and a little meadow blazes with wild roses and fireweed. This is one of the loveliest spots in the entire loop and a prime area to spend the night.

Do not follow the track that fords the stream at this point. The main trail stays to the north of the brook, climbing up and over a rocky ridge, and descending back down to Lost Creek. Make your way through the willows and nettles until you cross Lost Creek by a three-log bridge.

Take the trail to the left, ascending through aspen and huge rock outcroppings. After a while, you get a good view of a V-shaped drainage cut between granite pinnacles high on the mountain

ridge to the south. This indicates the trail's general direction of travel.

Drop down to a series of tiny ponds. Above you towers the gully that the trail climbs in its longest and most arduous ascent of the loop.

The aspen blanketing the hillsides are particularly spectacular when autumn tints them gold in concert with the red of the occasional Rocky Mountain maples.

The trail crosses a stream via stepping stones, then switchbacks upward, gaining altitude quickly as it clings to the left side of the narrowing ravine.

Gradually, the granite outcroppings, jutting above, creep nearer and nearer. After a long, long hike, the valley opens into McCurdy Park, a broad meadow strewn with bushy cinquefoil, orange paintbrush and alpine avens. Mushrooms of all kinds and colors thrive in this moist environment.

The trail weaves through groves of bristlecone pine, easily identified by their needles, which grow in distinct bundles of five.

At last it reaches the top of the nameless pass at an elevation of 10,900 feet, where the Brookside-McCurdy Trail #607 merges from the right.

Brookside-McCurdy Trail Junction to Lake Park Trail Junction

Continue straight, descending through large old-growth conifers. The trail crosses the infant Hay Creek in a willow-choked pasture and heads back into the spruce on the left flank of the valley.

There are several good camp spots on both sides of the creek in this area. This is also the last reliable water source until you descend into Hankins Gulch—several miles and many hours away.

After a short ascent, the trail arrives at a junction.

Lake Park Trail Junction to Hankins Pass

Head left on the Lake Park Trail #639, switchbacking eastward. Continue to climb past a saddle between two unnamed summits. Finally, at almost 11,600 feet in altitude, you reach the highest point of the hike.

The stiff climb rewards you with a stupendous panorama east over the Lost Creek Wilderness Area and the foothills to the gray-green distant plains. Granite outcroppings to the left of the trail provide perfect seats for spectators. This would be a wonderful place to watch the sunrise. Unfortunately, there is no water nearby, so camping is inadvisable. The delicate blossoms of James' saxifrage stand out like jewels in crevices in the pinkish rock formations.

The trail now descends amid huge serrated ridges into Lake Park, which, despite its name and the appearance of the topographic map, has neither ponds nor streams during the

latter part of the summer. Handsome specimens of Parry gentian adorn the wide, peaceful meadow.

A final short ascent out of Lake Park brings you to the beginning of a long, winding downhill stretch to Hankins Pass. Views to the west reveal the Tarryall Valley, backed by the Kenosha Mountains and the vast flat depression of South Park.

The trail swoops downward to Hankins Pass, where it intersects the Hankins Pass Trail #630.

Hankins Pass to Trailhead

Turn left at the junction and meander down through tall aspen and spruce. Shortly, a stream begins to trickle alongside the trail, but the presence of grazing cattle is a deterrent to sampling its murky water.

The spruce gradually give way to ponderosa pine, Douglas fir and dwarf juniper as altitude is lost. Numerous wildflowers speckle the occasional meadows.

The trail bridges back and forth across the creek as the valley alternately narrows and widens.

Finally, 4.2 miles from Hankins Pass, you reach the junction with the Goose Creek Trail, where you started your three-day hike. The trailhead is a mere 0.2 mile uphill to your right.

Vail & Environs

The ski resort of Vail nestles in the long, narrow Vail Valley

Located 100 miles west of Denver along Interstate 70, Vail sprawls in a deep valley flanked by two awe-inspiring wilderness areas. Along with its reputation as a world-class ski resort, Vail is also a popular destination for summer adventurers. The Gore Range, cradling the

Eagles Nest Wilderness Area, towers to the north. To the southwest, the Holy Cross Wilderness Area surrounds the distinctive Mount of the Holy Cross. Both regions are studded with crystal-clear alpine lakes and crisscrossed by rushing streams. Numerous trails lead through colorful forests to open tundra, providing hikers with the opportunity to enjoy pristine beauty.

Hike 22 approaches the Gore Range from the east. Passing through one of the most diverse bird sanctuaries

in Colorado, it follows an old road to the site of a late 19th-century mine.

Hikes 23 and 24 originate from the town of Vail itself. They penetrate deep into the Gore Range, culminating at tarns huddled beneath 13,000-foot summits.

Hike 25 winds through the spectacular Holy Cross Wilderness Area to a unique basin dotted with 14 lakes.

Vail is well supplied with accommodations, restaurants and other amenities. The Gore Creek Campground

lies to the east of town at the beginning of the bike path over Vail Pass, and several other Forest Service campgrounds border US Highway 24 to the south.

left: The flamboyant Parry's primrose adorns high-altitude stream banks

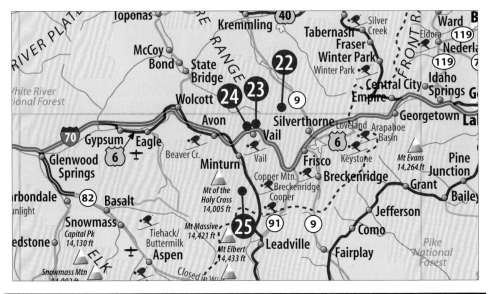

Other Hikes in the Vail Area

Two Elk National Scenic Trail

Shuttle day hike, 11 miles one way
Elevation gain: 2,300 feet
Rating: Moderate
USGS Topographic map: Red Cliff, Colo. and Minturn, Colo.

Few hiking paths achieve the designation of National Scenic Trail, a title given only to the most varied, historic and panoramic of routes. Starting by ascending a narrow ravine to the west of Vail Pass, the Two Elk National Scenic Trail meanders through the famous bowls on the back of Vail Mountains before descending to Minturn via a luxuriant valley. Expansive views of the Gore Range and Holy Cross Wilderness, flower-strewn meadows and the experience of hiking across one of Colorado's prime ski areas without its winter coat of snow provide a refreshing contrast to the typical wilderness hikes.

Holy Cross City

Day hike or overnight, 3.9 miles one way
Elevation gain: 2,049 feet
Rating: Moderate
USGS Topographic map: Mount of the Holy Cross, Colo.

In 1879, gold was discovered near the Mount of the Holy Cross. Numerous mining communities sprang up, including Holy Cross City, just four miles south of the mountain. Despite that fact that it boomed for only four years, at its peak this town boasted two general stores, two saloons, the Timberline Hotel and 300 inhabitants.

The Holy Cross City Trail follows the route of the old stagecoach road to the now-crumbling ghost town. Hikers choosing to examine the mining remains littering the hillsides should exercise extreme caution.

Notch Mountain

Day hike, 5.0 miles one way
Elevation gain: 2,937
Rating: Difficult
USGS Topographic map: Mount of the Holy Cross, Colo.

Since 1873, when the famous Western photographer William Jackson took his inspirational photographs of Mount of the Holy Cross, this peak has been a popular destination for religious pilgrimage. The summit of 13,237-foot Notch Mountain, rising just across the valley to the northeast, provides an unequaled view of the cross on this sacred mountain and of the lake below known as the Bowl of Tears.

The trail climbs by means of a series of switchbacks to the Notch Mountain Shelter, a large rock building constructed in 1924 to house the hordes ascending this peak. The summit of Notch Mountain lies 0.5 mile to the north of the shelter.

The valley of Rock Creek past the Boss Mine site penetrates the Gore Range

~ 22 ~ Rock Creek

Through popular hike in the Eagles Nest Wilderness Area follows an old mining road to the remains of the Boss Mine. Along the way, it passes through the

Alfred M. Bailey Bird Nesting Area, one of the most biologically diverse bird sanctuaries in Colorado. Grassy meadows, abundant wildflowers, trembling aspen, beaver ponds, rich streamside scenery, spectacular vistas and a chorus of exuberant birdsong are all features of this gentle stroll.

The Rock Creek Trailhead is one of the major access points for the Gore Range Trail, which runs for 54.5 miles along the eastern side of the Gore Range.

Trailhead to the Gore Range Trail

Although the trailhead is in Arapaho National Forest, the mining road almost immediately enters White River National Forest.

A sign indicates that this is the Alfred M. Bailey Bird Nesting Area, founded by the Denver Field Ornithologists in 1971. An unusual

Trailhead

Take Exit 205 from Interstate 70 at Silverthorne and head north on Colorado Highway 9 for 7.7 miles. Turn left on Rock Creek Road, just across from the Blue River Campground. Drive southwest for 1.2 miles and turn left following the brown sign for Rock Creek Trailhead. The last 1.5 miles is along a rough dirt road. While unsuitable for trailers, it is passable by cars. The trailhead is at the southwestern tip of the parking lot.

Route

Day hike; 1.7 miles one way; easy

Route	Elevation (ft.)	Distance (mi.)
Trailhead	9,500	0
Gore Range Trail Crossing	9,620	0.5
Boss Mine	10,200	1.7

USGS Topographic map: Willow Lakes, Colo.

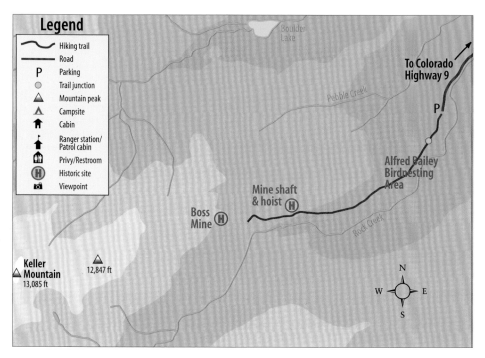

Legend

〰	Hiking trail
──	Road
P	Parking
○	Trail junction
△	Mountain peak
▲	Campsite
⌂	Cabin
⛨	Ranger station/ Patrol cabin
🏠	Privy/Restroom
Ⓗ	Historic site
📷	Viewpoint

Boulder Lake

To Colorado Highway 9

Pebble Creek

P

Alfred Bailey Birdnesting Area

Mine shaft & hoist Ⓗ

Boss Mine Ⓗ

Rock Creek

Keller Mountain
13,085 ft

△ 12,847 ft

N W E S

number of species breed in this site because of its wide variety of habitats.

The abundance of aspen among the lodgepole pine makes this hike up the North Rock Creek drainage particularly attractive in early fall. The mesh of golden leaves shimmering atop the whitish trunks provides a stunning contrast to the dark green of the evergreens and the cobalt blue of Colorado's autumn sky.

Gore Range Trail Crossing to Boss Mine

After 0.5 mile, the Gore Range Trail crosses the road. Continue straight for the Boss Mine. By turning right or left, you may hike to several scenic alpine lakes in the Eagles Nest Wilderness Area.

Beaver ponds, along with many ponds lining the stream, glisten below to the left.

The road descends briefly and passes an expansive meadow dotted with bushy cinque-foil, alpine avens, aspen daisies, harebells and clover. At its western end stands a tiny abandoned house.

North Rock

Creek meanders alongside the meadow, offering a soothing backdrop for a leisurely picnic. This is a perfect place to rest while children explore the lush streamside environment.

Streaks of yellowish tailings on the evergreen-clad hillside to the south are signs of the mining that took place here a

above:
A howling
coyote

The trail follows an old mining road through lodgepole pines and aspens

cabin are being swallowed by the forest a little to your left.

The trail exits the trees, and a vast hillside blanketed by tailings indicates the location of the once-fruitful Boss Mine. Fireweed and wild raspberry, often the first plants to reclaim a patch of disturbed land, speckle the barren slope.

Magnificent views extend up the glacier-carved valley to the rugged Gore Range. The ridge of Keller Mountain, looming above the tailings, is the only peak in the region bearing a name.

After crossing the mine site, the road swoops around to the right, only to fade out after climbing a few hundred yards.

From the bend in the road, a faint track continues along the northern side of the valley, offering a challenge for intrepid hikers and determined fisherfolk.

The Boss, Josie and Thunderbolt mines produced silver in the valley of North Rock Creek from 1881 into the early 1900s. At one time, the miners lived in the settlement of Naomi, at the junction of Rock Creek Road and Colorado Highway 9. They commuted the five miles to the mines by horse and pack mule and used these animals to transport the ore back to the highway. In June 1897, *The Denver Republican* stated that the Boss and Thunderbolt had yielded almost $500,000 in silver ore.

hundred years ago.

The trail now rushes uphill, clinging to the right flank of the valley. It leaves the creek and its cheerful melody far below to the left. Aspen clothe the right-hand slope. Ahead, the distant bare summits of the Gore Range protrude above the aspen.

Brilliant orange butterflies flit back and forth in the colorful display of arnica, wild roses, thistles, pearly everlasting and western yellow paintbrush growing on the grassy verge.

Just before the road narrows, the ruins of an old mine shaft and hoist house hide in a depression over a bank to the right. The remains of a

The Continental Divide Trail

The Continental Divide is an 8,000-mile-long watershed that runs through North America from Wales, Alaska to the Panama Canal. The Continental Divide National Scenic Trail (CDNST) journeys along this natural partition for the 3,100 miles that it meanders through the United States.

Many consider the 759 miles passing through Colorado's Rocky Mountains to be the most breathtaking section. It is only in Colorado that the trail reaches altitudes of above 12,000 feet and, in fact, it climbs to its highest point on top of 14,270-foot Grays Peak. In the San Juan Mountains, it remains in the realm of the alpine tundra for 120 miles of sensational panoramas. As it travels through pristine landscapes of majestic peaks, awesome ridges and deep-carved valleys, it explores Colorado's rich variety of ecosystems and weaves through 11 designated wilderness areas.

After spending much of his life working to make his dream of the Appalachian Trail a reality, 87-year-old Benton Makaye envisioned a pathway connecting existing wilderness areas along the Continental Divide. He presented his idea to Congress in 1968, but it was not until 1978 that the CDNST received official recognition under the National Parks and Recreation Act. Despite the fact that most of the route uses well-marked, long-established pathways, only 90 percent of the CDNST is currently complete in Colorado. The final realization of Makaye's dream will require considerable funding and volunteer effort for the next few years.

The majority of the CDNST passes through National Forest land. However, it is the responsibility of the non-profit membership Continental Divide Trail Alliance (CDTA) to raise the funds needed to protect, build, maintain and manage the trail.

Alfred M. Bailey Bird Nesting Area

The Alfred M. Bailey Bird Nesting Area is located in the Rock Creek drainage on the east side of the Gore Range in the Eagles Nest Wilderness Area.

The site was founded by the Denver Field Ornithologists in 1971 to protect the numerous birds nesting in its widely diverse habitats. Subalpine forest, aspen, alpine tundra, beaver pond, meadow and cliff environments are all represented in the area.

Ongoing research is being carried out by the Colorado Bird Observatory in cooperation with the Colorado Division of Wildlife. Birds are carefully caught, weighed and measured, and information about their age, sex and condition are recorded. Individuals are also marked with an aluminum U.S. Fish and Wildlife Service band.

Birds nesting in the area in-

clude broad-tailed hummingbirds, Western and olive-sided flycatchers, wood pewees, violet-green and tree swallows, mountain chickadees and pine siskins. The area contains one of the few known breeding sites in Colorado of the "dusky" fox sparrow.

The site was named in honor of Dr. A.M. Bailey, director of the Denver Museum of Natural History for more than 40 years.

Pitkin Lake huddles in a cirque at the head of the valley

~ 23 ~ Pitkin Lake

T he aquamarine teardrop named Pitkin Lake rests in a cirque directly below two 13,000-foot summits of the Gore Range in the Eagles Nest

Wilderness Area. The hike to this tarn is a favorite of local residents as it starts in the town of Vail itself. Winding along a glacial valley, the trail passes through aspens, conifers and flower-strewn meadows, and offers views of two spectacular waterfalls.

Anglers tell tales of 10- to 12-inch brook and native trout lurking in Pitkin Lake and Pitkin Creek.

Trailhead

Turn off Interstate 70 at Exit 180 for Vail East Entrance. Head east along the North Frontage Road for 0.2 mile. A small parking area lies to the north (left) of the road immediately after you have crossed Pitkin Creek. The road ends just past the trailhead at some condominiums and townhouses. Don't forget to sign in at the Forest Service trail register.

Trailhead to Lower Pitkin Creek Falls

After a brief climb from the trailhead, the Pitkin Creek Trail #2012 bridges Pitkin Creek next to a gauging station and winds around the back of some townhouses. For the next 1.0 mile, a lung-popping ascent takes you up the hot, south-facing wall of the Vail Valley. Scattered strands of aspen promise good fall foliage

Route

Day hike; 5.0 miles one way; easy

Route	Elevation (ft.)	Distance (mi.)
Trailhead	8400	0
Lower Pitkin Creek Falls	9960	2.5
Upper Pitkin Creek Falls	10520	3.5
Pitkin Lake	11400	5.0

USGS Topographic map: Vail East, Colo.

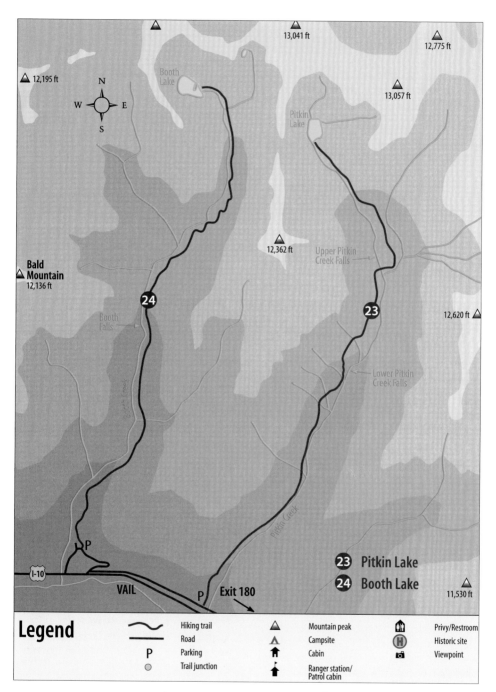

Legend

Symbol	Description	Symbol	Description	Symbol	Description
∿	Hiking trail	△	Mountain peak	🚻	Privy/Restroom
—	Road	⚑	Campsite	Ⓗ	Historic site
P	Parking	🏠	Cabin	📷	Viewpoint
●	Trail junction	⬆	Ranger station/ Patrol cabin		

23 Pitkin Lake
24 Booth Lake

viewing. The trail becomes less steep as it enters the glacier-carved hanging valley of Pitkin Creek. The roar of traffic charging along Interstate 70 finally fades into the distance, providing welcome peace and quiet. Throughout this hike, the terrain provides ample evidence of the work of glaciers active in the Rocky Mountains during the major

Parry's primrose, Parry's gentian, Parry's sunflower, Parry's harebell, Parry's clover—an extensive list of Colorado wildflowers bears the name of the botanist Charles Christopher Parry (1823-1890).

Parry was born in England, but emigrated to New York with his parents at the age of nine. He studied medicine at Columbia University and, shortly after establishing a practice in Davenport, Iowa, he participated as surgeon-naturalist in an expedition to survey the U.S. and Mexico boundary from Texas to San Diego. He spent the next 40 summers researching flora throughout the West, sending many of the specimens he collected to the well-known botanists John Torrey and Asa Gray. It was these gentlemen who bestowed the genus *parryi* on many of these plants.

Parry visited Colorado many times during the 1860s and '70s, discovering hundreds of new plant forms. He also made the first documented ascents of a number of high peaks and named them after his friends or colleagues. These included Grays and Torreys peaks and Mount Audubon. The first surveyor-general of Colorado Territory named a 13,344-foot peak on the Continental Divide above Empire in honor of Parry. From 1867 to 1870, Parry served as the first botanist to the U.S. Department of Agriculture, spending much of his time cataloging the plant collection at the Smithsonian Institute.

The striking Parry's primrose or *Primula parryi* graces the banks of alpine streams in the Colorado Rockies at an elevation of around 10,000 to 11,000 feet. The 12- to 15-inch-high, leafless stems produce several bright magenta blossoms with a yellow eye in the center. Several erect, fleshy leaves grow at the base of the stem.

ice ages. Between five million and about 11,000 years ago, deep snow compacted into ice and then flowed down preexisting drainages. Gouging rock from the canyon walls, the glaciers created the typical U-shaped valleys visible today, while depositing debris as they moved. Climactic changes forced their retreat up the canyons, and the ridges of detritus, or moraines, which lie in the glacier's wake, form distinctive escarpments, steps and convolutions in the valley floor.

This hike is characterized by a series of steep ascents to crest these false summits, which alternate with gently sloping, flower-strewn meadows.

As you parallel the rippling brook, aspen groves alternate with lush, grassy pastures blanketed with harebells, chimingbells, aspen daisies and arnica. Look for the delicate Rocky Mountain red columbine, which blooms in June, and its close cousin, the Colorado blue columbine, dotting the slopes in July. Gradually, lodgepole pines and Engelmann spruce begin to mingle with the aspens, and willows bow over the creek. The trail crosses a series of side streams and the valley broadens, becoming wilder, rock-strewn and more dramatic.

After about 2.5 miles, steep switchbacks reveal the first of two waterfalls on Pitkin Creek. Two hundred yards to the east of the trail, Lower Pitkin Creek Falls tumbles through a notch in a rock wall. Toward the base of the cascade, the water spreads out into a braided horsetail of shimmering rivulets. Many hikers choose this spot for a leisurely picnic before descending the 1,560 feet back to the trailhead.

Lower Pitkin Falls to Pitkin Lake

Past the falls, the trail continues its pattern of arduous ascents interspersed with squelchy marshes choked with Richardson geraniums, larkspur, fireweed and chest-high cow parsnip. Sometimes it rises through strands of huge old-growth Engelmann spruce and subalpine fir. Wild blueberry covers the ground beneath the conifers, creating a brilliant rust-red carpet in the early fall.

As you traverse the base of a scree slope beneath towering gray cliffs, watch for pikas and yellow-bellied marmots among the chunks of talus. The difficult-to-spot pika spends the summer frantically harvesting large amounts of vegetation for sustenance during the long winter, when it remains awake beneath the snow. Unlike this industrious little creature, the more easily observed marmot lazes its life away on a rock near its den, interested only in acquiring enough body fat to see it through its winter hibernation.

About 3.5 miles into the hike, cross Pitkin Creek by way of stepping stones. Upper Pitkin Creek Falls streaks the moraine, blocking the valley to the left. The stiff climb rewards you with a panoramic view back down the canyon, over the ski slopes to the south of Vail and to the peaks of the Holy Cross Wilderness.

Only scattered patches of conifers relieve the generally rocky slopes as the trail weaves through pond-speckled meadows. Flora enthusiasts will rejoice in the profusion of ephemeral wildflowers, which change both with the elevation gain and the passage of the summer months.

Fremont and Richardson geraniums, as well as rosy and orange paintbrush, decorate the meadows, while the regal Parry primrose flourishes on tiny islets in Pitkin Creek. Pitkin Lake huddles in a cirque at the head of the valley. Its crystal-clear water reflects the barren summits of the Gore Range, rising abruptly from the shoreline. Although nameless on U.S. Geological Survey topographic maps, two peaks bear unofficial names popularized by Colorado Mountain Club veteran Robert Ormes. The 13,041-foot "West Partner" stands vigil to the north of the tarn and 13,057-foot "East Partner" rises to the east. Patches of snow linger on the gray slopes well into the summer and the tarn is usually frozen until early July.

The first two falls on Pitkin Creek

The terrain around Pitkin Lake harbors picnic sites too numerous to mention, each one prettier than the last. However, the popularity of the hike guarantees that you will have company.

A multitude of brilliant pink elephant's head thrives among the boulders and outcroppings. If you inspect these flowers closely you will see that each blossom resembles a totem pole of elephant heads, each one with an upturned trunk. Pitkin Lake was named in honor of Colorado Governor Frederick W. Pitkin (1837-86), who served during the 1870s and '80s.

Booth Lake is a peaceful setting

~ 24 ~ Booth Lake

Flower-decked meadows, an attractive waterfall, breathtaking panoramas and a gem of a tarn tucked beneath the summits of the Gore Range are all components of this popular hike in the Eagles Nest Wilderness. As the trail begins in the town of Vail itself, the first stretch is favored by joggers and strolling residents.

Trailhead to Booth Falls

The pathway shoots uphill from the trailhead, quickly snaking its way up the steep north wall of the Vail Valley. To the left, Booth Creek cuts a deep gash in the landscape, fervent in its endeavor to join Gore Creek in the canyon below. This south-facing slope, only sparsely dotted with aspens, makes for a hot beginning to the hike. The grade moderates after 1.0 mile as the trail enters the hanging valley of Booth Creek. A board indicates the Eagles

Trailhead

From Interstate 70, take Exit 180 for Vail East Entrance and proceed west along the North Frontage Road (toward the center of Vail) for 0.8 mile. Turn right (north) on Booth Falls Road. Drive straight for about 0.25 mile, passing a soccer field, tennis courts and condominiums, to Booth Falls Trailhead. Parking space is at a premium here. Arrive early, or you may be out of luck.

Route

Day hike or overnight; 6.0 miles one way; moderate

Route	Elevation (ft.)	Distance (mi.)
Trailhead	8,400	0
Booth Falls	9,400	2.0
Piney Creek Trail Jct	10,300	4.0
Booth Lake	11,480	6.0

USGS Topographic map: Vail East, Colo.

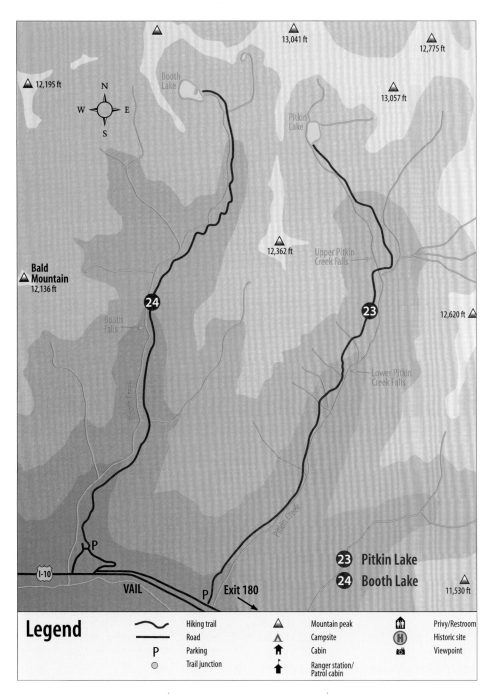

Legend

〰 Hiking trail	△ Mountain peak	🏛 Privy/Restroom
— Road	⛺ Campsite	Ⓗ Historic site
P Parking	🏠 Cabin	📷 Viewpoint
○ Trail junction	Ranger station/Patrol cabin	

23 Pitkin Lake
24 Booth Lake

Nest Wilderness boundary.
Sharp ascents alternate with gentle gradients as you surmount a succession of glacial terraces, deposited during the retreat of ice age glaciers. Old-growth Engelmann spruce and Douglas fir preside over the footpath, tall and proud reminders of the forests once prevalent in this region. The leaves of Rocky

The trail to Booth Lake runs through flower-strewn meadows

Vail

Lying just 100 miles west of Denver on Interstate 70, Vail is one of Colorado's most easily accessible ski areas. This picture-perfect village nestles in a seven-mile-long valley at the foot of the spectacular peaks of the Gore Range. Designed in 1962 after a typical Bavarian ski town, Vail rapidly skyrocketed to the forefront of international fame. It sealed its reputation as one of the ultimate ski mega-resorts in 1989 when it hosted the World Alpine Ski Championships.

With 4,644 acres of skiable terrain, Vail boasts the most extensively developed single ski mountain in North America. Hidden behind Vail Mountain are the legendary back bowls, providing what many consider to be the quintessential skiing experience. The altitude, dry air and sun combine to create perfect "champagne powder." Vail also has one of the largest ski and snow board schools in the country with more than 1,500 instructors. Its Mountain Activities Center, the first on-mountain hub of non-skiing activity in the state, offers plenty to keep the nonskier occupied, including snowshoe and snowmobile tours, ice skating and snowbiking.

Scores of hotels and restaurants cater to the throngs converging from all corners of the globe. It is important to remember, however, that this little community is one of the playgrounds of the rich and famous and prices can reflect this clientele.

Mountain maples turn shades of orange and red in the fall, competing for magnificence with the golden hues of the trembling aspens. Thimbleberry shrubs, decorated with tiny white flowers in July and fat scarlet berries in August, thrive in moist areas alongside the numerous side streams.

The trail journeys through a succession of open meadows, blanketed during the short summer by a multitude of wildflowers—butter and eggs, goldenrod, monkshood, clover and the Colorado blue columbine to name but a few. A rugged wall of black rock blocks the valley ahead and an awesome roar announces the presence of Booth Falls off to the left of the trail. Constricted to foam, the magnificent cascade crashes through a stingy cleft, almost too narrow for the copious amount of water gushing downward. The welcome cool spray from the falls is most refreshing after the hot climb. The area around the cascade makes a wonderful rest spot for those continuing to Booth Lake, or a fulfilling final destination for less ambitious hikers.

Booth Falls to Piney Creek Trail Junction

Zigzag up the headwall through thickets of aspens, willows and evergreens. Naked gray cliffs enclose the narrowing canyon as the trail hugs its right-hand perimeter. The predominant species of wildflowers change with the rapid gain in altitude. Stonecrop, bistort, alpine

Bears, the world's largest terrestrial carnivores, are unmistakable with their heavy build, thick limbs, close-set eyes, tiny tail and rounded ears. The *Ursus americanus*, or American black bear, is the most widely distributed and the smallest species of North American bear. It is believed that about 8,000 to 12,000 black bears live in Colorado today. The largest populations inhabit regions dominated by Gambel oak and aspen, where there is a rich supply of serviceberry and chokecherry bushes.

At one time the grizzly reigned supreme throughout the Colorado Rockies. Early settlers found this creature to be incompatible with civilization and systematically destroyed the animals. In 1979, the last grizzly to be killed in the state was shot when it attacked a hunter in the San Juans. Today, no one knows for sure if there are still grizzlies in Colorado.

The black bear weighs from 175 to 400 pounds, measures about three feet tall at the shoulder and may be up to five feet in length. Despite the name "black" bear, their color varies between black, cinnamon and blond. The muzzle is often brown and the animal may sport a white spot on its chest. Bears have keen senses of smell and hearing but poor vision. They are agile on land, strong swimmers and they climb trees readily. Despite their slow, ponderous gait, they can gallop in bursts of up to 35 mph.

These solitary animals may roam up to 15 miles a day in search of food. While primarily nocturnal, black bears are often also active during the morning and evening. Bears are true omnivores, enjoying a diet of grasses, berries, fruit, fish, insects, eggs, carrion, rodents, garbage and whatever else they can procure. During early fall, the bear seeks food with particular determination. Intent only on acquiring sufficient body fat to see it through its long winter hibernation, it may feed for up to 20 hours a day and take in as many as 20,000 calories.

Bears locate their dens in caves, hollow logs, rotten trees and rocky crevices, and line them with soft grasses, ferns or leaves. They breed in June or July every other year, but the fertilized egg does not implant itself into the female's uterine wall until November. Two to four blind, naked young are born in midwinter. The cubs grow rapidly from a birth weight of about 12 ounces to 15 pounds before they leave the den in mid-May. They stay with their mother for at least a year and are mature enough to breed by age three or four. A normal life span in the wild is about 20 years.

Signs of the Presence of Bears

Bears inhabit many of the areas traversed by the trails in this book. Shy, cautious animals by nature, they generally avoid encounters with humans and only become a nuisance once they learn to associate people with food.

The best way to determine whether or not bears are present is to watch for tracks, droppings, claw marks on logs or fur adhering to tree bark. Bear tracks are easy to recognize as they look almost exactly like the footprints of a small human, complete with five toes.

Bear Etiquette

Black bear attacks on humans are rare. Generally, a bear will perceive you before you see or hear it and will leave the area. Always keep children within

Black bear

sight and make sure your dog is on a leash. If you suspect the presence of a bear, talk, sing or tread loudly as you hike to avoid a surprise encounter.

If you do meet a bear, stay calm. Do not run or make sudden movements. Speak softly to the creature to let it know that you are there and that you mean it no harm. Do not show fear. Back away slowly while facing the animal. Avoid direct eye contact as bears interpret this as a sign of aggression. Females can be particularly dangerous if you approach a cub or come between them and their young. If a black bear attacks you, fight back with rocks, sticks, binoculars, a camera or even your bare hands.

Camping in Bear Country

There are several rules that you should always follow when camping either in a campground or in the backcountry.

• Keep your campsite clean and free of food residue or scraps.

• Cook away from your tent.

• Always store food and coolers in the trunk of your car or suspended from a branch 10 feet above the ground and four feet away from the tree trunk. Scented toiletries like soap and toothpaste may attract bears. Store these with your food.

• Get rid of garbage correctly. Either dispose of it in the bear-proof trash cans provided in campgrounds or, in the backcountry, hang it with your food and pack it out. Do not burn or bury it.

Aspens and conifers along the Elk River

avens and pretty Rocky Mountain gentians begin to make an appearance in the pastures.

At the point where two drainages converge, a track splits off to the left to climb alongside Piney Creek. Continue straight ahead for Booth Lake.

Piney Creek Trail Junction to Booth Lake

The trail switchbacks incessantly upward to the right of the stream through Engelmann spruce and subalpine firs. An outcropping of bedrock causes an abrupt halt in the upward momentum. This provides a good spot to catch your breath while enjoying the stupendous views back down the canyon, across the ski slopes on the south side of the Vail Valley and as far as the peaks of the Holy Cross Wilderness.

The trail continues more gently, crossing babbling brooks and traipsing through marshy meadows adorned with fireweed, harebells, pearly everlasting, heartleaf arnica and several varieties of Indian paintbrush. Now and again, tiny waterfalls trickle over rocky ledges, and ponds glitter in grassy depressions.

At timberline, the trees become sparse and stunted, and uninterrupted panoramas of the Gore Range are an apt reward for the effort it requires to reach this high alpine paradise. Notice an old metal drum rusting just to the left of the trail—a reminder of the mining activity of the late 1800s.

The final 0.25 mile to the tarn is an unrelenting slog between rocky outcroppings and scattered boulders. With dramatic suddenness, Booth Lake appears, nestled in a tight cirque at the foot of the

nameless summits of the Gore Range. You would be hard pressed to find a more peaceful setting than this pristine body of water. Gray crags fall to vivid green slopes above the lake, meadows studded with elephant's head nudge the shoreline and a minute island completes the perfection of the scene. Here's an added bonus: fishers marvel at the big trout just waiting to be caught in the tarn.

Fireweed

In September, 1988, fire swept through Yellowstone National Park, devastating large tracts of forest. The following summer, primary colonizing fireweed transformed much of the cauterized landscape into a sea of flaming magenta.

The numerous blossoms of this widespread member of the evening primrose family are each composed of four irregularly spaced petals which crowd the top of an unbranched two-to three-foot-tall stem. The narrow, lance-shaped leaves alternate along the lower part of the stalk. The flower eventually develops into a pod which splits, releasing a mass of seeds. Attached to cottony hairs, these seeds travel far in the wind.

Botanists have identified 100 different species of *Epilobium angustifolium* in the Northern Hemisphere. Twenty-five of these thrive in the Rockies, bearing such common names as blooming Sally, great willow herb or willowweed. Fireweed

plays an important role in nature. As one of the first plants to invade an area disturbed by fire, deforestation or avalanche, it aids in preparing the soil for the growth of other vegetation.

Fireweed also has many uses to man. A flavorful tea results from infusing its leaves with tea leaves. The new spring shoots can be boiled and eaten like asparagus. At one time, parts of the plant were harvested as a remedy for asthma and whooping cough. It is believed that the

Russians made beer and vinegar by fermenting the shoots. This vibrant flower blooms throughout the summer in wet, sunny locations from the lowlands to the high mountains. It is often seen alongside highways and trails.

The dwarf fireweed, *Epilobium latifolium*, graces the slopes of the alpine tundra. Despite the fact that it grows only a few inches tall, its flowers are bigger and its leaves are wider than those of its lower-altitude cousin.

Lazy Missouri Lakes nestle at the base of Holy Cross Ridge

~ 25 ~ Missouri Lakes and Pass

Cradled in a pristine alpine basin in the Holy Cross Wilderness, the 14 Missouri lakes and ponds form a wonderful destination for those who desire

peace and quiet. This moderate hike follows the route of Missouri Creek as it tumbles through dramatic gorges and meanders over meadows sprinkled with wildflowers. The summit of Missouri Pass, 0.5 mile beyond the upper lake and an additional 436 feet in elevation, commands excellent views to the northwest and southeast.

Trailhead to Lower Missouri Lake

From the trailhead, the pathway tunnels through a shady coniferous forest, passing the

Trailhead

From Interstate 70, take Exit 171 at Dowd Junction and drive 12.8 miles south through Minturn on Colorado Highway 24. Turn right (west) on Homestake Road (County Road #703). Pass Blodgett and Gold Park campgrounds, where there are many good spots for free camping. After 8.0 miles, turn right onto County Road #704, following the sign on Homestead Road for Missouri Creek Trail. Continue for 2.2 miles to a large black pipeline (to the left) and parking area (to the right) in front of a pit toilet. The trailhead is behind the pipe—the aqueduct for the Homestake I water project. Don't forget to sign in the trail register.

Route

Day hike or overnight; 4.4 miles one way to Missouri Pass; moderate

Route	Elevation (ft.)	Distance (mi.)
Trailhead	10,000	0
Trail Junction	10,300	0.5
First Stream Crossing	10,440	0.8
Second Stream Crossing	10,620	1.1
Lower Missouri Lake	11,380	3.5
Upper Missouri Lake	11,550	3.9
Missouri Pass	11,986	4.4

USGS Topographic maps: Mount Jackson, Colo., Mount of the Holy Cross, Colo.

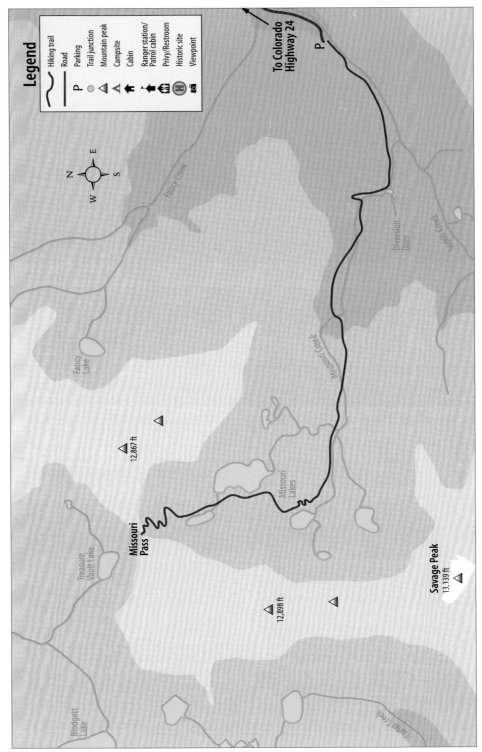

Legend

~~~ Hiking trail
— Road
P Parking
○ Trail junction
▲ Mountain peak
⌂ Campsite
↟ Cabin
🏠 Ranger station/ Patrol cabin
🚻 Privy/Restroom
Ⓗ Historic site
📷 Viewpoint

N
W E
S

Fancy Creek

Fancy Lake

Treasure Vault Lake

Blodgett Lake

Missouri Pass

▲ 12,867 ft

▲ 12,898 ft

▲

Missouri Lakes

Missouri Creek

Savage Peak
13,139 ft ▲

Diversion Dam

Squaw Creek

Carter Creek

To Colorado Highway 24

P

The 14 Missouri Lakes and ponds nestle in a pristine alpine basin in the Holy Cross Wilderness

remains of a wooden cabin—a reminder of the mining operations taking place in this area in the late 1800s.

After 0.5 mile, the trail exits the trees where a track joins from the left and hastens upward across a grassy opening to a diversion dam and pipeline. Reentering the forest, it continues to ascend steeply, often clambering over

Mount of the Holy Cross

The Mount of the Holy Cross, jutting to 14,005 feet just southwest of Vail, is considered by many to be one of the most sacred peaks in the United States. An impressive cross scars its northeastern face, formed by snow and ice in intersecting gullies measuring 1,500 vertical by 750 horizontal feet. For years, mystery enveloped the "Cross of Snow." Legends recount sightings of this cross by Ute Indians, Spanish explorers, mountain men and lost priests. The first official sighting was by William H. Brewer on August 29, 1869. In 1873, the Western photographer William Henry Jackson took the first pictures of the cross, which were widely publicized. At the same time, J. T. Gardner and W. H. Holmes made the first ascent of the peak.

The Mount of the Holy Cross was now catapulted into the media limelight, and several noted artists traveled to Colorado to paint the famous peak. In 1880, gold was discovered just to the east of the mountain, giving rise to the Holy Cross Mining District. Several small towns sprang up in the area, including Holy Cross City. For a brief four years, this community boasted two general stores, a school, the Timberline Hotel, two saloons and 300 inhabitants.

Gradually, the entire region around the mountain took on a religious aura and became the focus of pilgrimages. In 1912, three Episcopal priests celebrated Eucharist on the top of nearby Notch Mountain. By 1932, 2,000 people converged there for this annual ritual.

Many pilgrims reported miraculous healings. A snowfield to the right of the cross was christened the Supplicating Virgin and a lake at the foot of the peak became known as the Bowl of Tears.

Today, the Mount of the Holy Cross is popular with climbers, not only because of its religious significance, but due to its status among Colorado's celebrated "Fourteeners."

naturally stepped or polished outcroppings of rock. It crosses Missouri Creek by a lengthy two-log bridge with no handrails. This can be somewhat intimidating and precarious, especially when the timber is wet.

The climb continues to the left of the stream. Wild blueberry covers the ground beneath the thick canopy of subalpine firs and Engelmann spruce.

Shortly, a track veers to the right to a spectacular viewpoint. Revealing its true force, Missouri Creek has cut into the sheer bedrock to create a deep gorge. On both sides, orange- and black-streaked walls drop vertically into the river. An old mine shaft penetrates the cliff just above the water level.

On several occasions throughout the hike, the footpath makes use of carefully constructed log walkways to traverse sections of bog.

The trail skirts to the north of a meadow vibrant with rosy paintbrush, elephant's head, monkshood and mountain figwort. Pan-sized trout skim through the clear water of the lazy stream. Vistas open westward to snow-flecked Savage Peak and Holy Cross Ridge looming at the head of the valley above the basin that contains the unseen Missouri Lakes.

Once again back into the evergreens, the trail traverses several side streams by way of stepping stones. After about 1.1 miles, it recrosses to the north of Missouri Creek on a substantial plank bridge overlooking a miniature canyon through which the exuberant river cascades over a series of low falls. The grade soon moderates as the trail rounds an expansive meadow choked with willows. American bistort, brookcress, chimingbells and a host of other marsh-loving flowers thrive in this wet environment. Look especially for the striking Parry's primrose growing alongside the stream. Each of the vivid magenta blossoms bears a bright yellow eye.

Maintaining a gentle pace, the trail saunters through alternating patches of conifers and flower-dotted meadows. Although easy to follow, it can be very muddy in places. Watch for delicate Colorado blue columbines decorating a talus slope that tumbles to the right of the pathway.

The USGS topographic map shows a trail splitting off to the left to the lowest Missouri Lake, which lies at an elevation of 11,380 feet. An avalanche in 1995 buried this path.

Greenback Cutthroat Trout

The greenback cutthroat trout is one of the very few creatures to have been removed from the endangered species list without becoming extinct. It is currently classified as threatened and will, hopefully, be downlisted to non-threatened status within the next couple of years.

The greenback originally inhabited the cold, clear lakes and headwater streams of the Arkansas and South Platte drainages of eastern Colorado. Early European settlers called it the "black-spotted native" because of the dark, round spots on its sides and tail. Around 1890, it gained its present-day name. It is unknown why it was christened the "greenback" as its back is no more green than that of any other trout. "Cutthroat" is an apt appellation for a fish with colorful blood-red stripes decorating each side of its throat.

The greenback population declined during the early 1900s due to unregulated fishing, the stocking of non-native rainbow, brook, brown and Yellowstone cutthroat trout, and the widespread loss of habitat due to logging, livestock overgrazing, water diversion projects and industrial pollution. A cooperative recovery effort of the U.S. Bureau of Land Management, Colorado State University, the U.S. Fish and Wildlife Service, U.S. Forest Service, National Park Service and the Colorado Division of Wildlife was initiated in 1959. In 1973 the Endangered Species Act was passed, which listed the greenback as endangered. A group of biologists called the Greenback Cutthroat Trout Recovery Team systematically removed non-native trout from streams and lakes in Rocky Mountain National Park, several national forests and sections of BLM land, and reintroduced the greenback into the reclaimed habitat. By 1978, this trout had established a sufficient quantity of stable populations that it was downlisted to threatened status.

Today, the greenback is present in 52 locations in the Arkansas and South Platte drainages. Nineteen of the populations are believed to be self-sustaining.

Missouri Creek boasts a series of breathtaking cascades

Lower Missouri Lake to Upper Missouri Lake

After a short but steep rise, the trail reaches the second lowest lake, sprawling at timberline near the foot of Savage Peak. Occasional clumps of conifers decorate the otherwise barren shoreline. Passing to the right of the tarn, the path wanders upward from pond to pond and lake to lake, sloshing through bogs crisscrossed by streams. Marsh marigolds, globeflowers and Parry clover stand out like jewels in the emerald meadows.

The trail rounds the largest lake, a steely gray sheet of water that appears quite vicious when afternoon winds riffle its surface. Snow banks linger around its perimeter into mid-August. Now, only scattered islands of *krummholz*, or stunted trees, provide limited shelter from the elements. This is a very exposed area and no place to be in an afternoon thunder and lightning storm.

The final tarn huddles at the base of gray Holy Cross Ridge, with its scree falling below snow-speckled cliffs to its western and northern shoreline. Adequate rocky outcroppings protruding from the tundra near the water's edge act as comfortable benches to relax on and enjoy this tranquil setting.

Upper Missouri Lake to Missouri Pass

From here, the trail shoots steeply uphill to Missouri Pass, switchbacking sharply to gain 400 feet in a mere 0.5 mile.

The stiff climb to this high vantage point rewards you with excellent panoramas. Only now can the immensity of this great alpine basin containing the 14 Missouri lakes and ponds be perceived, despite the fact that only the upper few are visible. To the south, the rounded summit of Savage Peak, adorned by its permanent snowfield, presides over the dramatic scene of barren rocks, gray bodies of water and marshland.

Immediately to the northwest, Treasure Vault Lake nestles on a tundra-clad bench above the yawning chasm of the Cross Creek drainage. The western ridge of the Sawatch Range rises beyond this canyon, enhancing the grandeur of this stark and austere setting.

The trail continues down the northwestern side of Missouri Pass to join the Cross Creek Trail. Backpackers who have planned a car shuttle can hike the 15.5 miles from Treasure Vault Lake down this drainage to Tigiwon Road, just south of Minturn. Those desiring a shorter loop can choose to return via Fancy Pass, a little to the northeast. This drops to Fancy Lake and follows the Fancy Pass Trail back down to County Road #704, covering a distance of 3.5 miles from Treasure Vault Lake.

Aspen

Openings in the trees reveal views of Maroon Lake

Aspen, the premier ski resort, natural playground and genuine mountain community, huddles in a box canyon amid some of the most majestic peaks in Colorado. It began as a mining camp in 1879 and rapidly developed into one of the world's wealthiest silver-producing areas. When the silver market crashed in 1893, Aspen's first boom ended, but by the 1940s it had established a reputation as a major ski resort. Although it is best known for its winter attractions, Aspen provides plenty of activities to occupy the summer visitor. Lying within the White River National Forest, it is surrounded by seven wilderness areas, including the Maroon Bells-Snowmass, Collegiate Peaks and Hunter-Fryingpan regions. Numerous hiking trails lead to scenic alpine lakes or culminate atop high peaks or passes.

Hike 26 directs the hiker to the summit of 14,433-foot Mount Elbert, the monarch of Colorado's prestigious Four-teeners. Not only does this giant boast the honor of being the state's highest peak, but it is also the second tallest mountain in the contiguous United States.

Looping between two trailheads just to the west of Independence Pass, Hike 27 explores the tundra environment of the Hunter-Frying-pan Wilderness. Hike 28 leads through an expansive vale in the Collegiate Peaks Wilderness to an alpine tarn tucked at the base of forbidding Grizzly Peak.

Hikes 29 through 33 explore drainages in the Maroon Bells-Snowmass Wilderness, providing vistas of some of the most-often photographed peaks in the state—the Maroon Bells, Pyramid and Capitol peaks, and Snowmass Mountain. In summer, meadows sustain a profusion of wildflowers while, in early fall, the aspen-clad hillsides turn brilliant shades of gold. Anyone who enjoys a hot springs will relish backpacking to Conundrum Hot Springs.

left: Aspens light up the countryside with brilliant shades of yellow

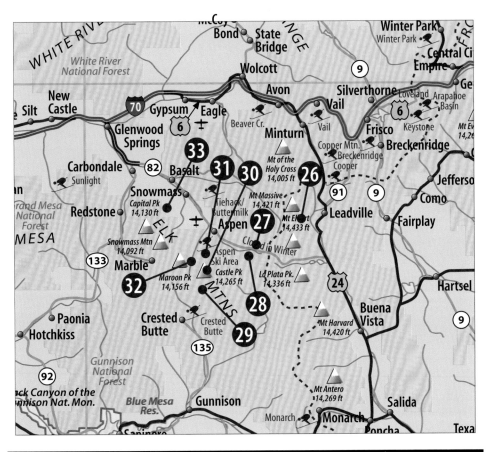

Other Hikes in the Aspen Area

Snowmass Lake

Long day hike or overnight, 8.5 miles one way
Elevation gain: 2,586 feet
Rating: Difficult
USGS Topographic maps: Snowmass Mountain, Colo. and Capitol Peak, Colo.

The hike up Snowmass Creek to Snowmass Lake is one of the most popular in the Maroon Bells-Snowmass Wilderness. This jewel of a tarn huddles at timberline at the foot of 14,092-foot Snowmass Mountain.

Backpackers desiring a longer trip have the choice of several extended excursions using Snowmass Lake as an overnight camp. These include the 21-mile Snowmass Creek-East Snowmass Creek loop and the 16-mile Snowmass Creek-Maroon Lake shuttle hike. Both of these routes offer spectacular vistas of the majestic scenery in the Aspen area.

From Aspen to Crested Butte by West Maroon Pass

Day hike, 11.0 miles one way
Elevation gain: 2,950 feet
Rating: Difficult
USGS Topographic maps: Maroon Bells, Colo. and Snowmass Mountain, Colo.

This popular trail leading from Maroon Lake over 12,500-foot West Maroon Pass to Schofield Park is the shortest hiking route from Aspen to Crested Butte. Traveling through the heart of the Maroon Bells-Snowmass Wilderness, the path passes beneath magnificent Pyramid Peak and the well-photographed Maroon Bells. Many hikers call the Crested Butte Chamber of Commerce to arrange taxi transportation back from Schofield Park to Aspen.

Views from Mount Elbert extend in all directions

~ 26 ~ Mount Elbert

The massive hulk of Mount Elbert, topping out at a mighty 14,433 feet above sea level, boasts the honor of being the tallest peak in both Colorado

Trailhead

Drive south of Leadville for 4.0 miles on US 24 and turn right (west) on Colorado Highway 300 following the sign for Halfmoon Campground. After 0.8 mile, take a left as directed for Halfmoon Campground and, 1.3 miles later, hang a right onto a gravel road. Continue for 5.3 miles, passing Halfmoon and Elbert Creek campgrounds. The Mount Elbert Trailhead parking lot lies to the left of the road.

Two other trails lead to the summit of Mount Elbert. Both the South Mount Elbert and the Black Cloud trails originate from Colorado Highway 24 in the vicinity of Twin Lakes and climb to the top in 5.5 miles. The North Mount Elbert Trail, which this book describes, is the shortest and quickest route and involves the least elevation gain. No technical skills are necessary.

and the Rocky Mountains. Only California's Mount Whitney, claiming an additional 62 feet, is higher in the contiguous United States. This elevated status has made it one of the most popular climbs in Colorado. Fourteener-baggers religiously choose this as one of their first summits. Colorado visitors, intent on conquering

Route

Day hike; 5.0 miles one way; strenuous

Route	Elevation (ft.)	Distance (mi.)
North Mount Elbert Trailhead	10,060	0
North Mt. Elbert Trail Jct	10,500	1.5 (Approx.)
Tree line	11,900	3.0 (Approx.)
Summit	14,433	5.0

USGS Topographic maps: Mount Elbert, Colo. Mount Massive, Colo.

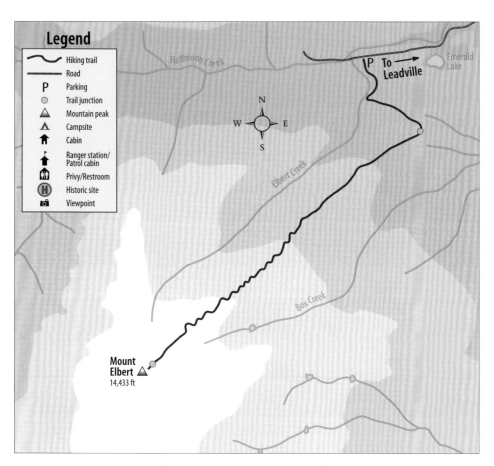

Legend

- ～ Hiking trail
- — Road
- P Parking
- ○ Trail junction
- △ Mountain peak
- ▲ Campsite
- ♠ Cabin
- Ranger station/Patrol cabin
- Privy/Restroom
- Ⓗ Historic site
- Viewpoint

Halfmoon Creek

P To →
Leadville

Emerald Lake

N
W — E
S

Elbert Creek

Box Creek

Mount Elbert △
14,433 ft

---

only one peak, favor this tiring but non-technical ascent. You are, therefore, unlikely to find solitude on Mount Elbert. The summit presents one of the most extensive and breathtaking views in the Rockies.

Trailhead to North Mount Elbert Trail Junction

From the south end of the parking lot, the North Mount Elbert Trail heads through a forest of lodgepole pines, passing the trail register. Shortly, it bridges Elbert Creek and then starts to climb briskly, skirting some old

cabin remains. Switching to the left by the stream, it clambers rapidly out of the drainage, offering occasional glimpses of the Arkansas Valley through the conifers. At 10,600 feet, the trail reaches the crest of Mount Elbert's northeastern ridge, which it will follow to the summit. The trail drops toward the drainage of Box Creek and soon reaches a Y-junction. Go right at the sign for Mount Elbert.

North Mount Elbert Trail Junction to Tree Line

The broad, well-used footpath continues to descend

briefly and then commences its true assault on the mountain. Shooting straight upward, it employs no switchbacks or curves to moderate its rate of ascent.

Only scattered patches of blueberry decorate the otherwise barren ground beneath the tall, erect lodgepoles. After a while, views open southward over the Box Creek drainage to the tree-clad eastern ridge of Elbert and the tundra slopes towering above. The trail hastens up the south-facing slope of the northeastern ridge with the music of Box Creek emanating from the valley to the left.

Using a couple of bends to

Breathtaking vistas surround the hiker on Mount Elbert

the ridge, the footpath levels briefly, then continues its rapid ascent. After a long stretch of huffing and puffing, you come to the first clearing. Here, among the dead timbers and wildflowers littering the grassy meadow, a rest is in order as you enjoy the first extensive views of the trip.

Huge Mount Massive dominates the scene to the north. To the south, the Arkansas River Valley, enhanced by the sparkling waters of Twin Lakes Reservoir, fades into the distance. Ahead rises the first of the series of knobs on the ridge leading to the top. Don't be fooled. This false summit is much farther than it looks; the real summit is a considerable distance beyond it. As you climb over the open meadow, vistas increase to the east, encompassing the entire Arkansas Valley as it stretches from north to south. The former mining boomtown of Leadville is visible, nestling at the foot of the gray peaks of the Mosquito Range. With an elevation of 10,152 feet, Leadville is the highest incorporated city in the United States.

Back in the forest, the trail resumes its hurried climb. Subalpine fir and Engelmann spruce have taken over from the lodgepole pines, and figwort has replaced blueberry as the dominant ground cover.

Suddenly, the trail exits the trees and only scattered islands of krummholz or banner trees mar the unobstructed panoramas over the alpine tundra. Hummocks marking the spine of the

readjust its position near the ridge's prow, the trail marches directly upward, stumbling over the clutter of rocks and roots in its path. Engelmann spruce mingle with the lodgepole pines as altitude is swiftly gained. Reaching the crest of

A Word of Caution

Climbing Mount Elbert can be an exhilarating experience. Nevertheless, it should be regarded as a serious undertaking—something not to be attempted by the unprepared.

Always start your trip early in the day so that you can be off the exposed slopes before the arrival of afternoon thunder and lightning storms. If you see large, dark clouds approaching, get down as quickly as possible, even if you haven't yet reached the top.

Despite the fact that it may be a hot day in Leadville, temperatures are unlikely to be much above 50 degrees Faren-

heit on the summit. Dress in layers, being sure to bring rain gear, a spare sweater or jacket, warm gloves and a hat.

Altitude sickness is a common problem on Mount Elbert, especially for out-of-state visitors. If you experience severe headaches, dizziness or sickness, the only cure is to descend.

Last but not least, the dry, high-altitude air causes rapid dehydration. Expect to drink at least two quarts of water during your ascent. Don't rely on the streams unless you plan to filter or boil the water.

ridge tower ahead, enticing the hiker on toward the unseen summit.

Tree Line to the Summit

As you hike across the tundra, marvel at the magnificent display of vibrant wildflowers—often minute versions of their low-altitude cousins. Harebells, globeflowers, stonecrop and sandwort stand out like jewels among the gray rocks and emerald mosses. Panoramas now grow more expansive with every step. You can see Turquoise Lake stretching to the west of Leadville and Mount Sherman rising to the east of the town. The ragged summits of the Gore Range jut majestically, far to the north. To your right, the terrain drops sharply to Elbert Creek, with Elbert's north ridge rising beyond. Further to the north, Mount Massive crowds the landscape.

The trail maintains its position just below the crest of the ridge. After a long slog, it bends to the left. Upon reaching the prow of the escarpment, it swerves right to continue its upward momentum just to the left of the ridge's backbone. Once more, it repeats this pattern.

Tiny patches of moss in between the fragmented boulders blanketing the slope nurture miniature gardens of alpine anemones, Western yellow paintbrush and sky pilots. Watch for the conspicuous yellow old-man-of-the-mountain sprouting alongside the trail. The two- to four-inch blossoms of this large alpine sunflower always face east, providing hikers with a reliable compass.

The trail snakes between the rocks, clambering toward the first distinct knob on the ridge. To the left, cliffs and scree tumble into Box Creek cirque, which is occupied by a tiny green lake. Nearing the top of the first false summit, the footpath veers to the right, skirting around the north and northeast flanks. As it scrambles back onto the prow of the ridge, a second protrusion looms ahead.

The trail weaves back and forth while Mount Massive gradually shrinks in size. This peak, aptly named because of its bulky three-mile summit crest, suffers the indignity of falling short of Colorado's highest point by only 12 feet.

Abruptly, the summit of Mount Elbert appears, looming at the southern end of the final rocky ridge. The path veers left, passing the junction with the South Mount Elbert Trail and several rock shelters. At last, you are standing on top of Colorado.

From this lofty perch, the 360-degree view seems to reach the limits of the continent. All around, Colorado's Fourteeners and "High Thirteeners" parade toward the horizon, rising to majestic heights above neighboring ranges and canyons. The Arkansas Valley cuts a deep rift to the east, with the gray, scree-covered peaks of the Mosquito Range blocking its eastern edge. Past Twin Lakes Reservoir and beyond the depression of South Park, Pikes Peak protrudes in the distance.

La Plata Peak rises to the south and, beyond that, mounts Oxford, Belford, Harvard and numerous others of the Collegiate Peaks point skyward. To the north, past Mount Massive, jut the jumbled summits of the Gore and Ten Mile ranges. Snowmass Mountain and the other giants surrounding Aspen peer above their deep drainages to the west.

Samuel Elbert

Mount Elbert was named in honor of Samuel H. Elbert who was appointed by President Abraham Lincoln in 1862 as secretary of the Colorado Territory under Governor John Evans. In 1865 he married Evans' daughter, Josephine. In 1873, while Elbert was serving a brief term as territorial governor, he succeeded in creating Elbert County. Later, he was elected to the Supreme Court after Colorado achieved statehood in 1876.

Waist-high cow parsnip and subalpine larkspur thrive along the trail

Tall chimingbells bloom alongside streams

Shrubby cinqefoil grows along the trail and on the alpine tundra

Old Man of the Mountain

The old man of the mountain, one of relatively few alpine plants endemic to the Rocky Mountains, is one of the largest and most majestic flowers on Colorado's tundra. It is also known as *Rydbergia grandiflora*, alpine sunflower and graylocks. The name "old-man-of-the-mountain" derives from the whitish hairs covering its foliage that protect it from the extreme cold, dehydration and strong ultraviolet radiation of the tundra climate.

Each plant consists of one or more fat stems bearing a two- to four-inch yellow blossom. The flowers are unusual in that they always face east toward the rising sun and away from the prevailing wind.

The old-man-of-the-mountain builds a store of nutrients for several years until it has sufficient energy to bloom. After it produces seeds, the whole plant withers and dies.

173

Colorado's Fourteeners

Colorado boasts 54 peaks which rise higher than 14,000 feet above sea level.
Coloradans lovingly call these giants "Fourteeners."

1.	Mount Elbert	14,433
2.	Mount Massive	14,421
3.	Mount Harvard	14,420
4.	Blanca Peak	14,345
5.	La Plata Peak	14,336
6.	Uncompahgre Peak	14,309
7.	Crestone Peak	14,294
8.	Mount Lincoln	14,286
9.	Grays Peak	14,270
10.	Mount Antero	14,269
11.	Torreys Peak	14,267
12.	Castle Peak	14,265
13.	Quandary Peak	14,265
14.	Mount Evans	14,264
15.	Longs Peak	14,255
16.	Mount Wilson	14,246
17.	Mount Shaveno	14,229
18.	Mount Princeton	14,197
19.	Mount Belford	14,197
20.	Crestone Needle	14,197
21.	Mount Yale	14,196
22.	Mount Bross	14,172
23.	Kit Carson Peak	14,165
24.	El Diente Peak	14,159
25.	Maroon Peak	14,156
26.	Tabeguache Peak	14,155
27.	Mount Oxford	14,153
28.	Mount Sneffels	14,150
29.	Mount Democrat	14,148
30.	Capitol Peak	14,130
31.	Pikes Peak	14,109
32.	Snowmass Mountain	14,092
33.	Mount Eolus	14,083
34.	Windom Peak	14,082
35.	Mount Columbia	14,073
36.	Missouri Mountain	14,067
37.	Humbolt Peak	14,064
38.	Mount Bierstadt	14,060
39.	Sunlight Peak	14,059
40.	Handies Peak	14,048
41.	Culebra Peak	14,047
42.	Mount Linsey	14,042
43.	Ellingwood Peak	14,042
44.	Little Bear Peak	14,037
45.	Mount Sherman	14,036
46.	Redcloud Peak	14,034
47.	Pyramid Peak	14,018
48.	Wilson Peak	14,017
49.	Wetterhorn Peak	14,015
50.	North Maroon Peak	14,014
51.	San Luis Peak	14,014
52.	Mount of the Holy Cross	14,005
53.	Huron Peak	14,003
54.	Sunshine Peak	14,001

Lost Man Lake stretches in a rock-strewn basin at the foot of the Continental Divide

~ 27 ~ Lost Man Loop

With an elevation gain of only 1,300 feet, the Lost Man trail lacks the endurance-testing climbs of many of the hikes in this book. The trailhead

lies above timberline, making for excellent panoramas of the 13,000-foot peaks of the Continental Divide right from the start. The route circles through two drainages in the Hunter-Fryingpan Wilderness, skirting a couple of pretty alpine lakes and a reservoir,

and surmounting a 12,800-foot pass.

It is important to start your hike early in the day. This exposed terrain is no place to be caught in an afternoon lightning storm.

Trailhead

As 4.5 miles separate the beginning and ending of this hike, a car shuttle is advisable. The hiker can follow the route in either direction, but because the upper Linkins Lake Trailhead is 1,000 feet higher than the lower, most people prefer to start there.

From Aspen, head southeast for 18.5 miles on Colorado Highway 82. The hike starts from a parking area to the north of the road at the last switchback below Independence Pass. The hike finishes in the parking lot opposite Lost Man Campground, 14 miles southeast of Aspen.

Route

Shuttle day hike; 8.8 miles one way; strenuous

Route	Elevation (ft.)	Distance (mi.)
Last Switchback Trailhead	11,506	0
Independence Lake	12,490	1.8
Lost Man Pass	12,800	2.6 (Approx.)
Lost Man Lake	12,450	3.0 (Approx.)
South Fork Trail Jct	11,660	4.8 (Approx.)
Lost Man Reservoir	10,660	8.0
Lost Man Campground	10,506	8.8

USGS Topographic maps: Independence Pass, Colo., Mt. Champion, Colo.

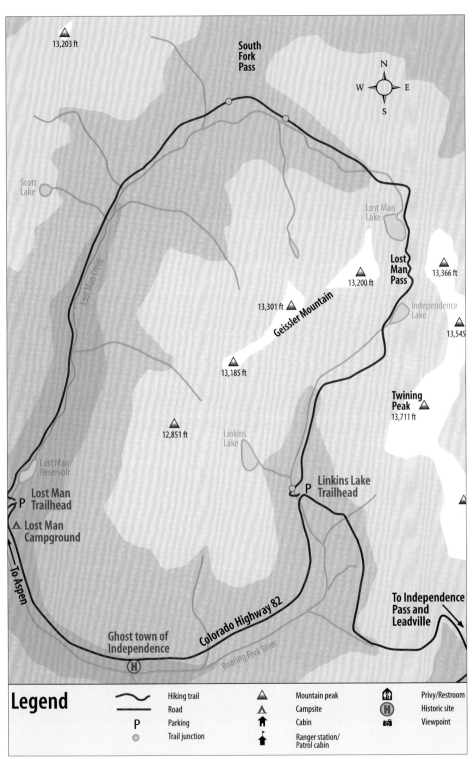

13,203 ft

South Fork Pass

N
W   E
S

Scott Lake

Lost Man Lake

Lost Man Creek

Lost Man Pass

13,366 ft

13,200 ft

13,301 ft

Geissler Mountain

Independence Lake

13,545

13,185 ft

Twining Peak
13,711 ft

12,851 ft

Linkins Lake

Lost Man Reservoir

Lost Man Trailhead
P

Linkins Lake Trailhead
P

Lost Man Campground

To Aspen

Colorado Highway 82

Ghost town of Independence
(H)

Roaring Fork River

To Independence Pass and Leadville

Legend

〰 Hiking trail	▲ Mountain peak	🏠 Privy/Restroom
— Road	⌂ Campsite	(H) Historic site
P Parking	🏠 Cabin	📷 Viewpoint
● Trail junction	▲ Ranger station/ Patrol cabin	

Trailhead to Independence Lake

The loop starts at the trailhead for Linkins Lake Trail #2183. After heading through low willows for about 200 yards, the route reaches a Y-junction. The left fork climbs to Linkins Lake, which lies in a cirque about 0.5 mile to the west. Keep right for Independence Lake. Soon, the trail crosses the headwaters of the Roaring Fork River. From here, this fledgling waterway descends to drain the entire Aspen area before journeying to join the Colorado River at Glenwood Springs.

The pathway now ascends steadily, maintaining a position about 50 yards to the right of the brook. The dominant vegetation quickly changes from willow-choked marsh to rock-strewn meadows. A rainbow palette of wildflowers colors the landscape. Elephant's head, chimingbells, American bistort and several varieties of paintbrush stand out in the emerald tundra. Watch especially for the magenta Parry's primrose growing in clumps on tiny islands in the many side streams feeding the Roaring Fork River.

To either side of the valley, barren, scree-covered slopes fall beneath forbidding gray cliffs. Snowfields hang under the skyline of many of the ridges.

The trail recrosses the river once again and metallic-colored Independence Lake stretches ahead—a small, kidney-shaped tarn nestled in a grassy basin. Snow banks linger around its perimeter and ice decorates its surface until midsummer.

The Ghost Town of Independence

On July 4, 1879, Leadville prospector Billy Belden and his partner discovered gold about 4.0 miles west of what later came to be called Independence Pass. They named the claim "Independence" to honor its discovery date. A tent city sprang up which, by the following summer, was home to 300 people.

By 1881, the newly established Farwell Mining Company had acquired most of the mines in the area and had constructed the Farwell Stamp Mill, which produced $100,000 worth of gold that year, and a sawmill. A stage road was constructed, providing access from Aspen to Leadville over 12,095-foot Independence Pass. Today, this route is the highest regularly used crossing in Colorado. The population of the camp rose to 500, supporting four grocery stores, four boarding houses, three saloons and a newspaper, the In-

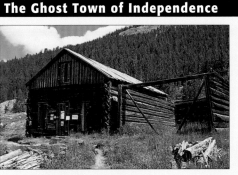

dependence Miner.

Prosperity continued into 1882, when the population peaked at 1,500. At its height, the town of Independence supported three post offices and 40 businesses, including several hotels, gambling halls, saloons and brothels.

Life at an elevation of 10,880 feet was not easy. Snow covered the ground from October to May. The treacherous journey over Independence Pass from Leadville to Aspen required 10 to 25 hours, a $0.25 toll and several changes of horses. Travelers, missing the trail in winter, sometimes rolled off the steep embankment. One story told of a man who spent five days attempting to get over the pass to Leadville.

Between 1881 and 1882, gold output valued $190,000. The next year, production plummeted to $2,000. By 1888, the Denver and Rio Grande Railroad had reached Aspen and the majority of the inhabitants of Independence had moved down to the new boomtown.

Nowadays, the ghost town of Independence is a National Register Historic Site, maintained by the nonprofit Aspen Historical Society. Many of the original buildings still stand in an alpine meadow both above and below the highway. Brochures, a picnic table and privies are available at the site.

To get to the ghost town of Independence, travel southeast from Aspen for 16.0 miles on Colorado Highway 82. The parking lot lies to the right of the road.

Independence Lake to Lost Man Pass

Veering to the left of the lake, the trail climbs steeply during the remaining 310 feet to Lost Man Pass.

Precarious, bare-rocked ridges rise on either side of this narrow crossing. Lost Man Pass is a good vantage point with nearly unparalleled views for the altitude gained. To the north, cradled in a basin 350 feet directly below lies turquoise Lost Man Lake.

Many hikers end their excursion at the pass, returning by the same route and thus avoiding a car shuttle.

Lost Man Pass to South Fork Trail Junction

The trail tumbles in a series of switchbacks down the boulder-strewn northern flank of Lost Man Pass, meeting Lost Man Lake at its southeastern corner.

The early morning hiker is rewarded with first-rate reflections in its glassy waters of the dramatic profile of the Continental Divide looming above to the right. You would be hard pressed to find a more inviting setting for a picnic. It's a scene of stark and desolate beauty.

The footpath skirts the right-hand margin of the tarn, dodging between numerous outcroppings of lichen-splotched bedrock.

Listen for the high-pitched calls of pikas and marmots in this peaceful cirque. The litter of boulders provides prime habitat for these creatures.

Around the northern tip of

Independence Lake nestles in an alpine basin to the south of Lost Man Pass

the lake, bogs produce an abundance of moisture-loving wildflowers, including marsh marigolds, globeflowers and elephant's head. Dark penstemon and alpine avens speckle the drier patches of tundra.

The terrain drops abruptly to the north. The trail begins its long descent to the right of newborn Lost Man Creek, which it will follow for the remainder of its journey to Lost Man Campground. The route now degenerates to cairns as it rounds a rocky promontory to head in a northwesterly direction and enters the broad valley carved by Lost Man Creek. It crosses and then recrosses the stream, amidst a riot of Parry's clover and heartleaf arnica.

The trail descends, hugging the right wall of the valley through damp meadows decorated with chimingbells, ragwort, Richardson geraniums and brookcress. As altitude is lost, the grade of descent lessens and the stream begins to meander lazily down the wide valley base. At about 11,600 feet, conifers put in an appearance on the hillside to

the left. At about 4.8 miles into the hike, keep left on the Lost Man Trail when the South Fork trail merges from the right.

South Fork Trail Junction to Lost Man Campground

Now subalpine forest alternates with flowery meadows and areas of bog as the vale bends to the left, heading south toward its union with the Roaring Fork drainage. During the interminable slog down the valley, conifers become more predominant on the hillsides as the trail drops farther below timberline.

Finally, you reach Lost Man Reservoir and enter the domain of fishers and strolling families.

Keep to the right of this body of water and stay left when a spur trail splits off to the right for Midway Pass.

The pathway veers away from the stream and bends back to the left before bridging Lost Man Creek. It immediately arrives at the trailhead in the parking lot opposite Lost Man Campground.

The trail climbs toward rugged Grizzly Peak

~ 28 ~ Grizzly Lake

This pleasant hike leads through a picturesque valley in the Collegiate Peaks Wilderness to a tarn cradled in a barren pocket at the foot of Grizzly

Peak. Meadows sprinkled with wildflowers combine with sweeping panoramas to make this one of the most popular hikes in the Aspen region.

Trailhead

Head 10.0 miles east of Aspen toward Independence Pass on Colorado Highway 82 and turn right (south) on Lincoln Creek Road. Pass Lincoln Gulch Campground and several official free camp spots. Those with a city car should proceed very carefully along this rough dirt road. Veer left around Grizzly Reservoir after 6.1 miles, following the sign for "Portal Campground." A wooden fence and notices stating "No Trespassing" discourage one from clambering down to the shoreline. Two small parking areas lie to the left of the road, 0.3 mile further on, just before Portal Campground. A brown sign to the right of the road points to the trailhead.

Trailhead to Cabin Remains

Grizzly Lake Trail #1990 starts with a brisk climb through a forest of Engelmann spruce, passing the Collegiate Peaks Wilderness boundary marker. To the right, Grizzly Creek thunders in its hurried descent.

After about 0.5 mile, the grade moderates as the pathway enters the hanging valley of Grizzly Creek, emerging into an expansive meadow. For the next 1.5 miles, only narrow swathes of conifers mar the otherwise unobstructed vistas

Route

Day hike; 3.6 miles one way; moderate

Route	Elevation (ft.)	Distance (mi.)
Trailhead	10,560	0
Cabin Remains	11,400	2.0 (Approx.)
Grizzly Lake	12,520	3.6

USGS Topographic map: Independence Pass, Colo.

179

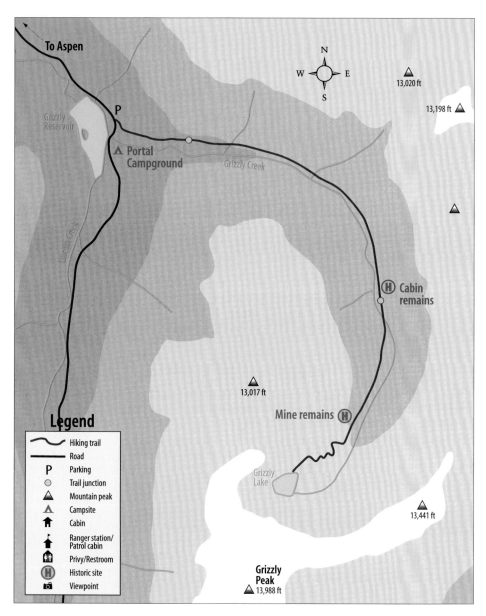

Legend

～	Hiking trail
—	Road
P	Parking
○	Trail junction
△	Mountain peak
▲	Campsite
♠	Cabin
♦	Ranger station/ Patrol cabin
🏠	Privy/Restroom
Ⓗ	Historic site
📷	Viewpoint

up the broad canyon to Grizzly Peak. Rising to 13,988 feet above sea level, Grizzly is only 12 feet shy of joining the ranks of Colorado's exalted Fourteeners. Snowfields streak this impressive mountain's gray flanks throughout the summer, and its bulky form is easily discernible

from atop distant high ridges and peaks. To its left, the long escarpment of the Continental Divide looms as a succession of nameless summits.

The most noticeable but not the highest of these is Peak 13,020. This craggy knob catches your attention as it juts to the north at the point

where the valley bends in a southerly direction. Grizzly Creek meanders along the valley base through a lush growth of willows. The radiant colors of fireweed, scarlet paintbrush and exquisite Colorado blue columbine decorate the meadow. About 2.0 miles into the hike, the remains of a log

Snow lingers throughout the summer in the gullies above Grizzly Lake

Mountain goat and kid

cabin hide within the final grove of conifers.

Cabin Remains to Grizzly Lake

The trail veers right and descends briefly to ford wide but shallow Grizzly Creek.

Its banks explode with Richardson geraniums, chimingbells and American bis-

tort. The canyon narrows and the footpath now starts its serious ascent along the right flank. The terrain becomes wilder as altitude is gained and only low willow shrubs stand above the myriad wildflowers carpeting the slopes.

An old mining tunnel pierces the embankment to the right of the trail. This, to-

gether with a rusting cast iron stove and a few scattered logs, are all that remain to tell the story of the miners who ventured into this remote alpine region during the 1880s. A headwall, streaked by cascading Grizzly Creek, exuberant in its escape from the tarn, blocks the valley in front. To the right of the stream rises a large rounded hummock. Grizzly Lake lies in a tight cirque to the west of this promontory.

Heading to the right, the trail shoots up the western perimeter of the valley only to moderate as it winds between outcroppings, contouring to the right of the rocky eminence guarding the lake. It squelches across a series of marshes dotted with tiny ponds.

Marsh marigolds, rosy paintbrush, elephant's head and Parry's primrose thrive in this moist environment.

181

Climbing beneath the towering cliffs of the ridge to the north of Grizzly Peak, the trail makes its final approach to the basin containing the lake.

Defiant sky pilots, king's crown and patches of columbine struggle among the chunks of talus, often seeming to survive without the benefit of soil.

The trail levels, penetrating a narrow depression between the ridge and hummock. Grizzly Lake appears suddenly, crouching in a tight cirque at the foot of inhospitable Grizzly Peak. Snow lingers throughout the summer on the scree slopes and gullies beneath the precipices tumbling from its summit. A low, grassy knoll to the right of the approach route provides plenty of picnic spots. Those who prefer to lunch with an eagle's eye view, not only of the lake but all the way back down the valley, can scale the rocky protrusion to the left. A sign states that Grizzly Lake is the spawning area for brook, rainbow and golden trout.

The appellation "Grizzly" is a popular name for streams, lakes and mountains in Colorado. It refers to the grizzly bear, once common in the state. There are seven Grizzly Gulches, five Grizzly Peaks, four Grizzly Lakes, three Grizzly Creeks and a Grizzly Mountain.

Globeflowers and March Marigolds

Two flowers familiar to every high-country hiker are the globeflower and the marsh marigold. Both of these members of the buttercup family are impatient to bloom at the first signs of summer. You will often see mixed beds thriving in bogs next to streams and receding snowbanks.

The globeflower has cream-colored sepals arrayed around a cluster of bright yellow stamens. Each blossom, rising on a single stem, grows from eight to 15 inches tall.

Like its partner, the marsh marigold lacks petals. Flowers consist of five to 12 narrow, white sepals emanating from a golden center.

The best way to tell the difference between these flowers is by looking at the leaves. Those of the marsh marigold are dark, glossy and heart-shaped, while the globeflower's are much smaller and have toothed edges divided into five or more segments.

Openings in the aspens reveal the picturesque Castle Creek Valley

~ 29 ~ Cathedral Lake

Bright-emerald Cathedral Lake nestles in a cirque beneath the rugged spires of Cathedral Peak, one of the summits in the Maroon Bells—Snow-

mass Wilderness. Starting from a trailhead about half an hour's drive from Aspen, this attractive hike is a popular half-day excursion for both locals and visitors.

In summer, myriad wildflowers blanket the tundra around the tarn and, in early fall, golden aspens light up the lower hillsides. Plenty of camp spots near the lake provide backpackers with a base for further explo

ration. The adventurous can continue to Electric Pass, the highest trail-accessible pass in Colorado. This excellent vantage point offers extensive views of the peaks around Aspen.

Trailhead to Electric Pass Junction

From the trailhead, Cathedral Lake Trail #1984 climbs gently through a shady forest of tall, stately aspens, traversing the slope to the west

Trailhead

Head west from Aspen on Colorado Highway 82 for 0.5 mile. Turn left (south) on Maroon Creek Road and, immediately, left (east) again onto Castle Creek Road. Pass the Elk Mountain Lodge and ghost town of Ashcroft. Watch for the 12-mile marker; just past it a brown "Trailhead" sign directs you along a dirt road to the right (west). Follow this road uphill for 0.6 mile to the Cathedral Lake trailhead parking lot.

Route

Day hike or overnight; 3.2 miles one way; moderate

Route	Elevation (ft.)	Distance (mi.)
Trailhead	9,900	0
Electric Pass Jct	11,800	2.6
Cathedral Lake	11,866	3.2

USGS Topographic map: Hayden Peak, Colo.

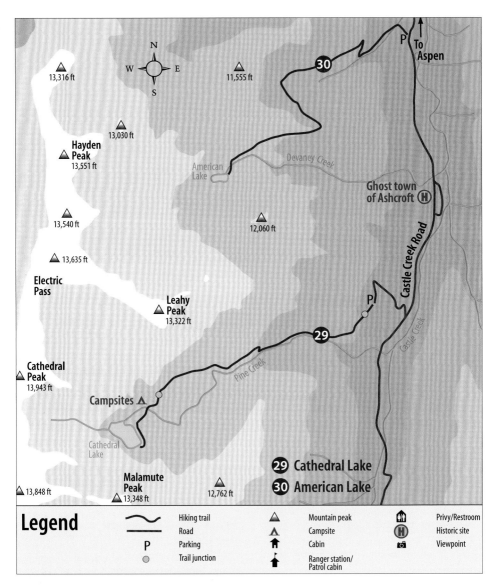

Legend

~~	Hiking trail	△	Mountain peak	🏠	Privy/Restroom
—	Road	⚑	Campsite	Ⓗ	Historic site
P	Parking	⬆	Cabin	📷	Viewpoint
⬤	Trail junction	⬆	Ranger station/Patrol cabin		

29 **Cathedral Lake**

30 **American Lake**

Peaks and features shown on map: 13,316 ft; 11,555 ft; 13,030 ft; Hayden Peak 13,551 ft; 13,540 ft; 13,635 ft; 12,060 ft; Electric Pass; Leahy Peak 13,322 ft; Cathedral Peak 13,943 ft; Campsites; 13,848 ft; Malamute Peak 13,348 ft; 12,762 ft; Cathedral Lake; Pine Creek; American Lake; Devaney Creek; Ghost town of Ashcroft; Castle Creek Road; Castle Creek; To Aspen.

of the Castle Creek Valley. Notice that most of the whitish trunks within arm's reach bear the scars of decades of graffiti. Unfortunately, this form of vandalism occurs in aspen groves along many of the popular trails in Colorado.

The footpath heads toward the gorge carved by Pine Creek, the stream emanating from Cathedral Lake. Open-

ings in the aspens reveal the southern end of the picturesque Castle Creek valley. Upon nearing the rambunctious stream, the path veers to the right and starts to climb steeply through the ravine. As the aspens make room for conifers, you pass the boundary marker for Maroon Bells-Snowmass Wilderness.

Above, a distinctive notch

marks the entrance to the hanging valley of Pine Creek. A gray summit, peeping between the "V," slowly increases in stature as one gains altitude. The trail alternates through aspens and conifers, sometimes passing between thickets of willows and occasional wild gooseberry bushes. It cuts across a talus slope falling from the rugged

The Ghost Town of Ashcroft

Two prospectors, C.B. Culver and W.F. Coxhead, found silver in the Castle Creek Valley in 1880. Immediately, a boomtown sprang up in the vicinity, taking its name from T.E. Ashcraft an early scout, mountain man and prospector. This community flourished for a mere three years.

At its height, Ashcroft boasted 5,000 inhabitants, two main streets, a school, a newspaper— *The Ashcroft Herald,* a post office, a jail, six hotels and numerous saloons and brothels. A number of silver mines such as the Montezuma, Tam O'Shanter and Empress contributed to the town's prosperity.

Stagecoaches provided transportation to Aspen in the north and Crested Butte to the south. At first, in order to make the difficult journey over Taylor Pass, wagons had to be disassembled at the top of the crossing and lowered piece by piece down 40-foot cliffs.

One of Ashcroft's most famous residents was Horace Tabor, the Leadville silver magnate. He poured millions of his Leadville profits into the Montezuma and Tam O'Shanter mines, which, despite producing about $20,000 of silver a month, generally operated at a loss. Tabor built a luxurious home in Ashcroft with gold-encrusted paper paneling in the living room. Whenever Baby Doe, his beautiful young wife, came to town, he always declared a 24-hour holiday, with free drinks for all in the saloons.

With the development of Aspen, Ashcroft began to decline. Many Ashcroft residents moved their homes and businesses to the new boomtown. By the 1890s, most of the mines had closed.

Today, the ghost town of Ashcroft is listed in the National Register of Historic Places. Several buildings have been beautifully restored to tell the story of the once-thriving mining community. A picnic area by Castle Creek is a wonderful place to relax and enjoy the magnificent scenery.

To get to Ashcroft, head west from Aspen on Colorado Hwy. 82 for 0.5 mile. Turn left on Maroon Creek Road and, immediately, left again onto Castle Creek Road. Follow this south for 11 miles. The ghost town sprawls in a wide meadow to the left of the road.

Several buildings in the the once-thriving mining community of Ashcroft have been restored

following pages: The trail switchbacks toward Buckskin Pass and through meadows decorated with waist-high flowers

cliffs towering to the right and switchbacks to maintain its position above the level of the Pine Creek. To your left, the exuberant stream tumbles in a series of cascades through a deep rift in the bedrock.

By a bend in the trail, a massive old-growth spruce stands vigil over the landscape.

At the beginning of a second set of switchbacks, about 1.5 miles into the hike, a track shoots down to overlook the most spectacular of the waterfalls. This provides a pleasant spot for a picnic. Vistas extend back down the drainage to the conifer-clad ridge on the other side of the Castle Creek Valley. This panorama is particularly spectacular in early fall, when the aspens and willows turn a brilliant, golden shade of yellow.

The trail continues to snake its way up the steep gully until, about 2.0 miles into the hike, it moderates upon penetrating the hanging valley and traverses a second talus slope. The vale now broadens with the brook meandering through a wide meadow.

The trail veers right, hugging the northern flank of the canyon, alternately tunneling through aspens, Engelmann spruce and subalpine fir.

As the footpath rises gently, it leaves the stream far below to the left. Looking backward, you can see the summits of the Collegiate Peaks Wilderness peering over the escarpment to the east of the Castle Creek drainage.

Approaching a headwall blocking the valley, the trail traverses a vast boulder field and then shoots up a grassy slope between the talus and a band of conifers via a succession of tight switchbacks. It then levels, passes through the evergreens and descends briefly to an intersection. The path to Electric Pass slants uphill to the right, climbing 1,700 feet to the top of the ridge separating the Conundrum Creek and Castle Creek drainages.

Electric Pass Junction to Cathedral Lake

Head left for Cathedral Lake, through extensive thickets of willows.

Due to the high altitude, catkins decorate these hardy shrubs late into the summer. The remains of a rock shelter crumble to the right of the pathway. Campers will notice several good spots to erect a tent off to the left.

The trail descends to Pine Creek, where a second track splits off to the left for Electric Pass. Cross the stream by jumping between the substantial outcroppings of bedrock protruding on either side.

As you ascend gently through the low willows, views open to the the northwest, revealing the trail as it snakes up to Electric Pass high above on the skyline.

As you come to the top of a short rise, Cathedral Lake stretches before you, crouching in the shadow of magnificent Cathedral Peak.

Rising to only 13,943 feet, Cathedral Peak does not qualify for inclusion in the list of Colorado's celebrated Fourteeners. Nevertheless, its fragmented north ridge and crumbling northeast face create an imposing spectacle. The ragged escarpment continues

Sunflower composites dot the meadows

to the south of Cathedral Peak, standing vigil over Cathedral Lake and climbing again to form Malamute Peak. Many hikers choose to linger in this tranquil setting, enjoying the beauty of the scenery while relaxing over a leisurely picnic.

The trail descends to the lakeshore, veers left and skirts the water in a clockwise direction before continuing up the grassy slope to the east of the tarn.

Streaks of yellow tailings and a couple of superficial holes in an embankment to the left indicate past mining activity. The top of the hillock above the tailings provides the best views of the lake and the rugged ridge between Cathedral and Malamute peaks.

If you continue past the tailings to the edge of the cirque, a vast panorama stretches to the northeast, encompassing the Pine Creek Valley and the distant summits of the Collegiate Peaks Wilderness.

American Lake nestles in a cirque surrounded by scree and conifers

~ 30 ~ American Lake

This half-day hike through forests and flowery meadows leads to a picturesque tarn cradled in a cirque just below timberline. The abundance of aspen groves along the first section of the trail makes it a favorite fall excursion for local residents.

Trailhead to First Band of Evergreens

The American Lake Trail #1985 begins by meandering along the slope to the west of the Castle Creek Valley, heading in a northerly direction. Shortly, it crosses a small, unnamed stream before it curves left to follow the brook's drainage up the hillside. The path enters an aspen grove and makes a beeline for a notch in the ridge high above. After a couple of minutes, it passes the Maroon Bells-Snowmass Wilderness boundary marker.

Gentle water music announces the presence of the creek off to the left.

Upon approaching the stream, the trail starts to hurry upward, gaining altitude quickly by means of a sequence of long switchbacks.

Trailhead

Drive 0.5 mile west of Aspen on Colorado Highway 82 and turn left (south) on Maroon Creek Road. Take an immediate left (east) and follow Castle Creek Road for 10 miles. The entry to the parking lot for American Lake Trail #1985 is to the right of the road just opposite the Elk Mountain Lodge.

Route

Day hike; 3.2 miles one way; moderate

Route	Elevation (ft.)	Distance (mi.)
Trailhead	9,400	0
First Band of Evergreens	10,500	1.5
American Lake	11,365	3.2

USGS Topographic map: Hayden Peak, Colo.

189

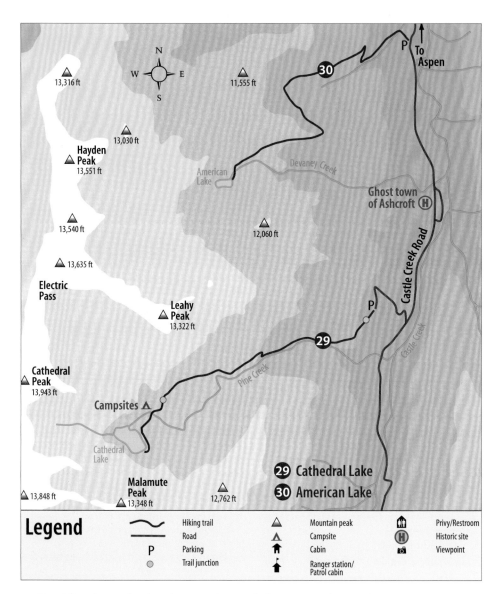

Legend

	Hiking trail		Mountain peak		Privy/Restroom
	Road		Campsite	Ⓗ	Historic site
P	Parking		Cabin		Viewpoint
⊙	Trail junction		Ranger station/ Patrol cabin		

29 Cathedral Lake
30 American Lake

Trembling aspens dot the slope. In September, the crisp air and shorter days indicate the approach of winter. This triggers the breakdown of chlorophyll in the small, rounded leaves, causing them to put on their showy display of yellow-gold. In Colorado, not every year provides excellent fall foliage viewing. Only Septembers with the correct mixture of sunny days and cool nights create the richest spectrum of colors.

This aspen grove has been scarred by vandals, as is the case along many of the state's most popular trails. The initials carved in all of the whitish trunks within arm's reach bear testimony to decades of travel and infatuation.

As the aspens thin out, views open eastward across the Castle Creek Valley to the scattered buildings of the Elk Mountain Lodge. In front of you, a couple of high peaks rear their heads over the indentation in the ridge above. On the other side of the nameless creek, the steep,

The trail meanders across open meadows toward American Lake

north-facing slope wears a thick cloak of conifers. After about 1.5 miles, the aspens make room for a band of thick evergreens. This provides welcome shade to hikers choosing not to start the excursion at the crack of dawn.

First Band of Evergreens to American Lake

The grade moderates as the trail soon exits the subalpine forest into a vast, sloping meadow chopped in half by a stand of aspens. In summer, yarrow, ragwort, several hybrid varieties of Indian paintbrush and many other wildflowers speckle the grass.

Reentering the evergreens, the broad, well-used trail stumbles over the roots cluttering its path.

Wild blueberry covers the ground beneath the trees, together with the occasional mushroom.

Now heading southward, the footpath makes a brief but steep ascent to the edge of the ridge overlooking the deep-cut canyon of Castle Creek.

Notice a different species of conifer among the subalpine fir and Engelmann spruce. The limber pine is easy to identify because of its bundles of five needles and its large, sappy pine cones. The trail crests the ridge and, changing direction yet again, veers to the right to enter the hanging valley of Devaney Creek. As it loses a little of its altitude, glimpses through the aspens reveal the summits and escarpments around the basin containing American Lake.

The path contours along the hillside, wandering through two more flower-strewn meadows, one of which contains a rough talus slope. It hurries upward through a forest of conifers, hugging the right flank of the Devaney Creek drainage. Devaney Creek, the outlet stream from American Lake, plays its cheerful music below to the left.

The trail drops momentarily through a second rockfall. Wild raspberries have somehow found a precarious footing in among the boulders. During late summer, the juicy red berries ripen within arm's reach, tempting the hiker to linger and sample some of nature's bounty. Listen for the peeps of industrious pikas and lazy marmots. These creatures are frequent residents of barren talus slopes such as this.

The trail ducks back into the forest and, abruptly, meets American Lake at its northeastern shoreline. Lying just below tree line, this little tarn nestles in a pretty cirque surrounded by scree and conifers. Rocks provide seats for hikers to relax and picnic in this pleasant setting. Anglers will want to try their luck with the small trout often visible in the shallows.

The trail crosses the outlet stream and circles to the left of the tarn. From here, it climbs through marshy meadows to a tundra-clad upper basin, which offers excellent views to the north and east.

Robert Ormes

Robert Manly Ormes—climber, author, map maker and college professor—was one of Colorado's greatest mountaineering legends. Ormes was born on September 27, 1904, in Colorado Springs. He attended Colorado College and earned a BA in English in 1926 and an MA in 1927. He became an English teacher at Fountain Valley School, where he also instructed rock climbing. During World War II, he taught mountaineering at Camp Hale with the Tenth Mountain Division. He held the post of Professor of English at Colorado College from 1952 until 1973 and received an honorary doctorate upon his retirement.

Ormes married Suzanne Viertel on December 25, 1937, in Colorado Springs. They had a daughter, Stephanie "Robin" Quizar, and a son, Jonathan. Suzanne passed away in 1988.

It is no surprise that Ormes became an avid hiker from an early age. His father, Manly Ormes, who was a librarian at Colorado College, had founded the Saturday Knights in 1904, a group that hiked every Saturday. The 9,728-foot Ormes Peak, rising just to the north of Pikes Peak, was named in honor of Manly Ormes.

Robert Ormes began his serious climbing career at the age of nine, when he made the first of his 40 ascents of Pikes Peak with his brother, sister and two friends. He joined the AdAmAn Club in 1929, a group that upheld a tradition of climbing Pikes Peak every New Years Eve to set off fireworks.

During the 1920s and 1930s Ormes became one of Colorado's pioneer mountaineers, climbing with such notables as Carl Blaurock, Albert Ellingwood, Eleanor Davis and Mel Griffiths. He made several first ascents, including the north face of Blanca Peak in 1927, Chimney Rock in 1934 and Needle Ridge between Sunlight Peak and Mount Eolus in 1931. He reached the top of all of Colorado's Fourteeners and many of the state's 13,000-foot peaks. Over the years he led numerous groups up these mountains.

In 1952, he authored *A Guide to the Colorado Mountains*, the first complete guide to the Colorado Rockies and, at the time of its publication, considered to be the hikers' bible. He also wrote an autobiography, *A Farewell to Ormes*, and produced a book on Colorado railroads and an atlas of Pikes Peak. Thousands of hikers have relied on his excellent maps of the state's mountain ranges.

Ormes was not only a member of the Colorado Mountain Club, the Saturday Knights and the AdAmAn Club, but also belonged to the American Alpine Club, the Recreational Trails Committee and the Colorado Division of Wildlife. He continued to be an active outdoorsman well into his 80s. Ormes died on December 23, 1994 in Longmont at the age of 90.

The trail follows Conundrum Creek up the long valley

~ 31 ~ Conundrum Hot Springs

Relaxation in the Conundrum Hot Springs is the major draw of this popular hike in the Maroon Bells-Snowmass Wilderness, closely followed by the

impressive wildflower displays alongside the trail. The route chooses a long but unhurried grade up the Conundrum Creek Valley, through forests of tall conifers and luxuriant meadows, revealing frequent panoramas of

rugged, snow-streaked peaks. Although it can be done as a lengthy day hike, the majority of people prefer to backpack to the hot springs and to camp overnight in one of the many designated campsites.

Trailhead

Head 0.5 mile west of Aspen on Colorado Highway 82. Turn left (south) at the stoplight at Maroon Creek Road and then take another immediate left on Castle Creek Road. Drive for 4.8 miles and go right (west) on Conundrum Creek Road. Proceed downhill for 0.2 mile and veer left in front of the gateway to the Bellcamp. Follow the dirt road uphill for 0.9 mile to the trailhead parking lot. Be careful to avoid entering any of the private driveways. A Conundrum Hot Springs Hiking Guide leaflet with a campsite map is available free of charge at the trailhead. Don't forget to sign in at the trail register.

Route

Overnight; 8.5 miles one way; strenuous

Route	Elevation (ft.)	Distance (mi.)
Trailhead	8,700	0
First Crossing	9,380	2.5
Rise	9,600	4.0
Second Crossing	10,240	6.0
Third Crossing	10,300	6.5
Old Cabin	10,800	8.0
Conundrum Hot Springs	11,200	8.5

USGS Topographic maps: Hayden Peak, Colo., Maroon Bells, Colo.

Trailhead to First Stream Crossing

For the first 2.5 miles of the hike, the trail follows an old mining road that parallels Conundrum Creek along the eastern side of the valley. It gains altitude slowly, with occasional ups and downs, passing across wide meadows and through woods of shady conifers or stately aspens. Sometimes the valley broadens, with the stream meandering sluggishly through the willow-choked base. At other times it narrows, with the river cutting a deep V-shaped gash in the floor.

Aspens streak the gentle slopes on either side of the drainage, creating a riot of gold in the fall. Wildflowers carpet the meadows right from the start. Brilliant yellow sunflowers, mauve aspen daisies and white Richardson geraniums grow in wild profusion. Thimbleberry shrubs, dotted with white blossoms in July and large red berries in August, thrive alongside the pathway.

After about 1.5 miles, a few planks and a well-defined doorway standing in the middle of a meadow indicate the remains of a tumbled-down cabin. The panorama improves with the gain of mileage along the valley. Hayden Peak is the closest gray summit, jutting above the ridge to the left. Rising to 13,561 feet, it is the lowest of a series of major peaks thrusting above the eastern margin of the canyon. Farther on, the hiker will gain good views of jagged Cathedral Peak (13,943 feet), Conundrum Peak (14,022 feet) and Castle Peak (14,265 feet). While the latter

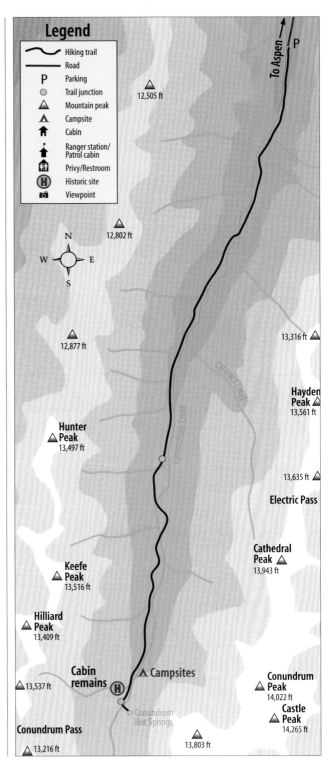

Legend

〰	Hiking trail
—	Road
P	Parking
○	Trail junction
△	Mountain peak
⛰	Campsite
🛖	Cabin
	Ranger station/Patrol cabin
	Privy/Restroom
Ⓗ	Historic site
📷	Viewpoint

To Aspen — P

12,505 ft

12,802 ft

N
W • E
S

12,877 ft

13,316 ft

Cataract Creek

Hayden Peak
13,561 ft

Hunter Peak
13,497 ft

Conundrum Creek

13,635 ft

Electric Pass

Cathedral Peak
13,943 ft

Keefe Peak
13,516 ft

Hilliard Peak
13,409 ft

Cabin remains Ⓗ

Campsites

Conundrum Peak
14,022 ft

Castle Peak
14,265 ft

13,537 ft

Conundrum Hot Springs

Conundrum Pass

13,216 ft

13,803 ft

Myriad wildflowers decorate the trailside

finds its place among Colorado's 54 prestigious Fourteeners, Conundrum Peak is considered only as its satellite.

From time to time, abandoned beaver ponds glisten among the thickets of willows clogging the valley floor.

Two and a half miles into the hike, the horse route veers right to ford Conundrum Creek. Continue straight ahead if you're on foot as, a little farther, the foot trail also heads to the right to cross the river. A sturdy double log bridge with a handrail makes the first stream crossing easy to accomplish.

First Stream Crossing to Rise

The trail now travels along the western flank of the drainage, winding through narrow bands of tall subalpine firs and Engelmann spruce, and sauntering across cheery meadows exploding with goldenrods and delicate fairy trumpets. Generally, it maintains its route 100 feet or so above the level of the creek. Waist-high cow parsnip and fireweed enjoy the abundance of moisture present in this lush environment.

Rise to Second Crossing

The gentle stroll ends about 4.0 miles into the hike. The valley sides constrict and the terrain rises abruptly. The trail shoots up the right hillside through the conifers and aspens. This breath-stealing ascent yields the first views to the north, back down the length of the broad defile.

Grassy pastures alternate with woods as the trail continues to slog upward, rapidly gaining altitude. After a while, the scenery opens as Conundrum Creek cascades through a gorge.

The trail traverses along the rim of the ravine, descending momentarily to cross a lively side stream by way of stepping stones.

Moss Campion

Standing out like a jewel against the bare gray rock, the moss campion is one of the most common plants found on the alpine tundra. Numerous star-shaped pink blossoms dot the plant. Its tiny stems and leaves are so close-knit that it resembles moss.

The moss campion, usually one of the first plants to colonize a barren slope, is well adapted to survive the severe conditions prevailing in the land of no trees. As it hugs the ground like a compressed pin cushion, a sturdy tap root holds it tight in the scant earth against the strong winds.

A young plant may measure only a few inches across. As it gets older, it spreads out, covering up to two feet of ground. The small, bright-green basal leaves dry and remain on the stem for up to 50 years. Therefore, much of the cushion may consist of dead material.

This debris creates soil, which in turn nurtures other tundra flowers. Eventually, the invading plants take over from the moss campion.

Two hikers relax in the largest and hottest of the three pools at Conundrum Hot Springs

Ahead, snub-nosed rocky summits look down on the Conundrum Creek Valley like spectators at a show, revealing their glacier-eroded gullies etched with snow and ice.

The predominant flowers change with the increase in elevation. Rosy and Western yellow paintbrush, harebells and Lewis flax clothe the meadows. The Colorado blue columbine and its white relative now make an appearance, adding richness to the display.

After 6.0 miles, the trail crosses Conundrum Creek by a secure two-log bridge with a handrail.

Second Crossing to Third Stream Crossing

The pathway skirts two pools, the larger one named Silver Dollar Pond, and hastens uphill through a coniferous forest. The grade quickly moderates and the trail continues its journey along the left flank of

Magpie

The black-billed magpie is one of the most commonly observed year-round residents of open woodlands, grasslands and cities in Colorado.

This crow-family member is easy to identify due to its black and white coloring and metallic green-blue highlights. It measures 20 inches in length, has a 24-inch wingspan, a long tail and walks in a series of hops. It has a noisy demeanor and often makes a loud "cack" or harsh "yak yak yak" call.

Magpies are intelligent, bold, curious and adaptable birds. Their willingness to eat almost anything—including carrion—has led to their wide distribution throughout the Northern Hemisphere. Magpies build their large, dome-shaped nests in trees and reuse them year after year. The female lays from six to nine greenish blotched eggs and raises one annual litter of fledglings.

One of the most interesting features about the magpie is its "funeral" behavior. When an individual dies, all its neighboring magpies gather in nearby trees and make a great racket. One at a time, each bird flies to the deceased and calls its lament while all the others watch. When every magpie has taken a turn at "mourning," they all fly away.

Bull moose

the valley at a more forgiving pace.

To either side tower the orange-red cliffs, so typical of the Aspen area. Descend next to a sea of blue chimingbells, yellow ragwort and larkspur taller than the head of a six-foot man. Slosh through the mud on the valley floor and step across a patch of standing water.

Six and a half miles into the hike, you arrive at a log jam—the third stream crossing. Be especially careful at this point. Despite the fact that a jumble of tree trunks bridges Conundrum Creek, these timbers can be slick after a rainfall.

Third Stream Crossing to Hot Springs

Scramble up the slippery bank on the right side of the river and follow the track upstream. Logs clutter the ground among the thick conifers, but the forest service does an excellent job of keeping the pathway clear. The route resumes its previous pattern of burrowing through willow tunnels, squelching through bogs, weaving across lush flower meadows and ducking into the shade of dense evergreens. As has been the case throughout the trip, the melody of the creek remains the hiker's constant companion.

The trail exits a thicket of willows alongside a sizeable beaver pond. Strategically placed stones enable one to step across the southern end of the pool. Traversing a scree

slope, the path has been carefully flattened to make for easy travel amid the mass of rocks.

Columbines flourish among the boulders together with shrubby cinquefoil and wild gooseberry bushes.

The trail climbs moderately, crossing several tiny brooks by way of stepping stones, logs or planks, their banks resplendent with brookcress, ragwort and chimingbells. The trail ascends through a long stretch of forest before traversing a slope littered with timbers—debris resulting from repeated avalanches.

This tree graveyard is far from depressing as colorful primary colonizers have taken root among the devastation.

Shortly, the trail approaches a couple of brown signs pointing down a track to the left toward several backcountry campsites. These sites, where campfires are permitted, are in addition to the 16 stoves-only sites nearer to the hot springs.

Heading straight, the route climbs steeply through the forest, crossing a large side stream by way of logs and stepping stones.

As the trail continues its arduous ascent through scattered conifers, signs indicate several secluded campsites off to the left. It skirts a deep canyon, which Conundrum Creek has carved through the bedrock, and levels as it passes to the left of an old cabin.

After traversing an opening, the path reaches a signpost. Triangle Pass is straight ahead. The hot springs lies to

following pages: The trail crosses flower-strewn meadows on its long upward journey   **197**

the left across the creek. A single log spans the fast flowing stream. Intrepid hikers will perform a precarious balancing act to cross this obstacle. Others prefer to bushwhack upstream to utilize slippery stepping stones.

Three pools comprise Conundrum Hot Springs. The upper and larger one is the hottest, with an average temperature of around 98 degrees Farenheit. As approximately 2,000 people a year make the pilgrimage to this pleasant spot, most of them visiting between late June and the end of September, you are unlikely to find solitude. Nevertheless, the soaking pools provide a wonderful place for relaxing, conversing and enjoying the magnificent view extending all the way down the valley to the distant ridges north of Aspen. Castle Peak, the state's 12th highest summit, stands sentinel just to the east of the pools. Many hikers consider clothing to be optional here.

Snow lingers in the treeless basin above the hot springs late into the season, providing a source of water for the abundant wildflowers that carpet the open slopes in July and early August. Elephant's head, alpine avens, moss campion and myriad other tundra plants thrive in this high environment.

Ambitious hikers can continue up to Triangle Pass, which, at 12,900 feet is the second-highest named pass in the Elk Mountains. From here, a descent can be made to the East Maroon Trailhead or to Gothic near Crested Butte.

Conundrum Creek carves through a gorge

Cinquefoil

Flourishing from the foothills to the tundra, the shrubby cinquefoil is one of the most adaptable flowers in the Colorado mountains. Moreover, it blooms continuously from late June until early August. Vibrant yellow blossoms adorn this woody shrub, which grows from one to five feet tall. It is one of the many kinds of wild rose found in the state.

Cinquefoil comes from the French name for a similar European species with five finger-like leaflets.

Because it grows so easily, you will often see shrubby cinquefoil decorating flower gardens and city landscapes.

Switchbacks make for rapid altitude gain toward Buckskin Pass

~ 32 ~ Buckskin Pass

The sheer beauty and accessibility of the Maroon Bells region draws more visitors than any other area around Aspen. The reflection of North Maroon and Maroon peaks in the crystal-clear waters of Maroon Lake is, without a doubt, the most photographed scene in Colorado. These famous Fourteeners were named the Maroon Bells as they resemble two red bells. Wildflower enthusiasts will delight in the multitude of trailside wildflowers throughout this hike. In the fall, quaking aspens light up the hillsides.

This hike leads first to Crater Lake, a scenic

Trailhead

Head west from Aspen on Colorado Highway 82 and take a left (south) on Maroon Creek Road. Continue for 9.6 miles until the road dead ends in a spacious day-use parking lot.

Maroon Bells is such a popular tourist attraction that Maroon Creek Road is closed beyond the T Lazy 7 Ranch throughout the summer season from 8:30 a.m. until 5:00 p.m. During these hours, the Roaring Fork Transit Authority (RFTA) provides a shuttle bus to Maroon Bells from the Ruby Park Bus Terminal on Durant Street in downtown Aspen.

Call the local forest service office for current bus schedules. The Maroon Bells Trailhead lies at the western end of the parking lot. Restrooms and drinking water are available.

Route

Day hike; 4.7 miles one way; strenuous

Route	Elevation (ft.)	Distance (mi.)
Trailhead	9,580	0
Crater Lake	10,076	1.8
Buckskin Pass–Willow Pass Jct.	11,780	3.9 (Approx.)
Buckskin Pass	12,462	4.7

USGS Topographic map: Maroon Bells, Colo.

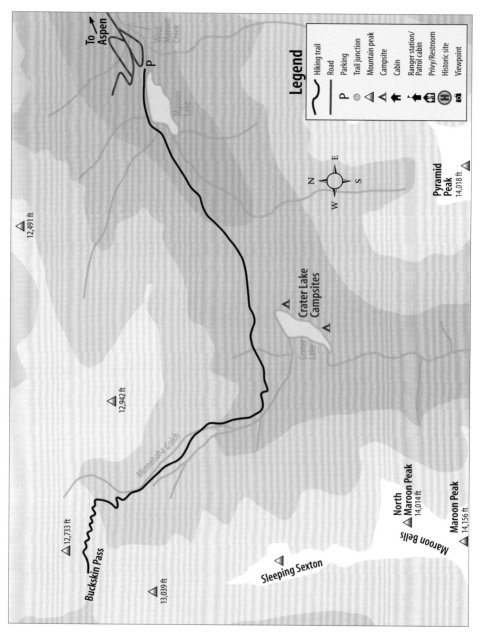

Legend

Hiking trail
Road
Parking
Trail junction
Mountain peak
Campsite
Cabin
Ranger station/Patrol cabin
Privy/Restroom
Historic site
Viewpoint

To Aspen

West Maroon Creek

Maroon Lake

12,491 ft

Pyramid Peak 14,018 ft

Crater Lake Campsites

Crater Lake

12,942 ft

Minnehaha Gulch

Buckskin Pass

12,733 ft

13,039 ft

Sleeping Sexton

North Maroon Peak 14,014 ft

Maroon Bells

Maroon Peak 14,156 ft

treasure set at the foot of the Maroon Bells and much favored by summer visitors. It then climbs a steep drainage to the right of North Maroon Peak and culminates at Buckskin Pass—one of the best viewpoints around.

Trailhead to Crater Lake

Leaving the parking lot, the trail to Crater Lake follows West Maroon Creek to the eastern tip of Maroon Lake. Passing the usual lineup of

tripods and photographers, it skirts the northern shore of the lake heading directly toward the corrugated flanks of the Bells.

The official trailhead and Forest Service bulletin board stand near the far end of the lake. A scenic path veers left at this point to meander between several pretty beaver ponds before rejoining the main trail higher up.

Keep right for Maroon-Snowmass Trail #1975, the route to Crater Lake and Buckskin Pass. The footpath continues through a profusion of Richardson geraniums, larkspur and cow parsnip. After hopscotching over a side stream by giant stepping stones, it starts to ascend through aspen groves, hugging the right flank of the valley.

Thimbleberry shrubs, easily identified by their huge lobed leaves, tiny white flowers in July and fat red berries in August, mix with the aspens. Beaver ponds glisten down to the left.

The trail runs through a band of Douglas fir, exiting into an opening with excellent views back to Maroon Lake and the surrounding aspen-clad hillsides. Photographers will find it hard to resist capturing this scene if the lighting is just right.

The scenic trail climbing from the beaver ponds

Maroon Bells

North Maroon and Maroon peaks, two Fourteeners known as the Maroon Bells, appear in more calendars and coffee-table picture books than any other mountains in Colorado.

They gain their characteristic bell-like shape from the conspicuous tilting ridges in their red sedimentary rock. These striations make them two of the most difficult Fourteeners to climb.

Although it is believed that a local boy first scaled Maroon Peak during the 1890s, the earliest documented ascents of both peaks occurred in August, 1908. Percy Hagerman, a 39-year-old Aspen businessman, and Harold Clark, a 46-year-old lawyer, climbed to the summit of North Maroon Peak by the north face. Three days later, Hagerman soloed Maroon Peak by the south ridge.

After these first ascents, the Maroon Bells rapidly became popular targets for Colorado Mountain Club parties. With the club's unrelenting focus on safe techniques, numerous members summited and descended safely. Unfortunately, several less experienced climbers were not so lucky.

Tragedy first struck in 1952 when Gordon Schindel lost his life, and his partner, Larry Hackstaff, was severely injured while descending a snow-filled gully on Maroon Peak.

The summer of 1965 and spring of 1966 have been called the year of the "Deadly Bells," when seven climbers died during a nine-month period. These included an Outward Bound instructor, three scientists from Los Alamos, New Mexico, and two Western State College students. The majority of the accidents occurred during the descent from Maroon Peak.

The most daring act on the Maroon Bells took place On June 24, 1971, when German skier and mountaineer, Fritz Stammberger, climbed the North Bell and skied down its north face in 48 minutes.

The Maroon Bells are located in the White River National Forest, just to the south of Aspen.

Buckskin Pass forms a dip in the skyline

merges from the left. The Maroon-Snowmass Trail, which we are following, makes a sharp right and shoots uphill, switchbacking to gain altitude quickly.

Penetrating a rocky basin, the trail assumes a more forgiving grade. It winds its way through a jumble of shattered talus, weathered from the crags towering to the right. Colorado blue columbines and shrubby cinquefoil have somehow found a precarious footing among the boulders.

Listen for the telltale peeps of marmots and pikas, who make their homes here. The obese marmot, intent only on acquiring sufficient body fat to withstand its winter hibernation, spends the summer sprawled on its favorite rock. The energetic pika, on the other hand, scurries hither and thither, harvesting enough flowers and grasses to see it through the long winter, when it remains awake beneath the blanket of snow.

The boulders provide picnic spots for the hordes of sandal- and sneaker-clad tourists trekking this stretch.

The trail drops slightly toward Crater Lake, yielding a delightful panorama over the tarn and south down the valley of West Maroon Creek. Three of Colorado's most celebrated Fourteeners preside over Crater Lake—North Maroon and Maroon peaks to the right and Pyramid Peak to the left.

Crater Lake to Buckskin Pass

Just before reaching the shore of Crater Lake, you arrive at a trail register and map showing the location of the 12 designated campsites around the tarn. The route divides, with the West Maroon Trail #1970 heading left to round Crater Lake on its southward journey to West Maroon Pass, 4.7 miles distant. Many hikers follow this path to Schofield Park near Crested Butte, arranging a car shuttle or taxi

service for the return trip to Aspen. For Buckskin Pass, go right on the Maroon-Snowmass Trail #1976.

As the path hurries upward, zigzagging now and again in its fervor to gain altitude, periodic openings in the aspens and willows frame vistas down to Crater Lake. Shortly, you enter the deep gorge carved by Minnehaha Gulch. The trail passes through a grassy meadow adorned with Richardson geraniums, dark penstemon, Lewis flax and Western yellow paintbrush and ducks through a band of shady evergreens.

Elbows on the sharp switchbacks reveal the deep V-shaped ravine gouged by the creek as it cascades down the drainage. North Maroon peak looms majestically to the left while an unnamed summit rises to the right. The dramatic profile of Pyramid Peak creates an imposing backdrop, rising in bold relief

Colorado's Wilderness Areas

The word "wilderness" has different connotations to different people. Some think of it as any wild place on earth that is uncivilized, uncultivated, uninhabited, empty and/or pathless. Others consider it to refer specifically to mountains or deserts.

In the "Wilderness Act" of 1964, Congress defined wilderness as being federal lands that have been set aside as part of the National Wilderness Preservation System.

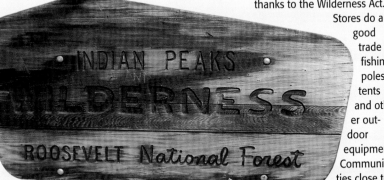

The act states: "A wilderness, in contrast with those areas where man and his own works dominate the landscape, is hereby recognized as an area where the earth and its community of life are untrammeled by man, where man himself is a visitor who does not remain."

The 1964 law designated five wilderness areas in Colorado covering a total of less than 300,000 acres. These were the Maroon Bells-Snowmass, Rawah, La Garita, Mount Zirkel and West Elk wilderness areas. In 1980, the Colorado Wilderness Act set aside 1.4 million acres as wilderness. The new areas included Holy Cross, Lost Creek and Mount Evans. The Colorado Wilderness Act of 1993 designated several more, most notably the Sangre de Cristo.

Today, there are 36 wilderness areas dotted throughout the Colorado Rockies, covering some 3.3 million acres. The Wilderness Act of 1964 prohibits logging, mining, permanent structures or installations, commercial enterprises, motorized equipment, mechanical transport (including bicycles and hang gliders) and the landing of airplanes. It permits hunting, fishing and livestock grazing.

Creating wilderness areas fulfills a number of functions and benefits many people. The first and most obvious value is the protection of large tracts of pristine land, thereby ensuring the preservation of vital and complex ecosystems.

The wilderness has a significant recreational value. Hikers, rock climbers, peak baggers, campers, fishermen and bird watchers can persue their favorite leisure-time activities there.

Many people feel spiritually uplifted or freed from stress through contact with nature. Organizations, such as the Col-orado Outward Bound School, build character through wilderness experiences. Educators and scientists use the wilderness to learn more about earth and life sciences.

Many people have jobs thanks to the Wilderness Act. Stores do a good trade in fishing poles, tents and other outdoor equipment. Communities close to wilderness areas flourish because of the influx of tourists. Outfitters provide an enjoyable backcountry experience for clients. Manufacturers of postcards and calendars profit from selling photographs of the spectacular scenery in the wilderness areas.

The old adage stated, "Take only pictures, leave only footprints." Today, we realize the environmental destruction that careless footprints can cause. It is important for all who enjoy Colorado's mountains to minimize impact by using the wilderness in an ethical manner and by adhering to the "Leave No Trace" conservation principles as outlined earlier in this book..

above: The trail passes the Indian Peaks Wilderness boundary sign

across the deep canyon of West Maroon Creek. At a bend in the trail, the hiker overlooks the junction of two branches of Minnehaha Gulch—one descending from Willow Pass, the other draining Buckskin Pass.

The trail climbs through alternating dense conifers and flowery meadows. It crosses the northern branch of Minnehaha Gulch.

Larkspur, arnica and ragwort thrive in the moist environment along the banks. Clumps of elegant Parry's primrose bow over the water, and brookcress and chiming bells decorate a midstream mini-island.

The trail continues to bustle upward, swerving back and forth between the two arms of Minnehaha Gulch. Eventually, it traverses the brow of the hanging valley and, leaving the coniferous forest behind, makes its way through a spacious alpine meadow. It follows the route of the left branch of the creek, through a riot of elephant's head, Parry's clover, king's crown, glacier lilies and globeflowers.

The path swerves to the right, crossing a side stream by way of stepping stones. Approaching the right branch of Minnehaha Gulch, it turns to the left and zigzags upward alongside the cascading water.

At an intersection, the Willow Lake Trail splits off to the right. Keep left for Buckskin Pass. Shortly, you can see the trail ahead snaking its way up to Buckskin Pass, a depression on the skyline 700 feet above. A white cornice hangs on the

Elegant sky pilots grow between the rocks on Buckskin Pass

ridge late into the season.

During the final climb up to the pass, flora enthusiasts will delight in the multitude of colorful wildflowers flourishing in this high-altitude environment. Ragweed, Western yellow paintbrush, bistort, purple fringe, sky pilot and tiny violets color the tundra. In early fall, when all the flowers have withered, the leaves of alpine avens paint the ground with a rich rust-red.

With the gain in altitude, the switchbacks grow progressively tighter. At last, the trail traverses beneath the crest of the ridge, bends to the right and arrives at narrow Buckskin Pass. To the right, a jumble of rocks provides ample picnic benches for the hikers congregating in this excellent vantage point. To the west, 14,092-foot Snowmass Mountain is easily identified by its

large snowfield. Snowmass Lake glistens at its foot. Behind and to the right of Snowmass Mountain rises Capitol Peak, another of Colorado's prestigious Fourteeners.

The trail zigzags down the western side of the pass into the valley of Snowmass Creek. Backpackers who have organized a car shuttle often head this way, camping overnight near Snowmass Lake. To the southeast, views encompass North Maroon Peak, the high point on the ridge to the south of Buckskin Pass, and Pyramid Peak towering on the other side of the West Maroon Creek Valley.

The dramatic north face of Capitol Peak towers over the lake like an impregnable fortress

~ 33 ~ Capitol Lake

Views of rugged, glaciated mountains lure hikers toward Capitol Lake, a jade-green jewel cradled in a rocky pocket at the base of 14,130-foot Capitol Peak. The lengthy trail gains elevation in fits and starts, strolling through flowery meadows and ascending through coniferous forests.

This route accesses the Avalanche Creek and West Snowmass trails, and is also popular with climbers heading for Capitol Peak. Because it passes through grazing allotments, expect to encounter cattle along the trail.

Trailhead to First Stream Crossing

The trailhead for the Capitol Creek Trail #1961 is a good vantage point for views of the deep-cut Capitol Creek Valley. Four hundred feet below, the stream wanders through the broad canyon. Here and there, ponds glisten in the

Trailhead

Head 14.0 miles west from Aspen on Colorado Highway 82 to Old Snowmass (not Snowmass Village). Go left (south) on Snowmass Creek Road for 2.0 miles to a T-junction, then turn right (west) on Capitol Creek Road. Continue for about 8.0 miles, passing St. Benedict Monastery and a large public parking lot. The last mile to the trailhead is a rough four-wheel-drive road. You'll need to walk this if you don't have a high-clearance vehicle. The trailhead is to the left of the road. Limited parking is available.

Route

Day hike or overnight; 7.3 miles one way; strenuous

Route	Elevation (ft.)	Distance (mi.)
Trailhead	9,400	0
First Stream Crossing	9,000	0.5
Second Stream Crossing	11,000	6.0
Third Stream Crossing	11,080	6.5
Capitol Lake	11,600	7.3

USGS Topographic map: Capitol Peak, Colo.

meadows. To your right, the valley makes a sharp left turn and carves a direct line toward Capitol Peak. One of the most difficult of Colorado's 54 Fourteeners to climb, Capitol gained its name from its similarity to the U.S. Capitol building.

The trail starts with an abrupt descent to the valley floor. Gambel oak and sweet-smelling sagebrush dominate this south-facing slope, together with a cheerful array of wildflowers. At first, horsemint nettleleaf and desert paintbrush color the hillside. Farther down, fairy trumpets and silvery lupines put on a show.

Just before the path reaches the canyon base, it enters an aspen grove and bridges a water diversion ditch via rickety tree trunks. It traverses a boggy meadow and approaches Capitol Creek. A boundary marker indicates that you are entering the Maroon Bells-Snowmass Wilderness.

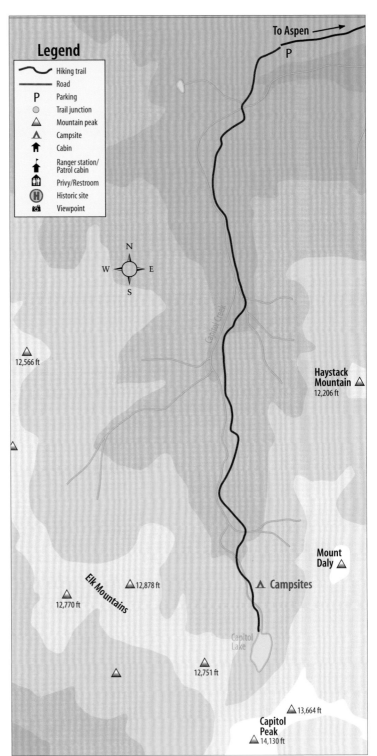

Legend

〜	Hiking trail
—	Road
P	Parking
○	Trail junction
△	Mountain peak
⛰	Campsite
♠	Cabin
⛺	Ranger station/ Patrol cabin
⛩	Privy/Restroom
Ⓗ	Historic site
📷	Viewpoint

To Aspen →

P

N
W — E
S

Capitol Creek

△ 12,566 ft

Haystack Mountain △
12,206 ft

Elk Mountains
△ 12,878 ft
△ 12,770 ft

Mount Daly △

⛺ Campsites

Capitol Lake

△ 12,751 ft

△ 13,664 ft
Capitol Peak
△ 14,130 ft

First Stream Crossing to Second Stream Crossing

After crossing the river by means of a sturdy single log, the trail rises briefly through conifers and reaches an intersection. Go right for Capitol Lake.

The footpath now begins to climb, hugging the left flank of the canyon with the stream meandering to the right. Shortly it winds to the left following the turn in the direction of the drainage. An opening provides panoramas across the braided creek and ponds decorating the flat valley floor to the gentle, aspen-clad hillside beyond. Far to the south, Capitol Peak barricades the end of the canyon, towering over its unseen tarn.

From time to time the trail sprints uphill, only to level or dip momentarily, and then resumes its upward journey at a moderate pace. Sometimes it climbs through thickets of willows or aspen groves, but more often it travels over flower-strewn meadows. Western yellow paintbrush, wild roses, sunflowers, yarrow and Richardson geraniums put on an ever-changing display.

The path hops over several side streams and burrows through a long tunnel of willows. Exiting into a vast meadow, it makes a leisurely traverse toward the right side of the valley. The lively music of Capitol Creek rises to a crescendo as the trail enters a subalpine forest of tall conifers and turns left to follow the right bank of the stream. It climbs through the trees before again venturing into an expansive meadow that offers excellent views of inhospitable-looking Capitol Peak and its neighbors.

Running along the foot of

Riparian Ecosystem

The term "riparian ecosystem" refers to the complex community of plants and animals thriving alongside watercourses, lakes and ponds. Numerous tiny creeks, originating on the alpine tundra, join forces to form larger streams, which in turn merge to create the major rivers of this country. Riparian ecosystems form corridors of varying width, which accompany these waterways on their long downhill journey to the eastern plains or western shrublands.

Riparian communities support the greatest diversity of plant and animal species found in any mountain habitat. Moisture-loving trees and shrubs dominate this environment.

The lower mountain valleys sustain a growth of narrowleaf cottonwood, willow, thin-leafed alder, aspen and river birch. Above 9,000 feet, these give way to shrubby willows and bog birch. The wildlife enjoys plentiful water, food and shelter provided by this lush habitat. Some make this their permanent home, while others visit to drink or to prey on the residents. Migrating birds build their nests in the shrubs and trees and raise their young here.

The beaver is perhaps the best-known inhabitant of the riparian ecosystem. Possessing technical skills rivaled only by man, this industrious creature plays a major role in altering the landscape. Beavers cut down the trees and shrubs, eating the inner bark of the twigs and using the larger branches to build their dams and lodges. They create ponds, which eventually kill large tracts of vegetation. After a number of years, beavers exhaust the local recourses and move elsewhere.

At one time, river otters frequented Colorado's mountain drainages, but trappers hunted them extensively for their fur. The Division of Wildlife recently transplanted dozens of otters from other parts of the country in an effort to reintroduce the animal into the state's rivers. This weasel-family member spends much of its time in and around the water and enjoys a diet of fish, crayfish and small mammals.

Other common animals are the muskrat, water shrew, montane vole, raccoon and Western jumping mouse. Coyotes, red foxes and other carnivores often hunt these tiny mammals.

One of the most entertaining riparian birds is the American dipper or water ouzel. This wren-like creature can often be seen bobbing on midstream rocks or diving underwater in search of insects and small fish. Nesting birds of the riparian ecosystem include yellow warblers, American goldfinches, willow flycatchers, western wood-pewees and black-capped chickadees. Hawks, owls and other raptors perch in the tall trees watching for prey.

following page: Capitol Lake is impounded by a jumble of boulders

the left flank of the vale, the trail passes a couple of abandoned beaver ponds. Several times it repeats a pattern of alternating through conifers and meadows, progressively gaining altitude as Capitol Peak creeps slowly closer, revealing the snow deep in its gullies.

Avoid the occasional track winding down to the creek.

The wildflowers gradually grow more profuse, until the meadows explode in a glorious display of floral fireworks. The Colorado blue columbine flaunts its beauty amid the orange sneezewood, larkspur and waist-high cow parsnip. Look for several varieties of Indian paintbrush coexisting in this lush environment.

Mount Daly, jutting to the left, presides over the landscape. This orange-red mountain is the destination for some climbers.

After crossing a side stream descending from Mount Daly, the trail bends right to traverse across a steep moraine blocking the valley. It tiptoes over another brook that tumbles down amid a cheerful array of Parry's primrose, chimingbells and brookcress. An opening in the tall conifers yields vistas down the long drainage toward Aspen and over the waves of light-blue ridges disappearing to the north.

The footpath switchbacks to gain altitude and, surmounting the top of the headwall, enters yet another open meadow. Logs aid in spanning both a tiny brook and Capitol Creek.

Second Stream Crossing to Capitol Lake

The trail continues its wearying ascent through conifers and bogs dotted with marsh marigolds. It climbs over a tree-clad ridge and drops briefly beneath a talus slope. Recross the Capitol Creek and a small side stream by way of stepping stones.

The first of several maps on posts by the trail indicates your exact location and the position of the 12 official campsites near Capitol Lake. The path slants up the left margin of the valley. The stream sings its joyful song at the foot of a rounded knoll rising to the west. Occasional cairns mark tracks veering off to the left or right to secluded tent sites. The trail steps over a wash where three miniature drainages converge. It ascends briefly

before jumping a stream. A single bend delivers you to the crest of the last moraine revealing an open valley.

As you traverse this final stretch before reaching Capitol Lake, enjoy the multicolored bouquets of columbine, kings crown, alpine anemone and bistort carpeting the meadow.

Just before a massive rock pile obstructs your forward progress, the path taking climbers to the saddle between Capitol Peak and Mount Daly splits off to the left.

The trail clambers over the boulders and, suddenly, Capitol Lake spreads in front of you, crouched at the foot of its namesake peak. No tarn could have a more impressive backdrop. The dramatic north face of Capitol Peak towers over the lake like an impregnable fortress. This 1,800-foot cliff, rising above a 700-foot scree slope, has provided a formi-

Capitol Peak

To reach the summit of 14,130-foot Capitol Peak, the climber must negotiate a 100-foot-long knife-edge ridge overlooking a 1,500-foot drop. The need to engage in such tricky maneuvering has earned Capitol the reputation of being one of Colorado's hardest Fourteeners to conquer.

Named for its similarity to the building in Washington D.C. where the U.S. Congress holds its sessions, Capitol Peak's regal demeanor makes it easy to identify from afar.

The earliest ascent of Colorado's 30th highest mountain was probably made by members of the Hayden Survey in

1873. But it is entrepreneur Percy Hagerman and attorney Harold Clark who are credited with the official pioneering climb on August 22, 1909.

The imposing north face, consisting of 1,800 feet of vertical rock, presented for years an irresistible challenge to technical climbers. Carl Blaurock, Elwyn Arps and Harold Popcorn were the first to scale this formidable obstacle in 1937. The initial winter ascent was made on March 10, 1972 by Fritz Stammberger and Gordon Whitmer, who summitted after spending 11 hours climbing the gigantic wall.

dable challenge to technical climbers over the years.

Impounded by an impossible jumble of boulders, Capitol Lake is devoid of picturesque alpine meadows. Its hard-edged shoreline is knotted tightly into the rockfalls and snowbanks that are reflected clearly in its green water.

The trail continues over the talus on the right-hand side of the tarn and winds up the grassy valley to the pass, visible 1.0 mile to the south. From there, many backpackers access the Avalanche Creek and West Snowmass Trails.

Ticks

The wood tick, *Dermacentor andersoni*, is one of the most annoying parasites present in the Colorado Rockies. Ticks resemble tiny, flattened spiders and are about 1/8 inch long. When they are engorged with blood, they can expand to more than twice their original size. Hikers may encounter ticks from March through July, although the arachnids are most prevalent from April through June. Wood ticks live in brush, grass and wooded areas in the foothills and montane zones. They are most abundant on south-facing slopes east of the Continental Divide.

This external, blood-sucking parasite embeds itself in the host by means of a dart-like anchor, making removal difficult without separating its head from its body.

Ticks go through four distinct stages in their life cycle: the egg, a six-legged larva, an eight-legged nymph and adult. The cycle takes up to two years as unfed adults and nymphs hibernate during the winter.

Ticks in Colorado can be carriers of Colorado tick fever and Rocky Mountain spotted fever. As tick bites are often unfelt, it is important to take measures to avoid being bitten.

Prevention
• Wear tight-fitting collars, sleeves and pant-leg cuffs.
• Cover your body with light-colored clothing so that you can see ticks easily.
• Check frequently for ticks on your clothing, scalp and exposed areas of skin.
• After your hike, thoroughly inspect your body for ticks.
• Use a repellent containing DEET on clothing and exposed areas of skin.

Removal
If you do encounter a tick embedded in your skin:
• Smear oil or ointment on the tick to cut off its air supply.
• Placing tweezers as close to the skin as possible, pull the tick straight out. Be careful to remove the head and mouth parts.
• Wash the affected area with soap and water and cleanse with disinfectant.

Tick-borne Diseases
Colorado tick fever is a viral disease transmitted to humans by the wood tick. While it is serious, this ailment is not life threatening. Ticks become carriers during their larval stage after ingesting the blood of an infected rodent. As adults, they pass on the illness to humans and large mammals during long hours of attachment.

Symptoms of Colorado tick fever start to appear three to six days after a person is bitten. These are headaches, body aches, abdominal pain, sensitivity to light and, occasionally, a skin rash. The illness usually lasts from five to 10 days, although this may be longer in persons over 30.

As yet, there is no vaccine against Colorado tick fever and 20 percent of patients may require hospitalization. There are from 100 to 300 cases reported in Colorado annually.

Rocky Mountain spotted fever is a very serious disease which is, thankfully, rare in Colorado. It is caused by *Rickettsia ricketsii*, a bacterium carried by the wood tick. As transmission of this microorganism requires from six to 10 hours of attachment, prompt removal of ticks can do a lot to prevent the likelihood of infection.

Symptoms of Rocky Mountain spotted fever begin two to four days after infection and include fever, headaches, nausea, vomiting, aches in the abdomen and muscles, and a spotted rash which starts at the wrists, ankles or waist and spreads over the entire body. If this disease is left untreated, complications develop which can result in death.

Treatment of Rocky Mountain spotted fever involves large dosages of antibiotics.

Steamboat Springs

Three Island Lake

Until the mid 1800s, the Utes made the Yampa Valley in northern Colorado their summer home, drawn as they were by the bison herds and the abundant mineral hot springs. They believed the springs were sacred places where the

Great Spirit lived deep below the earth's surface. After battles they would visit to rejuvenate their souls.

Today, Steamboat Springs boasts the title "Ski Town USA." Its non-glitzy resort, equipped with all the latest amenities, provides world-class conditions for skiers of all ability levels.

In summer, outdoor enthusiasts flock to this authentic Western town to enjoy the rich variety of diversions available, including hot-air ballooning, horseback riding, golf and rafting. The Routt National Forest is a paradise for hikers and backpackers. Its numerous trails cross flowery meadows and wind through forests of aspen and conifers.

The twin volcanic plugs crowning Rabbit Ears Peak stand like sentinels over the landscape. Hike 34 climbs to the foot of this unusual rock formation, affording some of the best views available in the Steamboat Springs area. Spectacular Fish Creek Falls, only three miles from the center of town, is a popular playground for picnickers. This is the starting point for Hike 35, which follows Fish Creek as it carves through a rugged canyon on its journey to Long Lake.

In October 1997, a sudden gale leveled more than four million trees in the Routt National Forest. Hike 36 offers an opportunity to witness some of the devastation caused by this Blowdown.

Steamboat Springs, which is located 166 miles northwest of Denver, is well equipped with motels, restaurants and other tourist facilities. Several National Forest campgrounds lie along Seedhouse Road to the north of town and along U.S. 40 on Rabbit Ears Pass.

left: The trail meanders alongside Fish Creek through a series of flowery meadows

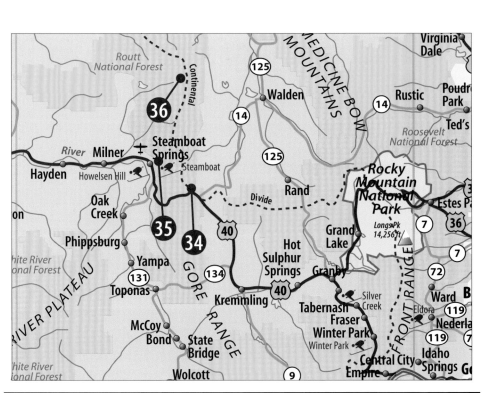

Other Hikes in the Steamboat Springs Area

Hahns Peak

Day hike, 1.5 miles one way
Elevation gain: 1,470 feet
Rating: Moderate
USGS Topographic map: Hahns Peak, Colo.

The trail to the old fire lookout tower on the summit of 10,839-foot Hahns Peak makes an excellent introductory climb for children and inexperienced hikers. The summit affords a 360-degree panorama of the forested ridges and wide valleys of the surrounding Routt National Forest and the Mount Zirkel Wilderness Area, as well as north all the way into Wyoming.

Abundant rock formations and wildflowers add interest along the way. The area is scattered with abandoned mine shafts and old cabins, so extra care is needed when viewing these mining remains.

The fire lookout tower crowning the peak was first built in 1912 and then reconstructed in 1942. It fell into disuse during the 1950s and is now listed on the Colorado Inventory of Historic Places.

Wyoming Trail

Day hike or multi-day backpack, 2.0 to 49.3 miles one way
Elevation gain: Along the route, elevations fluctuate between 8,000 feet and 11,880 feet.
Rating: Easy to difficult
USGS Topographic maps: Mount Werner, Colo., Buffalo Pass, Colo., Mount Zirkel, Colo., Farwell Mountain, Colo., Mount Ethel, Colo., West Fork Lake, Colo. and Dudley Creek, Colo.

The 49.3-mile-long Wyoming Trail is part of the interstate Continental Divide National Scenic Trail. It travels north from Base Camp, near Steamboat Springs, through the Mount Zirkel Wilderness to Medicine Bow National Forest, in Wyoming. As much of its route lies above tree line along the spine of the Divide, the hiker is often rewarded by extensive views to the east and west. Plenty of trails join the Wyoming Trail, making a wide variety of day hikes, overnight excursions and multi-day backpacking trips possible.

An excellent day hike starts at Buffalo Pass, near Steamboat Springs, and runs through flower-decked meadows along the crest of the Park Range for 4.0 miles.

Waves of peaks sweep toward the south

~ 34 ~ Rabbit Ears Peak

The two summit pinnacles of Rabbit Ears Peak—which resemble rabbit ears from a distance—form one of northern Colorado's most striking features.

This easy stroll through flower-strewn meadows to a fine viewpoint makes Rabbit Ears Peak an attractive choice for the whole family. Don't forget the sunscreen as little shade is available during the hike. Because the route follows a four-wheel-drive road for most of the way, you may encounter the occasional vehicle.

Trailhead

Drive 19 miles southeast of Steamboat Springs on US Highway 40. Turn north on Forest Road 315, following the signs for Dumont Lake and campground. Proceed 1.5 miles to a historic marker identifying the location of Old Rabbit Ears Pass. Head left (north) here and park in the spacious lot in front of the gate on Forest Road 311. If the gate is open, you may continue for 0.2 mile. Limited parking is available at the point where the four-wheel-drive Forest Road 291 veers off to the right.

Trailhead to Rabbit Ears Peak

Walk through the gate and continue along Forest Road 311 for 0.2 mile through a coniferous forest. As you exit the trees, look for the hard-to-spot indicator for Trail 291 and a post with a small hiking symbol, which direct you off to the right along a jeep road. The road skirts to the left of the forest, shortly entering the first of many cheery meadows that characterize this hike.

Pyramid-shaped Rabbit Ears Peak looms

Route

Day hike; 3.0 miles one way; easy

Route	Elevation (ft.)	Distance (mi.)
Trailhead	9,604	0
Rabbit Ears Peak	10,654	3.0

USGS Topographic map: Rabbit Ears Peak, Colo.

217

majestically ahead, crowned by its 100-foot-high rocky coronet. In the crystal-clear Colorado air, the mountain looks almost close enough to touch. Don't let it fool you. It is still quite a distance away.

The road swerves to the right to cross a small willow-choked brook. It then begins its meandering ascent toward the peak.

Throughout the summer, the meadow explodes with a glorious display of floral fireworks. The regal blue columbine, the state flower, flaunts its sovereignty over the other blossoms in massive clusters. Yellow sunflower composites, white Richardson geraniums, silvery lupines and scarlet paintbrush decorate the landscape. White totem poles growing in damp spots on closer inspection turn out to be bog orchids.

As the road continues its swerving amble over the rolling terrain, views improve steadily. Ahead, Rabbit Ears Peak dominates the scene. Looking back, you can see waves of turquoise ridges sweeping toward the south. Pointed Whiteley Peak, a well-known landmark to drivers approaching Rabbit Ears Pass from the south, rises above the valley of Muddy Creek. In the far distance jut the rumpled summits of the Gore Range.

After about 1.5 miles, the grade assumes an irregular pattern of rising and leveling and briefly dipping. Occasionally, the road ducks through a shady band of conifers, reemerging into the unrelenting sunshine of the meadow. A minuscule pond glitters off to the right.

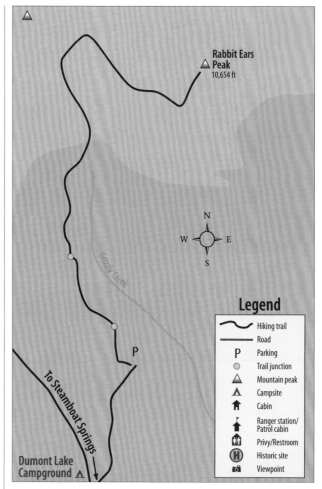

Rabbit Ears Peak 10,654 ft

Grizzly Creek

P

To Steamboat Springs

Dumont Lake Campground

Legend

〰	Hiking trail
—	Road
P	Parking
○	Trail junction
△	Mountain peak
⚊	Campsite
🏠	Cabin
	Ranger station/ Patrol cabin
🏛	Privy/Restroom
Ⓗ	Historic site
📷	Viewpoint

Elephant's Head

This common resident of wet meadows in Colorado's high country could not have a more appropriate name. Each pink-lavender inflorescence looks like a totem pole of elephant heads. An upward-pointing tube of petals, resembling a head, tapers down to an up-turned trunk. Protrusions on either side form perfect ears and a lower portion of the petal looks like a jaw.

Its stem is rod straight and grows from six inches to two feet tall. Its leaves are long, narrow and fern-like. Elephant's head thrives in bogs in the montane and subalpine zones and bloom in early summer.

Colorado blue columbines decorate the meadow in front of Rabbit Ears Peak

Montane Forests

The montane life zone extends from an elevation of about 6,000 feet to 9,000 feet in the Colorado Rockies. It contains several distinct ecosystems. Open ponderosa pine forests dominate sunny, dry, south-facing slopes. These tall conifers are characterized by their four- to seven-inch-long needles in bundles of two or three. Douglas fir and Rocky Mountain juniper often mix with the pines and the understory is rich with grasses and wildflowers.

Dense Douglas fir forests thrive on cool, moist, north-facing valley sides opposite the ponderosa-clad slopes. They are rarely found alone, often being accompanied by lodgepole pine, Engelmann spruce, subalpine fir and ponderosa pine. The Douglas fir is identified by its Christmas tree shape and distinctive cones with three-pronged bracts projecting from between the scales.

Aspens and lodgepole pines colonize areas that have been disturbed by deforestation, fire or avalanche. The aspen is the only major deciduous tree seen covering slopes in the mountains. Its rounded leaves tremble in the slightest breeze, thus the name "trembling" or "quaking" aspen. In fall, the leaves light up the hillsides with shades of brilliant yellow-gold, enticing thousands of visitors into the Rockies. The lodgepole pine is aptly named. Native Americans used the straight, tall trunks as poles for teepees and other such structures. Trees in a lodgepole pine forest are often of such uniform height that they look as if they are in a plantation.

The road descends to cross a tiny stream by way of stepping stones, then resumes its fitful climb.

It hastens up toward a saddle in the ridge extending to the left of Rabbit Ears Peak. A few hundred feet below the crest of the ridge, the track swerves to the right and continues its intermittent climb through a broad corridor in the coniferous forest. Suddenly, the road bends to the left and shoots up the southern flank of the mountain, paralleling the crags that fall beneath the summit pinnacles. This bend marks the limit of access by four-wheel-drive vehicles.

After a breath-stealing 300-foot ascent, the pathway reaches the base of the western rock tower. Be extra careful if you decide to follow the track that leads around the base of the Rabbit Ears or if you scramble up to the depression in between the spires. It is inadvisable to attempt to scale the pinnacles, as they are composed of brittle volcanic rock.

There are plenty of spots around the foot of the spires where you can relax while enjoying portions of the 360-degree panorama. Views include the Gore Range to the south, the Flat Tops Wilderness to the southwest, the Mount Zirkel Wilderness to the north and Rocky Mountain National Park to the east.

Steamboat Springs: Ski Town U.S.A.

Skiers, beware of the Yampa Valley Curse! An old Ute legend had it that this verdant vale in northwestern Colorado cast a spell upon its visitors, forcing them to come back year after year. Today, it's the world-class skiing and snowboarding that compel skiers to return to Steamboat Springs. Boasting the title "Ski Town USA," this ranching community nestles at an altitude of 7,000 feet in the heart of the Colorado Rockies. Unlike many glitzier resorts such as Aspen and Vail, Steamboat has successfully kept its Old West charm and small-town atmosphere while maintaining state-of-the-art facilities.

Steamboat is best known for its superlative snow conditions. An average of 335 inches of the fluffy white stuff falls each year, providing some of the best powder skiing in the world. A local rancher called Joe McElroy is credited with coining the term "champagne powder" in the 1950s.

Settlers of the late 1800s used skis as a means of winter transportation around the Yampa Valley. However, it was not until Norwegian cross-country and ski-jumping champion, Carl Howelsen, organized Steamboat's first Winter Carnival in 1914 that the townspeople began to ski for pleasure. The oldest ski area to be developed in Colorado (which lies adjacent to downtown Steamboat Springs) was named Howelsen Hill in honor of him.

By 1943, downhill skiing had become so popular that it was added to the school curriculum. Since the late 1940s, Steamboat Springs has spawned a total of 43 Winter Olympians, more than any other town in North America.

Steamboat Ski Area officially opened in 1963. It was originally called Storm Mountain and renamed Mt. Werner after hometown Olympian, Buddy Werner, died in an avalanche in Switzerland the following year.

Perhaps Steamboat's most famous hero is the legendary Billy Kidd. Kidd and teammate Jimmie Heuga became the first Americans to win medals in the 1964 Olympics in Innsbruck, Austria. Kidd was awarded a silver and Heuga the bronze in the slalom. Kidd went on to win both the Amateur and Professional World Championships in 1970 and was inducted into the Colorado Sports Hall of Fame in 1995. Today, Kidd serves as the resort's Director of Skiing, runs the Billy Kidd Performance Center and regularly offers free clinics.

Shannon Dunn, a 25-year-old Steamboatian, was the first female in the United States to win a medal for snowboarding in the 1998 Winter Olympics in Nagano, Japan.

Since its beginning, Steamboat Ski Area has grown to offer 140 trails, 3,668 vertical feet of skiing, seven on-mountain restaurants, 22 lifts—including the eight-passenger Silver Bullet and four quad chairlifts—and an uphill capacity of more than 32,000 people per hour. A total of 2,939 skiable acres spread over five peaks provides a wide diversity of terrain, attracting beginner, intermediate and advanced skiers and riders.

Steamboat offers a variety of clinics for all ages and ability levels. The Perfect Turn Learning Center holds specialty clinics in powder, style, bumps, racing and snowboarding, together with seminars for women and adaptive skiers.

Steamboat Springs lies in northwestern Colorado, 160 miles from Denver. Take Interstate 70 west through the Eisenhower Tunnel to Silverthorne, head north on Colorado Highway 9 to Kremmling and then go west on US 40 over Rabbit Ears Pass. The Yampa Valley Regional Airport in Hayden, just 22 miles from Steamboat Ski Area, provides flights from numerous cities nationwide. For more information, call Steamboat Central Reservations at (800) 922-2722 or (970) 879-6111.

Long Lake was constructed in the early 1900s as a water storage reservoir

~ 35 ~ Fish Creek Falls and Long Lake

In the early 1900s, whitefish and brook trout were abundant in the stream that later became known as Fish Creek. The entire population of Steamboat

Springs would make an annual fall pilgrimage to catch large quantities of fish with pitchforks, hooks and gunny sacks. They then salted and stored the catch in barrels for use during the long hard winter.

Today, Lower Fish Creek Falls, located near the trailhead, is popular with picnickers and hikers alike.

Trailhead to Lower Falls

Fish Creek Trail #1102 starts with a steep descent past a water pump and restrooms into the deep-cut canyon of Fish Creek, losing 120 feet in about 0.3 mile. It crosses a substantial footbridge spanning the river, which offers an excellent view of Fish Creek Falls.

Thundering through the narrow channel the falls have cut through the hard schist and

Trailhead

From the center of Steamboat Springs, turn north on 3rd from Lincoln (US 40), taking an immediate right on Fish Creek Falls Road. Drive 3.2 miles until it dead ends at the Fish Creek Falls Recreation Area. The first parking lot you come to is for overnight and horse trailer parking. The second is for day hiking and picnicking. The trailhead is at the far end of the lot.

Route

Day hike or overnight; 6.0 miles one way; strenuous

Route	Elevation (ft.)	Distance (mi.)
Trailhead	7,480	0
Lower Falls	7,560	0.3 (Approx.)
Upper Falls	9,000	3.0
Long Lake	9,850	6.0

USGS Topographic maps: Steamboat Springs, Colo., Mount Werner, Colo.

gneiss, a foaming torrent hurtles more than a 100 feet down a rock wall. At the foot of the falls, outcroppings split the white water. The clutter of boulders along the shore between the cascade and the bridge provides an attractive playground for picnickers.

Lower Falls to Upper Falls

Turning right, the trail starts its sinuous journey up the southern flank of the gorge, passing through a luxuriant growth of Rocky Mountain maple, Gambel oak, mountain ash, Utah juniper and tall Douglas fir. Wild rose mixes with Richardson and Fremont geraniums along the verge.

The grade moderates as the pathway leaves the deep canyon at the base of the falls and heads up the left side of the Fish Creek drainage. The trail rises through a long corridor of aspens. The quaking leaves turn brilliant shades of yellow-gold in the fall.

The trail exits the aspens and follows a route high above the level of Fish Creek. On both sides, giant cliffs enclose the narrowing valley, carved when glaciers gnawed through the landscape during the ice ages. The first panoramas of the hike reveal the rugged gorge ahead and the Steamboat Springs area behind.

Shortly, the trail recrosses Fish Creek by way of a sturdy wooden bridge.

Now hugging the left flank of the ravine, the trail continues its upward journey through the willows and aspens and a profusion of wild rose, cow parsnip and bedstraw.

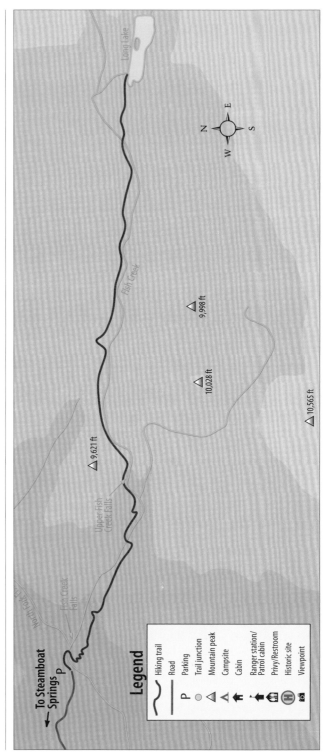

Long Lake

Fish Creek

△ 9,998 ft

△ 10,028 ft

△ 10,565 ft

△ 9,621 ft

Upper Fish Creek Falls

Fish Creek Falls

North Fork

To Steamboat Springs P

Legend

- Hiking trail
- Road
- P Parking
- Trail junction
- Mountain peak
- Campsite
- Cabin
- Ranger station/ Patrol cabin
- Privy/Restroom
- Historic site
- Viewpoint

Upper Falls to Long Lake

The trail zigzags up to the left of the waterfall through a riot of sunflowers and veers to the right by the head of the chute. Snaking back and forth, it quickly gains altitude.

To the right, rambunctious Fish Creek tumbles over a sequence of small but graceful cascades. The limber pines make an appearance among the scattered spruce and aspens.

The trail alternately approaches the brook and then switchbacks high above the level of the water. An abundance of rock slabs provides places to rest and enjoy the streamside scenery.

The vista westward grows ever more extensive, encompassing Steamboat Springs and the series of ridges and valleys behind the town.

At last, the trail climbs out of the canyon and enters a wide, open valley bordered on the south by a low, conifer-clad escarpment and to the north by a grassy slope scattered with boulders.

Fish Creek meanders lazily through thickets of willows. The entire meadow blazes with a multitude of vibrant blossoms. Flamboyant clumps of Colorado blue columbines flaunt their elevated status as the state flower, as decreed by law in 1899. Silvery lupines, rosy paintbrush, horsemint and heartleaf arnica bloom alongside the trail. Watch for the white candles of rare bog orchids thriving in marshes by the brook.

Favoring the left flank of the vale, the trail weaves

Ridges beyond Steamboat Springs

The trail swerves to the right to traverse near the base of a massive rock wall. Excellent views open all the way down the canyon to the hills around Steamboat Springs.

As the trail switchbacks upward, often clambering over easy-to-climb slabs of bedrock, tiny yellow clumps of stonecrop peek out from crevices.

After 3.0 miles, Upper Fish Creek Falls thunders into view quite suddenly. For many hikers, this is the final destination.

A side track leads down to plentiful picnic spots on the rocky ledges beneath the cascade. Chiseling a single channel through the bedrock, the cataract dances over several rocky obstacles as it thrashes into the chasm at its foot.

following pages: Pointed Whiteley Peak juts above the valley of Muddy Creek to the south

Colorado's Endangered Species

A sad fact of life is that more than 90 percent of all plant and animal species that ever existed on our planet are now extinct. Particularly alarming is the rapid acceleration in the rate of extinction that has taken place during the last few hundred years. In the 1600s, seven species of mammals disappeared from the face of the earth. The number increased to 11 in the 18th century and 27 in the 19th. During the 20th century, more than 70 types of mammals became extinct. And this is a direct result of the actions of the human race. Modern man's ever more complex lifestyle, unending desire for expansion and irresponsible pollution of the environment is depriving numerous creatures of the habitat they need for their continued survival.

Lists of endangered or threatened species are compiled by the U.S. Department of the Interior and the Colorado Wildlife Commission. The word "endangered" signifies an animal, insect, bird or plant that is in immediate danger of extinction. "Threatened" means that so few members of the species exist that it could become endangered. If recovery plans are successful, animals may be reclassified from endangered to threatened or even entirely removed from the lists.

The following is a description of some of the creatures that are currently on Colorado's endangered species list.

Grizzly Bear

The grizzly bear is perhaps the most feared of all North American wild animals. No wonder that authors have always depicted it as a terrifying beast. It is huge, standing up to eight feet tall and weighing more than 1,000 pounds. And, if it so desires, it can easily kill man or any other animal. The shape of its snout makes it easy to distinguish from the more common black bear. Its muzzle is concave, while that of the black bear is rounded.

The grizzly once roamed throughout the Colorado Rockies. During the late 1800s and early 1900s, settlers considered it to be incompatible with civilization and ruthlessly eliminated it from the state. The last documented grizzly to be killed in Colorado was shot in 1979. It is unknown whether there are still grizzlies here today.

Gray Wolf

The gray wolf, the largest member of the dog family, may exceed 170 pounds, although males generally average around 90 pounds. Wolf packs of from two to eight animals prey primarily on deer, elk and moose.

Once common inhabitants of Colorado, wolves were trapped for their fur during the 19th and early 20th centuries. The last of the state's native wolf population disappeared during the 1940s. Today there is considerable debate regarding the pros and cons of reintroducing the gray wolf into Colorado.

Lynx

This cat family member, which weighs about 30 pounds, is best identified by the tufts of long, stiff hairs growing on top of its ears. The lynx is an inhabitant of high elevations, and is well adapted to cold and snow due to its large, fur-covered feet that act as snowshoes.

While the lynx did live in Colorado, it was never as abundant here as it is in Canada and Alaska. Its presence in the state has been documented on four different occasions between 1969 and 1980.

Gray wolf

Colorado's Endangered Species

Wolverine

The wolverine is the largest member of the weasel family. It can be 33 inches long and weigh up to 60 pounds. It is a distinctive rich brown color with cream or yellow stripes along its sides. The wolverine is a brave hunter, sometimes attacking grown elk or even driving bears and mountain lions off a kill. Its favorite meal, however, is carrion.

The Colorado Rockies are the southernmost range of the wolverine. It is believed that it once inhabited densely forested mountain regions, but there is little evidence to suggest that it still exists in the state.

Black-footed Ferret

Wildlife experts consider the black-footed ferret to be the rarest mammal in North America. This 24-inch-long weasel family member is distinguished by the black mark over its eyes, its black tail tip and black legs.

The ferret preys on prairie dogs and makes its home in their burrows. The common practice of poisoning prairie dogs led to the near-extinction of the ferret. The last reported sighting of a black-footed ferret in Colorado was in 1943.

Whooping Crane

Cranes are among the largest birds on earth and are thought to be the oldest living species. Weighing from 11 to 16 pounds, the whooping crane stands about five feet tall and has a wingspan of seven feet. It is white with a long neck and long black legs. Whooping cranes pair for life.

Because of human encroach-ment on their nesting sites, populations dropped dramatically during the 19th and early 20th centuries. By 1945 there were only 19 whooping cranes left, 17 of which wintered at Arkansas National Wildlife Refuge and the other two of which were the lone survivors of a non-migratory flock in Louisiana. In the 1970s, a project was started to increase the population by placing whooping crane eggs under nesting greater sandhill crane foster parents at Gray's Lake National Wildlife Refuge in Idaho. The young whoopers successfully imitated the migration patterns of their foster parents, but failed to learn the correct mating dance necessary to breed with other whoopers. Today, there are less than 300 of these birds worldwide. Visitors to the annual spring crane festival at Monte Vista, Colorado, may be rewarded by a sight of one of the few remaining whoopers that still migrate from Idaho to New Mexico with the flock of sandhill cranes.

Peregrine Falcon

This medium-sized hawk family member used to nest throughout North America. Today, the peregrine falcon is limited to the western states. Population levels have declined due to the injurious effects of the pesticide DDT, which accumulates in the adults when they eat contaminated prey. This eventually leads to the thinning of the egg shells, which break before they hatch.

The peregrine is distinguished by its dark helmet, its dark blue back and striped, buff-colored front. Measuring from 15 to 22 inches in length, it has long, pointed wings and flies with strong, steady wing beats. This raptor's primary food is birds such as swallows, robins, doves, blackbirds and pigeons. Surprisingly, it puts up no resistance when other birds lie in wait to steal its food.

Two subspecies of peregrine falcons are seen in Colorado. Arctic peregrines migrate through the state. The American peregrine nests and breeds here. Considerable efforts are being undertaken to ban hikers and rock climbers from the vicinity of nesting sites during the breeding season.

Other Creatures Currently Listed as Endangered in Colorado

Amphibians
• Boreal toad

Mammals
• Kit fox
• River otter

Birds
• Plains sharp-tailed grouse
• Least tern
• Southwestern willow flycatcher

Fish
• Bonytail
• Razorback sucker
• Rio Grande sucker
• Lake chub
• Plains minnow
• Suckermouth minnow
• Northern redbelly dace
• Southern redbelly dace

through this floral paradise, sometimes following the stream bank, at other times making brief ascents through occasional copses of conifers.

About 5.5 miles into the hike, you reach the third stream crossing. During early summer, fording Fish Creek at this point will involve getting wet feet, so come prepared with rubber sandals.

The trail veers toward the right-hand side of the valley, rounds a grassy hummock and hops over a little side stream rippling through a bog that is covered in marsh marigolds and bog orchids.

Glacier lilies, anxious to bloom at the first signs of summer, poke their leaves through lingering snowbanks and adorn the surrounding terrain with their yellow blossoms.

The footpath contours around a marsh and comes to a trail junction. Keep straight ahead when a marker indicates that the Mountain View Trail #1022 branches to the right. The final stretch takes the hiker up the side of the valley through a subalpine forest. The trail meets Long Lake at its northwestern shore. This long, narrow lake, decorated by a solitary island, was constructed during the early 1900s as a water-storage reservoir. A dam stretches along its northern shore and an obvious bathtub ring reveals its former purpose. Due to its relatively low elevation, it is surrounded by thick conifers. Despite the fact that Long Lake is indeed a lengthy body of water, it gained its name from a prospector named Long.

Fish Creek Falls thunders through a narrow channel it has carved in the hard schist and gneiss

From Long Lake, the trail continues past Round Lake, Lake Percy, Little Lost Lake, Lake Elmo, Lost Lake, Fishhook Lake and Base Camp before it finally exits onto Forest Road 311 at Old Rabbit Ears Pass.

Three Island Lake lies snug in a basin bound on three sides by gentle hills

~ 36 ~ Three Island Lake

I n the early morning of October 25, 1997, a sudden gale tore eastward through the Routt National Forest, leaving a path of destruction in its wake.

It ripped trees from the ground and dropped them like toothpicks one on top of the other. During a mere two hours, the face of 20,000 acres changed forever.

The Three Island Lake Trail leads through an area affected by this "blowdown" to a tarn high in the Mount Zirkel Wilderness. It provides the hiker with an opportunity to witness how the forces of nature can shape the landscape.

Trailhead to Rocky Outcroppings

The trail ascends the embankment to the left of the road. After about 150 feet, it reaches the trail register, Mount Zirkel Wilderness Boundary marker, and a sign for Three Island Trail #1163. It switchbacks up the northern flank of the valley of the South Fork of the Elk River through aspen groves and scattered sunflowers, wild

Trailhead

Drive west of Steamboat Springs on US 40 for about 1.3 miles. Head north on Routt Country Road 129 toward Hahns Peak for 18 miles and turn right (east) just past Gleneden Resort. Travel 9.6 miles on Seedhouse Road (Forest Road 400), passing Seedhouse Campground. Go right on Forest Road 443. The trailhead is to the left after 3.0 miles. Limited parking is available.

Route

Day hike; 3.0 miles one way; moderate

Route	Elevation (ft.)	Distance (mi.)
Trailhead	8,400	0
Three Island Spur Jct	8,591	0.25
Rocky Outcroppings	9,050	1.5 (Approx.)
Three Island Lake	9,878	3.0

USGS Topographic map: Mount Zirkel, Colo.

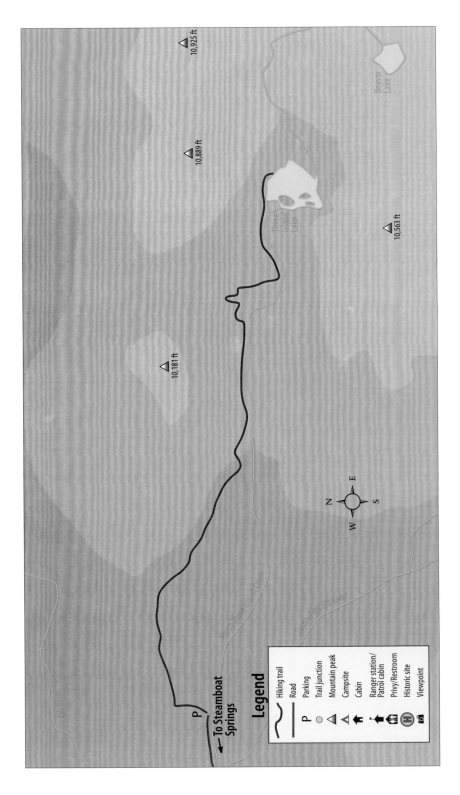

10,925 ft

Beaver Lake

10,889 ft

Three Island Lake

10,563 ft

10,181 ft

North Three Island Creek

South Fork Elk River

Elk River

P

To Steamboat Springs

N
W   E
S

Legend

⌇	Hiking trail
—	Road
P	Parking
○	Trail junction
◁	Mountain peak
◀	Campsite
🚶	Cabin
🏠	Ranger station/ Patrol cabin
🚻	Privy/Restroom
⚒	Historic site
📷	Viewpoint

Blowdown

Early in the morning of October 25, 1997, a most unusual phenomenon dramatically changed the face of the landscape just to the north of Steamboat Springs. Strong winds of more than 120 miles an hour blew from the east over the Continental Divide, devastating large tracts in 20,000 acres of the Routt National Forest.

It is estimated that the Routt Divide Blowdown destroyed more than four million Engelmann spruce and subalpine fir trees. It tore many from the ground, exposing entire root systems and leaving giant holes. In many places, toppled and broken trunks extend for acres, often piled thickly on top of one another. Many droop across streams or form unnatural bridges. Some are hung up in the forest canopy by their limbs or lean precariously against their neighbors. Others litter the gray hillsides like fallen toothpicks.

Through restoration projects, the forest service is progressively clearing trails and campgrounds blocked by the blowdown. However, because of the tremendous extent of the damage, it may be several years before all of the popular trails in the Routt National Forest are usable.

The trail leading to Three Island Lake (Hike 36) was one of the first to be reopened to the public. It passes through several areas of blowdown, providing a wonderful opportunity for hikers to witness the tremendous forces of nature and to observe

the exciting natural succession occurring in the forest.

It is, however, very important to realize that many of the downed trunks are extremely unstable, even along trails that have been reopened, and that dangerous conditions may persist for many years.

Information about the blowdown is posted at trailheads in the Routt National Forest. To find out more about the status of trails in the area, call the Blowdown Hotline at (970) 870-2192.

roses and fairy trumpets.

After 0.25 mile, the Three Island Spur Trail #1163 1A joins from the left; bear straight. The grade moderates as the footpath turns eastward, traversing along the hillside toward the drainage of North Three Island Creek.

Shortly, spruce, fir and pine begin to mingle with the aspens, rapidly developing into a thick forest of tall conifers.

The trail now passes through alternating aspens, evergreens and flower-strewn meadows. Richardson geranium, monkshood, dark penstemon and gigantic cow parsnip bloom by the path. Thimbleberry shrubs flourish in wet areas.

The footpath zigzags to gain altitude and crosses two tiny side streams by stepping stones. Periodic openings in the trees frame views across the South Fork of the Elk River Valley.

After about 1.5 miles, the trail passes several large outcroppings of bedrock, offering the best panoramas of the hike. From here, you can look southward to the snow-fretted summits of the Continental Divide and westward down the road that you drove along.

Rocky Outcroppings to Three Island Lake

A forest of old-growth fir and spruce encloses the trail as it veers left to penetrate the valley of North Three Island Creek. Suddenly, you enter an area devastated by the blowdown. Broken conifers crisscross the slope, resting where they fell, like skeletons

slowly decaying in the thin mountain air. Massive root systems lie exposed, leaving 10-foot-wide gashes where the wind wrenched them from the earth. In places, the pile of toppled timbers is so thick it's impassable. The forest service has done an excellent job of sawing a walkway through this desolate scene. North Three Island Creek sings its lively song as it cascades to the right. The water music grows louder as the trail approaches its banks and fades as it switchbacks far above the level of the brook.

The reader should note that the path remains on the left (north) side of the stream throughout the hike. The USGS topographic map inaccurately depicts the trail crossing and recrossing the creek.

The trail zigzags up the left flank of the valley, rapidly gaining altitude and leaving the waterway far below. A track leads off to the right to a big rocky slab, which provides a vantage point for vistas westward down the long valley carved by North Three Island Creek and the Elk River. Turquoise peaks rise far in the distance. Bare patches decorating the ridges on either side testify to the immensity of the damage caused by the blowdown.

About 2.5 miles into the hike, the terrain flattens. The trail meanders through swamps resplendent with marsh marigolds and glacier lilies. It traverses a treeless area with the creek sauntering through thickets of willows and crosses a little side stream

by way of stepping stones.

The path skirts to the right of a meadow blanketed with elephant's head, then plunges back into thick subalpine forest, passing more examples of blowdown damage.

Finally, you arrive at Three Island Lake, aptly named due to its three tree-clad islands. Lying snug in a basin, it is bound on three sides by gentle hills and on the other by a fringe of conifers. At the southeastern side of the tarn stretches a marsh speckled with Western yellow paintbrush, violets, globeflowers and dozens of other wildflowers.

Despite the fact that the lake freezes solid in the winter, it offers excellent fishing as the Colorado Division of Wildlife stocks it each summer with brook, cutthroat and brown trout.

The trail continues around the left of the lake, climbing toward the Continental Divide, Beaver Lake and the Wyoming Trail.

Strawberry Park

At Strawberry Park Hot Springs, four sculpted rock pools set in a narrow forested canyon are a great place for the hiker to relax and soothe sore muscles in a rustic setting.

Stunning views extend down the valley

Ponderosa Pine Forests

Ponderosa pines dot many of the slopes between 5,600 feet and 9,000 feet in Colorado's Rocky Mountains. They are particularly widespread in the foothills of the Front Range. Large strands are visible alongside Interstate 70 just to the west of Denver and on the low ridges on the east side of Rocky Mountain National Park.

The ponderosa is easy to identify by its olive-green, four- to seven-inch needles, which grow in bundles of two or three. It not only has the longest needles of any native conifer, but it is also the largest evergreen in the southern Rockies. Four-hundred-year-old individuals may measure more than 150 feet in height and have three-foot-wide trunks. Ponderosas are characterized by their straight, reddish trunk rising to a broad, open crown and rounded top.

Ponderosa forests occupy dry, sunny, south-facing slopes. At lower elevations they are often accompanied by Douglas fir, while higher up they mix with lodgepole pine, subalpine fir, Engelmann spruce and limber pine. The relatively large space between the trees in ponderosa forests allows for a profusion of understory grasses, shrubs and wildflowers, together with a diverse collection of animals and birds.

Flowers commonly seen decorating the ground beneath the pines include the pasque flower, golden aster, needle-and-thread, Sego lily, sulphur flower and Wyoming paintbrush.

One of the forest's most interesting residents is the Abert's squirrel. This dark, tassel-eared mammal is unusual in that it lives exclusively in the ponderosa habitat. Abert's squirrels feed on ponderosa pine cones in the summer, but depend on the inner bark of small twigs during the winter when these are not available.

Porcupines also enjoy the amenities offered by open ponderosa forests. These solitary, quilled rodents live on herbs in summer and the inner bark of the tree trunk at other times of the year.

Groups of mule deer congregate among the ponderosas during the winter to find respite from the harsh conditions prevalent at higher elevations.

Numerous birds inhabit ponderosa pine forests. Many, such as hairy woodpeckers, white-breasted and pygmy nuthatches, ravens and Steller's jays, can be observed at any time of the year. Mountain chickadees, pine siskins, dark-eyed juncos and American robins generally migrate to the plains in wintertime. Other birds often spotted during the summer are broad-tailed hummingbirds, yellow-rumped warblers, great horned owls, red-tailed hawks and goshawks.

Ponderosa forests are susceptible to periodic infestations by the bark-boring mountain pine beetle. An epidemic in the late 1970s is responsible for much of the standing, dead timber seen today on the east side of Rocky Mountain National Park.

The San Juans

A lovely backdrop for the beautiful flower-strewn meadows

The San Juan Mountains of southwestern Colorado comprise a staggering 10,000 square miles of formidable peaks, winding valleys, alpine lakes, abandoned mines and wilderness areas. The San Juans boast more land above 10,000 feet than any other mountain range in the contiguous United States. Thirteen of the state's majestic Fourteeners lie deep within the heart of this region.

Close to the San Juans are some of the prime tourist attractions in the country. At Mesa Verde National Park, a designated World Heritage Site, impressive cliff dwellings provide insight into the lives of the Ancient Puebloans who lived here from about 550 AD to 1300 AD.

The discovery of gold and silver in the 1800s saw the development of numerous mining camps throughout the San Juans. Silverton, Telluride and Ouray rapidly became the major centers of population. Today, many of the original Victorian buildings still line the streets of these Old West mining towns, offering clues to the original character of the communities.

Durango, with numerous motels, restaurants and other tourist amenities, is an excellent base from which to explore southwestern Colorado. Several private and national forest campgrounds line US Highway 550 to the north of town.

Many visitors enjoy a trip aboard the Durango & Silverton Narrow Gauge Railroad. This coal-fired train now offers a spectacular journey along the Animas River.

Hike 37 leads to Crater Lake, a magnificent high-alpine tarn. Excellent views right from the start and minimal elevation gain are hallmarks of this popular excursion. Hike 38 is undeniably a favorite of Colorado residents. One of the most remote backpacking destinations in the state, Chicago Basin is surrounded by majestic peaks, including three Fourteeners. Most hikers take the steam-powered train to the trailhead.

left: The magnificent peaks at the head of Chicago Basin

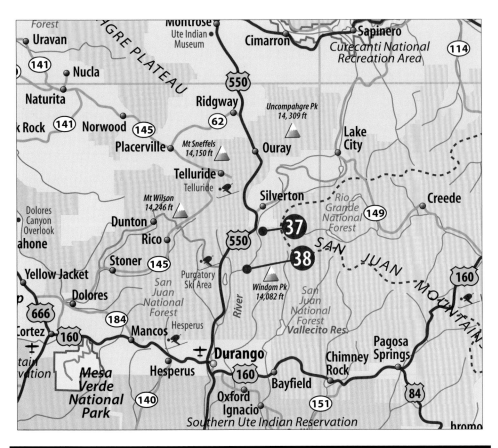

Other Hikes in the San Juan Area

Highland Mary Lakes
Day hike or overnight,
4.0 miles one way
Elevation gain: 1,720 feet
Rating: Moderate
USGS Topographic map:
Howardsville, Colo.

A favorite with both day hikers and backpackers, the three Highland Mary lakes recline in a picturesque basin above timberline in the heart of the Weminuche Wilderness. The trail begins just to the east of the old mining town of Silverton and follows the Cunningham Creek drainage as it winds south toward the formidable barrier of the Continental Divide. Abandoned mines speckling the hillsides attest to the frenzy of activity that took place here during the late 1800s.

Vallecito Creek–Pine River Loop
Multi-day hike, 38.5 miles one way
Elevation difference: 7,916 to 12,000 feet
Rating: Moderate
USGS Topographic maps: Vallecito Reservoir, Colo., Columbine Pass, Colo., Storm King Peak, Colo., Rio Grande Pyramid, Colo., Emerald Lake, Colo. and Granite Peak, Colo.

Colorado's largest wilderness area, the Weminuche Wilderness, encompasses more than 5,000,000 acres of dramatic peaks, tumbling waterfalls and hidden alpine tarns. Numerous trails wind throughout this vast region, connecting to provide backpackers with seemingly unlimited hiking options.

One of the most scenic and varied long-distance routes starts and ends near Vallecito Reservoir to the northeast of Durango. It travels north along the Vallecito Creek Trail, veers to the southeast via the Rock Creek and Flint Creek trails and returns by way of the Pine Creek Trail.

Crater Lake lies beneath the steep north face of North Twilight Peak

~ 37 ~ Crater Lake

E asy accessibility, expansive views of the San Juan Skyway and minimal elevation gain make this high-level hike a favorite of Colorado residents.

Crater Lake lies in a basin at the foot of 13,075-foot North Twilight Peak in the Weminuche Wilderness.

Trailhead to Crater Lake

From the Andrews Lake parking lot, the Crater Lake Trail #623 skirts around the west side of the lake, crosses the outlet stream and arrives at the trail register. After about 0.25 mile, it starts to switchback up a low ridge on the western flank of the West Needle Mountains. This 500-foot climb is the only serious ascent of the entire hike.

The scattered conifers on the hillside barely obscure the expanding panoramas. Near the top of the rise, rocky ledges provide perfect seats for spectators. Little Andrews Lake glistens like a jewel in the pistachio-green valley base. Behind the pool, US Highway 550 snakes its way north over Molas Pass to where it plunges down into Silverton. Predominant landmarks include the Twin Sisters, Jura Knob and Engineer Mountain.

The grade moderates as the trail heads toward the brow of the escarpment through the

Trailhead

Drive 45.0 miles north of Durango on US Highway 550 or 0.9 mile south of Molas Pass. Turn east following the sign for Andrews Lake and continue for 1.0 mile to the parking area. The trailhead is next to the restrooms at the south end of the lot.

Route

Day hike or overnight; 5.5 miles one way; moderate

Route	Elevation (ft.)	Distance (mi.)
Trailhead	10,744	0
Crater Lake	11,600	5.5

USGS Topographic map: Snowdon Peak, Colo.

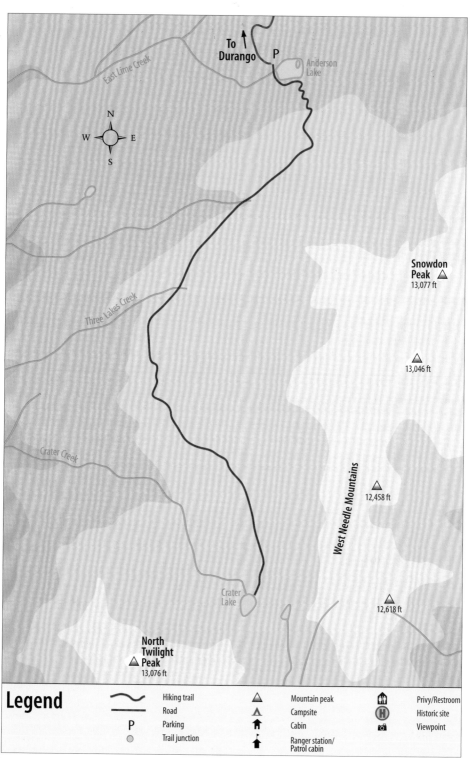

To
Durango

P

Anderson
Lake

East Lime Creek

N
W   E
S

Snowdon
Peak ◮
13,077 ft

◮
13,046 ft

Three Lakes Creek

West Needle Mountains

◮
12,458 ft

Crater Creek

◮
12,618 ft

Crater
Lake

North
Twilight ◮
Peak
13,076 ft

Legend

〜	Hiking trail	
—	Road	
P	Parking	
⬤	Trail junction	

◮	Mountain peak
◭	Campsite
⌂	Cabin
⬛	Ranger station/ Patrol cabin

⌂	Privy/Restroom
Ⓗ	Historic site
📷	Viewpoint

first of many flowery meadows. Goldenrod, Colorado blue columbine and several varieties of paintbrush decorate the grassy opening. As the footpath tops the ridge, views open eastward to the cliffs falling from Snowdon Peak.

The trail then begins its pattern of rolling up and down through a sequence of miniature drainages as it continues southward along the range of mountains. Dropping down behind the ridge, it passes a couple of ponds, traverses a little saddle and descends through a shallow valley chockablock with skunk cabbage. This gangly four- to eight-foot-tall plant, which also goes by the names California corn lily and false hellebore, is extremely poisonous to both humans and animals.

Still dipping, the trail ducks through a subalpine forest and then continues through a grassy ravine. It crosses a brook via stepping stones and, as it clambers steeply up the other side of the little valley, it passes the Weminuche Wilderness boundary marker. The path works its way along the side of

A Few Colorado Trees

Pinyon-Juniper Woodlands

Extensive groups of pinyon pine and juniper sprawl along mountain flanks and on low mesas throughout western and southern Colorado. Occurring at elevations from around 5,000 to 7,000 feet, these companion trees mark the transition zone between lower shrublands and higher forests of Douglas fir and ponderosa pine.

The Colorado pinyon has one- to two-inch-long needles growing in bundles of two. Its small cones produce the largest nuts of any pine, forming a favorite fall food for birds such as the pinyon jay. The Rocky Mountain juniper, like the pine, rarely exceeds 30 feet in height. Its branches are gray-turquoise in color and display tiny, waxy, berry-shaped cones. Its leaves differ from those of other evergreens in that they are composed of small scales, not needles.

Native Americans depended on the pinyon pine and juniper for a number of purposes. They relied on pinyon nuts for nourishment and enjoyed the juniper berries fresh or in cakes. They used the timber as firewood and for construction, and employed pinyon pitch as glue and as a waterproofing agent.

Cottonwood

Narrowleaf cottonwoods line the banks of major watercourses in mountain valleys. These willow-family members have a narrow, conical crown of upward-pointing branches and grow to be up to 50 feet tall. The trees produce two- to three-inch, reddish catkins in spring before the leaves develop. The lance-shaped leaves are shiny green on top and paler underneath. Like its cousin, the aspen, the cottonwood grows in "clones," or stands of genetically related individuals. Reproduction is generally from root suckering rather than pollination.

The name Alamosa derives from the Spanish word for "cottonwood grove." When this town was established in 1878, a large cottonwood standing alongside the Rio Grande acted as the local lynching post. Early travelers aboard the Denver and Rio Grande Railway were often welcomed by a corpse hanging from this makeshift gallows.

Douglas Fir

Douglas fir forests form dense, dark green strands on north-facing slopes between elevations of about 5,600 to 9,000 feet in the Colorado Rockies. In the Pacific Northwest, where moisture is abundant, Douglas fir grow to heights of more than 300 feet. In fact, this elegant conifer holds the world height record of 417 feet for a tree felled in British Columbia in 1895. In Colorado, however, it rarely exceeds 100 feet.

Douglas fir trees can be identified by their flat, short, round-tipped needles that protrude from the branch singly in all directions. The distinctive two- to three-inch-long cones display three-toothed bracts between the scales and hang down from the branches or scatter on the ground underneath the tree. The bark is reddish-brown and is often deeply furrowed.

Today, the Douglas fir is the most popular tree to use as a decoration in homes at Christmas. For many years, it was also an important source of lumber, being used mainly for the construction of settlements, mines and bridges.

The tree is named in honor of David Douglas (1798-1834), a Scottish botanical collector who sent back its seeds to Europe in 1827.

the mountains, overlooking the deep canyon through which the highway carves a circuitous route on its journey south toward Durango.

Leveling briefly, the trail again travels between tall subalpine firs and Engelmann spruce, and squelches through occasional muddy patches. It switchbacks downhill, hopping over a couple of side streams, and rises once more through the conifers.

As it surmounts a ridge, views again open over the deep gash in the earth to the gray ridges far to the southwest. North Twilight Peak, rounded and brown, stands like a sentinel to the south of the side valley of Crater Creek.

The path weaves over a broad, open shoulder of land, gradually veering left to penetrate this drainage.

The trail climbs gently through woods and a series of cheery meadows dotted with skunk cabbage, sunflowers, Colorado blue columbines, Parry's clover and bistort. Downed tree trunks litter the slopes beneath the living conifers and standing dead, but forest service rangers have cleared a pathway through the fallen wood.

Far below, through a thick mantle of conifers, Crater Creek pounds its way down toward its union with the Animas River.

The trail skirts to the right of a marsh full of elephant's head. It scampers over a low ridge and makes its final short descent to Crater Lake.

Hunkered in the shadow of the steep north face of North Twilight Peak, the tarn reposes in a boggy bowl just

Skunk cabbage is poisonous to humans and animals

below timberline. The surrounding conifers conceal good camp spots for those who choose to linger and take advantage of the fly- and spin-casting fishing opportunities.

The saddle just above the lake provides good views of the Needle Mountains to the southeast. Ambitious climbers may scramble up the col and along the ridge south to the top of North Twilight Peak, climbing an additional 1,475 feet in about 1.2 mile.

Yucca

The dense, sharp-tipped leaves and creamy blossoms of the yucca or "Spanish bayonet" are a familiar feature of the Southwest. The yucca is not a cactus but a member of the lily family. Its leaves are narrow to minimize water loss, a necessary adaptation in the semiarid high-desert environments of Colorado.

Native Americans had many purposes for the yucca. They soaked the leaves in water and used the fiber for making rope, sandals, baskets and mats. They obtained salicylic acid, the main ingredient in aspirin, from the leaves and also fashioned brooms from bundles of leaves tied together. They crushed the roots and rubbed them in water to procure suds for shampoo or soap. Native Americans also made a meal of the yucca; they roasted the fruit, eating it whole like a potato or grinding it into flour.

Kaleidoscopic wildflowers adorn this alpine meadow

~ 38 ~ Chicago Basin

Many outdoor enthusiasts think a trip into Chicago Basin is Colorado's quintessential backpacking experience. Sprawling in the heart of

the San Juan Mountains, this remote box canyon is surrounded by magnificent 13,000- and 14,000-foot summits. Wildflowers carpet the expansive meadows and a herd of

mountain goats calls this area home.

This hike starts at the mouth of the Needle Creek drainage, a point so far from a highway that most backpackers access the trailhead by steam train. Many "peak-baggers" use Chicago Basin as a base camp for ascending 14,083-foot Mount Eolus, 14,059-foot Sunlight Peak and 14,082-foot Windom Peak. There are lots of

Trailhead

Take the Durango & Silverton Narrow Gauge Railroad (D&SNG) north from Durango to the Needleton stopover, where this hike begins. Since not every train halts at Needleton to drop off passengers, when you make your advance reservation, it is important to explain that you are planning to hike into Chicago Basin. Be sure to find out what time to catch the train for your return journey to Durango.

An alternative exists for backpackers who wish to avoid the train trip. You can park by the Purgatory Campground on US Highway 550 and hike along the Purgatory Trail to its junction with the Needle Creek Trail.

Route

Two-day backpack or longer; 8.0 miles one way from train; strenuous

Route	Elevation (ft.)	Distance (mi.)
Needleton	8,000	0
Purgatory Trail Jct	8,280	1.0
New York Creek	9,240	2.0 (Approx.)
Lower Chicago Basin	10,800	7.0 (Approx.)
Upper Chicago Basin	11,200	8.0 (Approx.)

USGS Topographic maps: Snowdon Peak, Colo., Mountain View Crest, Colo.

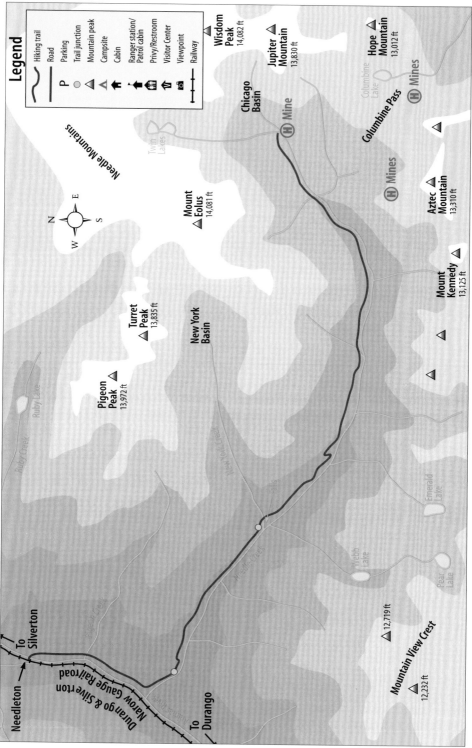

Legend

- Hiking trail
- Road
- P Parking
- Trail junction
- △ Mountain peak
- ▲ Campsite
- ⌂ Cabin
- Ⓗ Ranger station/Patrol cabin
- Privy/Restroom
- Visitor Center
- Viewpoint
- Railway

Needle Mountains

Wisdom Peak 14,082 ft

Jupiter Mountain 13,830 ft

Hope Mountain 13,012 ft

Chicago Basin

Ⓗ Mine

Columbine Pass

Columbine Lake

Ⓗ Mines

Ⓗ Mines

Aztec Mountain 13,310 ft

Mount Eolus 14,081 ft

Mount Kennedy 13,125 ft

Turret Peak 13,835 ft

Pigeon Peak 13,972 ft

New York Basin

Twin Lakes

Ruby Lake

Ruby Creek

Pigeon Creek

New York Creek

Emerald Lake

Webb Lake

Pear Lake

△ 12,719 ft

Mountain View Crest

12,232 ft

Needleton

To Silverton

Durango & Silverton Narow Gauge Railroad

To Durango

N E S W

New York Creek cascades over a spectacular waterfall

Needle Mountains

Sequestered deep within the San Juans, the gigantic Needle Mountains thrust skyward to create one of the most dramatic landscapes in Colorado. The range contains three of the most remote Fourteeners in the state. These, together with several 13,000-foot summits, impound Chicago Basin in a precipitous amphitheater of rock.

Franklin Rhoda, a member of the Hayden Survey, first saw the Needle Mountains from atop 14,309-foot Uncompahgre Peak in 1874. He wrote, "In the distance appeared a group of very scraggy mountains, about which the clouds were continuously circling, as if it was their home." Later, upon reaching the top of Mount Sneffels, he wrote:

We have never yet seen the group from any station (and we have viewed it from all sides) without feeling both deep respect and awe for their terrible ruggedness. The fact already stated, that the storm clouds seemed to hover about them before starting their meandering way, only served to add to our other feelings…

secluded spots to pitch tents among the thickets of conifers that line the valley. However, as 60 or more backpackers camp here each night, choice sites are sometimes hard to come by.

Trailhead to New York Creek

After leaving the train platform at the Needleton stopover, cross the large bridge spanning the Animas River. Turn right and follow the footpath that parallels the river's east bank, past several private cabins.

After a while, the trail veers to the left and starts to head up the Needle Creek drainage. At the 1.0-mile mark, The Purgatory Trail merges from the right, and you reach the trail register and Weminuche Wilderness boundary marker. Continue straight ahead.

The Needle Creek Trail climbs steadily up the north side of lively Needle Creek, following the route of a mining road dating from the late 1800s. A variety of types of deciduous trees and shrubs thrives in this lush valley. In August, wild raspberries ripen alongside the trail, tempting the hiker to sample their sweet fruit. In the fall, aspens and Rocky Mountain maples light up the canyon with brilliant shades of red and yellow. Wildflowers speckle the verge. Look for Fremont geraniums, clover, harebells, horsemint, cow parsnip and various sunflower composites.

The trail ascends steeply, sometimes hugging the bank of Needle Creek, at other times maintaining a position about 100 feet above the

following page: Peaks rise majestically from the flower-strewn meadow

Durango & Silverton Narrow Gauge Railroad

One of the highlights of a visit to southwestern Colorado is a ride aboard the Durango & Silverton Narrow Gauge Railroad (D&SNG). Pulled by a coal-fired, steam-powered locomotive, this train treats travelers to a breathtaking 45-mile journey through the rugged San Juan Mountains from Durango to the well-preserved mining town of Silverton.

Penetrating a remote region only accessible by railway or on foot, the D&SNG accompanies the Animas River through a deep-cut canyon. The spectacular, snow-streaked peaks of the Needle Mountains and Grenadier Range tower one mile above the valley floor.

Along the way, passengers enjoy a historical adventure as the train passes the ghostly sidings at Hermosa, Rockwood and Needleton, together with numerous other reminders of Colorado's mining era. It was in the early 1860s that prospector Charles Baker first discovered gold in the San Juans. Miners quickly flooded the area, establishing the remote boomtown of Silverton. While they found little gold, they dug up "silver by the ton."

The Denver & Rio Grande Railway Company expanded its narrow gauge system to the growing mining camp in 1882, in order to haul ores from the San Juans to Denver. Before the mines played out, more than $300 million worth of precious metals traveled along this branch line.

By the 1960s, tourists were flocking to Durango to take the scenic rail trip. On June 1, 1967,

the National Park Service designated the line as a National Historical Landmark and in March, 1968, the American Society of Civil Engineers labeled it a National Historic Civil Engineering Landmark.

In 1981, Florida orange grower, Charles E. Bradshaw, Jr., purchased the railway and christened it the Durango & Silverton Narrow Gauge Railroad. Determined to continue its historic steam operation, he bought 1920s locomotives and 1880s-era cars, which he carefully renovated and put into service. In March, 1997, First American Railways, Inc. of Hollywood, Florida bought the D&SNG. Throughout its long history, numerous rock slides, avalanches, floods and other mishaps have temporarily halted the train. Perhaps the greatest catastrophe was the fire of February 10, 1989, which devastated the 1882 Durango Roundhouse and badly damaged six vintage engines. Now, a rebuilt roundhouse contains the brand-new D&SNG Railroad Museum and the restored locomotives are in good working order.

Today, more than 200,000 people a year enjoy a leisurely, romantic ride in the orange and black coaches or open-air, roofed gondola cars aboard the D&SNG. The round-trip from Durango to Silverton takes all day with a two-hour lunch layover in Silverton. Snacks are available on the train. The D&SNG makes flag stops at Needleton and Elk Park for backpackers, fishermen and hikers to get on and off. The D&SNG runs daily from early May until late October, with four trains operating out of Durango during peak season. A Winter Train travels the stretch from Durango to Cascade Canyon Wye from late November to early May. To make your advance reservation, call (970) 247-2733.

water. The stream sings a lively song as it tumbles over a series of pretty miniature waterfalls. Tall conifers gradually take over from the aspens as the path leaves the montane for the subalpine zone. Now,

the tiny, plum-colored fruits of wild blueberries mature close to the ground beneath the forest canopy. Red thimbleberries, similar in appearance to raspberries, decorate the large-leafed shrubs by the

path. Although deer, birds and bears enjoy thimbleberries, humans usually find them tasteless.

A flat opening to your left is the only suitable campsite in the lower valley.

The trail drops briefly to the level of the stream, where a crystal cataract gleams diamond-like against the dark rock. Beneath the falls, the clear water swirls with liquid grace over the polished surface of the bedrock. Plenty of outcroppings and boulders provide benches for hikers to rest and enjoy this tranquil setting.

About 2.0 miles into the hike, the path spans New York Creek.

New York Creek to Chicago Basin

From a sturdy footbridge, you get a close-up view of New York Creek as it tumbles over a spectacular waterfall. A sheet of white water hurls itself down a sequence of cascades, dancing over ledges and pouring through channels it has carved in the rock. As the trail proceeds up the valley, panoramas extend westward over the forest stacked high on either side of the Needle Creek drainage to the ridge rising to the west of the Animas River. Ahead, a gray peak rears its head through the V-shaped gorge.

The trail tiptoes across a 20-foot-wide landslide zone, the first of several encountered on this hike. Massive boulders, the size of Volkswagen beetles, recline alongside the broad pathway as it tunnels through a shady forest of subalpine fir and Engelmann

Indian Paintbrush

The Indian paintbrush is one of the most common wildflowers in the Colorado Rockies. Because there are so many different species, each with its own subtle coloring, individual identification can prove extremely difficult. The wide variety of colors results from variations in habitat and from hybridization with other paintbrushes. Botanists believe that the majority of paintbrushes are parasites. They steal much of their nutrition from other plants by connecting their roots to other plants' root systems.

The bright-hued part of the plant is not its real flower. This is, in fact, a bract which completely conceals the tiny, inconspicuous blossom. The scarlet paintbrush is perhaps the most widespread Indian paintbrush in Colorado. This tall, reddish-orange species thrives in damp

woods and openings in forests in the montane and subalpine environment. The sulfur paintbrush, displaying a greenish-yellow inflorescence, grows in tufts six to 18 inches high. It thrives in wet meadows or open forests from the valleys to the subalpine zones. The Western yellow paintbrush is often confused with the sulfur variety. The Western yellow rarely grows more than four inches tall and is found only at high elevations on the alpine tundra. The rosy paintbrush, often seen in the subalpine and tundra zones gains its hue from hybridization with yellow paintbrushes.

The Indian paintbrush belongs to the figwort family. Other members of this lineage frequently seen in Colorado include butter and eggs, elephant's head and dark penstemon.

spruce. Splotches of green moss decorate these huge chunks of fallen rock.

From time to time, the trail runs along a wide bench high above the base of the valley. An overlook provides good views of the boulder-choked stream and of the rugged cliffs towering over the entrance to Chicago Basin.

At this point, the route divides. Logs across the right fork indicate that this section of trail has been destroyed by avalanche. Take the left fork.

The footpath winds away from the stream and zigzags upward. It swings left to round the channel gouged by the landslide, crossing a side stream by way of stepping stones. Below, you can see where the original footpath was swept away.

The trail drops briefly through the conifers and, as it again starts to climb, it rejoins the original path. Rambunctious Needle Creek announces its presence far off to the right. Austere stumps and broken tree trunks dot wide corridors of naked earth where avalanches have ripped down the hillside. These huge deforested areas are

evidence of the tremendous forces of nature constantly working to change the face of the landscape. Even in these scenes of devastation, signs of nature's rebirth are everywhere. Baby aspens push their heads up between the debris of rocks and logs. Ragwort, fireweed, Fremont geraniums and other primary colonizers decorate the barren ground.

After a final steep climb through the evergreens, the trail moderates upon entering Chicago Basin. The forest breaks into disjointed thickets and open meadows become the order of the day. Secluded tent sites hide among the conifers. forest service rangers do an excellent job of removing fire rings and other evidence of past human occupation. These are remarkably clean and trash-free considering the fact that so many people camp here. Remember, fires are not

permitted anywhere in the Needle Creek drainage.

The trail wanders through meadows that become progressively more expansive. Scenic vistas reveal the splendid summits of the Needle Mountains.

Three of Colorado's esteemed Fourteeners loom to the north. Mount Eolus, rising to 14,083 feet above sea level, is the massive mountain directly to your left. On the knife-edge ridge blockading the valley ahead, 14,059-foot Sunlight Peak and 14,082-foot Windom Peak reign over Chicago Basin like a pair of monarchs. Mount Kennedy, at 13,125 feet, and Aztec Mountain, at 13,310 feet, dominate the gray ridge to the south of the valley.

The profusion of wildflowers in the meadows is reason enough to visit this region. In fact, so many kinds

Needle Creek cascades down from the upper valley containing Twin Lakes at the head of Chicago Basin

containing the Twin Lakes. The area around these tarns makes a good base camp for climbs to the three summits.

A people-habituated herd of mountain goats inhabits this wild upper cirque. Because they crave the salt found in human urine, they will often dig up the spots where people have relieved themselves. The forest service asks hikers to urinate only on rocky surfaces to prevent the goats from destroying fragile plant communities.

From the head of Chicago Basin, many backpackers continue up the southern flank of the canyon to 12,800-foot Columbine Pass, gaining 1,600 feet in about 1.5 miles. This vantage point provides seemingly unlimited views of the ranges of the San Juan Mountains.

Several trails radiate south and east from the pass. One extended hiking possibility is to descend past Columbine Lake, along the Johnson Creek Trail and to exit the wilderness by means of Vallecito Creek Trail.

bloom in this high-alpine paradise that hikers often choose to bring a flower-identification book. The long list of species common here includes skunk cabbage, queens crown, sandwort, mountain bog gentian, goldenrod, monkshood, larkspur, dark penstemon and the Colorado blue columbine.

Needle Creek tumbles down the north flank of Chicago Basin, reaching the valley floor by means of a pretty waterfall. Rocks near the foot of this cascade make good picnic spots. Peak baggers, intent on conquering the three Fourteeners, forge a rugged route alongside Needle Creek to an upper basin

left: Ground squirrels

The Sangre de Cristos

Blanca Peak towers above the San Luis Valley

The Sangre de Cristos form the southernmost range in the long chain of the Rocky Mountains. Averaging no more than 10 to 20 miles wide, they extend for 220 miles from Salida, Colorado, to Santa Fe, New Mexico. The 115 miles of the Sangre de

Cristos lying within Colorado are flanked on the west by the San Luis Valley and the east by the Wet Mountain Valley and Huerfano Park.

The Sangre de Cristos jut 7,000 feet above the San Luis Valley, rising abruptly in a series of sharp ridges cut by deep, tapering gorges. These mountains create an almost impenetrable barrier to the east of this high basin. The range contains nine of the state's most difficult Fourteeners.

Unlike most of Colorado's mountain ranges, which were explored by Anglo miners during the 1800s, the history of the Sangre de Cristos revolves around the expansion of Spanish culture into the Southwest. It is believed that Francisco Coronado traveled through the San Luis Valley in 1540, although it was not until 1694 that Don Diego de Vargas made the first recorded European visit. In 1851, the Spanish founded San Luis, the first permanent settlement in Colorado.

The words "Sangre de Cristo" translate into "Blood of Christ." Legend has it that an unknown Spanish missionary christened the range after watching a sunset's rosy-hued reflection on the peaks.

The Great Sand Dunes, the country's tallest dunes, rise 700 feet at the foot of the Sangre de Cristos. Hike 39 leads to the top of the highest of these massive mounds of sand.

Hike 40 begins near Crestone and climbs steeply through a ravine that lies to the north of 14,165-foot Kit Carson Peak, and leads to picturesque Willow Lake. This tarn features a pretty cascade, which tumbles over a sheer cliff directly into its crystal clear water.

left: The dunes are wonderful for hiking all year round

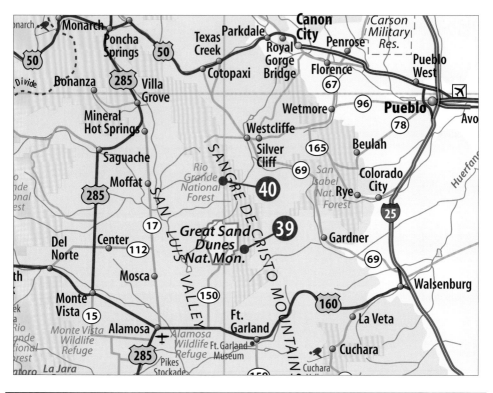

Other Hikes in the Sangre de Cristos

North Crestone Lake

Day-hike or overnight: 6.0 miles one way
Elevation gain: 3,040 feet
Rating: Moderate
USGS Topographic map: Rito Alto Peak, Colo. and Horn Peak, Colo.

North Crestone Lake lies within a high alpine basin beneath the magnificent summits of the Sangre de Cristo Range. The North Crestone Trail starts from Crestone, a tiny community to the east of the San Luis Valley. During its journey up the North Crestone Creek and the Lake Fork drainages, the footpath encounters aspen groves, spruce and fir forests, spectacular waterfalls and views of the valley. Mount Adams, topping out at 13,931 feet, and Fluted Peak, at

13,554 feet, stand sentinel over this large tarn.

South Crestone Lake

Day hike or overnight, 3.0 miles one way
Elevation gain: 2,640 feet
Rating: Moderate to Difficult
USGS Topographic map: Crestone, Colo., Rito Alto Peak, Colo. and Horn Peak, Colo.

Starting from the Willow Lake Trailhead just to the east of Crestone, the South Crestone Lake Trail climbs steeply up a drainage on the western flank of the rugged Sangre de Cristo Range. It passes through aspens, conifers and open meadows before reaching little South Crestone Lake, located at the foot of 13,931-foot Mount Adams.

Mosca Pass Trail

Day hike, 3.5 miles one way
Elevation gain: 1,463 feet
Rating: Moderate
USGS Topographic map: Mosca Pass, Colo.

The Mosca Pass Trail originates from within the Great Sand Dunes National Monument and is a popular day hike from late spring until early winter. It ascends the Mosca Creek drainage to Mosca Pass, following the route of an early toll road across the Sangre de Cristos. Passing through flowery meadows and forests of pine-juniper, spruce-fir and aspen, it provides excellent views of the Great Sand Dunes and the San Luis Valley.

The sand dunes rise 700 feet above the San Luis Valley

~ 39 ~ The Great Sand Dunes

Huddled at the base of the Sangre de Cristo Mountains, the Great Sand Dunes rise 700 feet above the San Luis Valley. These, North America's

tallest dunes, form a natural playground for adults and children. They present excellent year-round opportunities for hiking, sledding, snowshoeing and skiing on the sand. In the summer, splashing in the cool waters of shallow Medano Creek can provide welcome relief after a vigorous climb in the unrelenting sun. It

is inadvisable to walk barefoot, as the sand can become unbearably hot.

There are no trails on the dunes and you may explore wherever you want. As hiking in the soft sand can be deceptively difficult, climbing to the summit of the tallest dune may seriously test your powers of endurance.

Trailhead

Head 14 miles east of Alamosa on US Highway 160. Turn left onto Colorado Highway 150 and drive 19 miles north to the visitor center at the Great Sand Dunes National Monument. Hikes to the dunes start from the Dunes parking lot. To get to the Dunes Parking and Picnic Area, about 0.5 mile from the visitor center, go north for a few hundred yards and then turn left (west), following the sign. Ample parking is provided in the spacious lot.

Route

Day hike; 1.0 mile or more one way; moderate

Route	Elevation (ft.)	Distance (mi.)
Dunes Picnic Area	8,000	0
Foot of Dunes	7,990	0.3
Top of High Dune	8,690	1.0 (Approx.)

USGS Topographic maps: Zapata Ranch, Colo., Liberty, Colo.

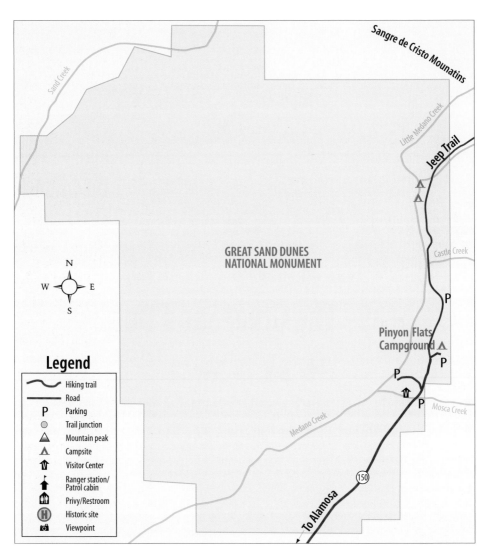

Legend

∼	Hiking trail
—	Road
P	Parking
○	Trail junction
△	Mountain peak
⌂	Campsite
⬆	Visitor Center
♦	Ranger station/Patrol cabin
⌂	Privy/Restroom
Ⓗ	Historic site
◻	Viewpoint

Dunes Picnic Area to the Top of High Dune

From the Dunes Parking Area, walk west through a line of cottonwoods and cross the broad expanse at the foot of the dunes. If Medano Creek is flowing through this flat drainage at the time of your visit, fording this stream will require getting wet feet.

Ahead, you will see a num-ber of ridges tapering to-ward the summit crest of the dunes. The most elevated point, known as High Dune, juts at the left end of the main escarpment. An ascent to this pointed peak involves a 700-foot elevation gain from the level of the creek. The Star Dune, a slightly lower protru-sion, is actually the tallest dune in the Western Hemisphere, rising 750 feet from base to top. However, it is less accessi-ble than High Dune and few people trek to its summit.

You can choose to follow the prows of any of the ridges to the top of the dunes, al-though finding the perfect pathway can be quite a chal-lenge. Unforeseen breaks in the continuity of the crests of-ten necessitate brief descents followed by steep upward scrambles. However, the view and sense of accomplishment gained from reaching the top

Great Sand Dunes National Monument

The gigantic piles of wind-sculpted sand forming North America's tallest dunes have fascinated people for thousands of years. The Folsom Indians camped and hunted near the Great Sand Dunes more than 10,000 years ago. It is likely that they hiked on the sand for pleasure, just as numerous Coloradans and out-of-state visitors do today.

As time passed, Utes, Spanish conquistadores, explorers, mountain men, prospectors, pioneers, ranchers and stagecoach travelers all marveled at this unusual and breathtaking landscape. President Herbert Hoover recognized the unique environment found at the dunes and designated the area as a national monument in 1932.

The Great Sand Dunes nestle in a pocket between the towering peaks of the Sangre de Cristo Range and the vast expanse of the San Luis Valley. They were formed by Rio Grande-eroded sand, which was blown northeastward across the flat basin and trapped by the mountain barrier. Nowadays, the sand dunes rise up to 750 feet and cover about 39 square miles.

Despite the harsh conditions prevailing on the dunes, a few tough life forms manage to survive. These include the kangaroo rat, three kinds of insects found nowhere else on earth, blowout grass, Indian rice grass and, in moist years, the occasional prairie sunflower.

Medano Creek defines the eastern edge of the dune field. During fall and winter, its dry, sandy creek bed usually absorbs the water before it reaches the monument. At the height of spring snow melt in the Sangre de Cristos, its strange surging action is a major feature of the park. Every 30 seconds or so, rip-ples gush down the creek, created by sand ridges built up on the bottom.

Attracting more than 300,000 visitors a year, the sand dunes are one of Colorado's favorite playgrounds. Hiking, sledding, cross-country skiing, snowshoeing and picnicking, together with enjoying the spectacular views of the Sangre de Cristos and San Luis Valley, are all popular activities.

The Pinyon Flats Campground, dunes and picnic area are open daily, year round. The visitor center is closed only for winter federal holidays. Park Service rangers offer a variety of talks, nature walks and slide programs during the summer. The Medano Pass four-wheel-drive road, leading north toward Medano Pass in the Rio Grande National Forest, is open from May through September.

Other Hikes at the Dunes

The Great San Dunes National Monument boasts many popular trails.

Visitor Center Nature Trail
This wheelchair-accessible trail leads past labeled natural history exhibits.

Montville Nature Trail
This self-guided trail penetrates the lower section of Mosca Canyon.

Little Medano Creek Trail
This 5.5-mile, one-way trail enables hikers to experience a variety of terrain.

Mosca Pass Trail
Gaining 1,463 feet in 3.5 miles, this trail leads to Mosca Pass, an early crossing of the Sangre de Cristos.

Castle Creek
The Castle Creek Trail follows the base of the dunes for 2.5 miles.

Wellington Ditch Trail
This more-or-less level trail runs alongside a ditch that was dug by a local 1920s homesteader named Wellington.

Backpacking
Ten backcountry campsites provide pleasant places to rest for hikers who are destined for trails between 0.5 to 10 miles in length. Backpackers need to obtain a free permit from the visitor center.

Zebulon Pike at the Dunes

During his expedition to take possession of the Southwest for the United States government, Captain Zebulon Pike first saw the Great Sand Dunes on January 27, 1807. The account in his journal describes what he saw as he descended from Mosca Pass, an old crossing of the Sangre de Cristos (known to him as the White Mountains).

"…after marching some miles, we discovered…sandy hills. The sand hills extended up and down at the foot of the White Mountains, about 15 miles and appeared to be about five miles in width.

"Their appearance was exactly that of the sea in a storm (except for color) not the least sign of vegetation existing thereon."

Wildlife at the Dunes

One of the attractions of the Great Sand Dunes National Monument is its rich variety of animals and birds. The following areas are particularly good for wildlife spotting.

As you drive along Colorado Highway 150, look for Swainson's, red-tailed and Cooper's hawks perching on telephone poles and fence posts. A bright blue flash in the grassy flats signals the presence of a mountain bluebird. Evening is the best time to see mule deer alongside the road. Drive carefully as a coyote, jackrabbit or kangaroo rat may cross in the path of your car.

Visitors staying in the Pinyon Flats Campground are likely to encounter many of the local inhabitants. Both chipmunks (stripe on the face and back) and ground squirrels (larger, no stripe on the face) dart from fire pits to picnic tables, scrounging for left-over scraps of food. Brazen mule deer amble between the campsites, confident in the park's no-hunting policy. As you sit outside your motor home or tent, listen for the trilling whistle of a broad-tailed hummingbird as it hovers above a nearby flower. Black bears exist in this area, but are rarely seen. However, campers should always store food in a bear-proof place like the trunk of a car.

The region around the Dunes Parking Lot is home to several species of birds. You can easily recognize the black-billed magpie by its raucous cries and iridescent green tuxedo. Listen for the hoarse, robin-like voice of the male Western tanager, singing to claim his territory in the picnic area.

As you view the monument's creatures in their natural habitat, do not feed or disturb them in any way. Animals that learn to rely on humans for food lose the ability to forage for themselves and may die when handouts are not available. Remember that wildlife is meant to stay wild.

Willow Lake lies at timberline

~ 40 ~ Willow Lake

T he monumental 14,000-foot summits of the Sangre de Cristos display a wild grandeur rarely seen in the Colorado Rockies. These mountains

tower 7,000 feet above the San Luis Valley, one of the largest valley basins in the world.

Exquisite Willow Lake lies snug beneath the lofty crags of 14,165-foot Kit Carson Peak. A spectacular waterfall tumbles over a cliff directly into this tarn. Many climbers use the

Willow Lake Trail to access Kit Carson Peak. However, the superb views of the San Luis Valley, the myriad wildflowers alongside the path and the dramatic setting of the lake are good reasons to take this popular hike.

Trailhead

Take Colorado Highway 17 north from Alamosa to Moffat and turn east toward Crestone. Follow this road for 12.5 miles and go right (east) at the four-way stop sign in the center of the small town. Take this forest road for 2.3 miles to the trailhead. Ignore a turnoff to the right just after you leave the blacktop and three unmarked jeep tracks heading off to the left. The trailhead lies a few hundred yards upstream to the east of the parking lot.

Route

Day hike or overnight; 3.9 miles one way; moderate

Route	Elevation (ft.)	Distance (mi.)
Trailhead	9,200	0
Crest of Ridge	9,880	1.5 (Approx.)
Lower Willow Creek Lake	11,564	3.9

USGS Topographic maps: Crestone, Colo. and Crestone Peak, Colo.

Trailhead to Willow Creek Park

The Willow Lake Trail #865 starts at the mouth of the wooded canyon of South Crestone Creek. From the trailhead marker, it heads to the right and crosses the stream by way of slippery logs. After bridging a second brook, the footpath leaves the forest and makes a sharp left turn as it enters a meadow. Ignore the trail that continues straight on at this bend.

The sandy path hurries uphill, passing a trail register for the Sangre de Cristo Wilderness Central Region.

A few junipers and aspens dot the grassy expanse, together with fairy trumpets, dark penstemon, silvery lupines and thistles. The first views of the hike extend westward across the broad San Luis Valley.

The trail enters a montane forest of Douglas fir and juniper and, shortly, begins to switchback up the north-facing flank of a miniature drainage.

Finally, the trail reaches the crest of a ridge separating the Willow Creek and South Crestone Creek gorges.

The vegetation changes abruptly. Leaving the forest behind, the trail traverses along the northern side of the Willow Creek Valley, crossing an open slope dotted with yucca, juniper, mountain mahogany and aspen.

Below to your right stretches Willow Creek Park, a brilliant-emerald expanse of grass. Willow Creek wanders to the left of this meadow. Rocks scattered on the sunny hillside make good vantage

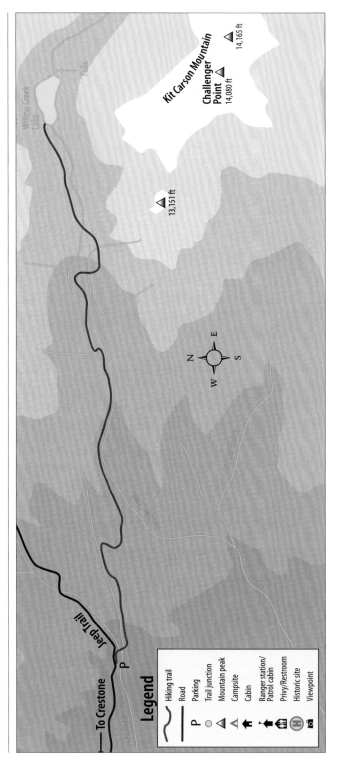

Kit Carson Mountain 14,165 ft

Challenger Point 14,080 ft

13,151 ft

Willow Creek Lake

Falls

Jeep Trail

To Crestone

Legend

Hiking trail
Road
Parking
Trail junction
Mountain peak
Campsite
Cabin
Ranger station/ Patrol cabin
Privy/Restroom
Historic site
Viewpoint

Views grow ever more extensive over the San Luis Valley

points to rest and enjoy the wonderful panorama of the Willow Creek drainage ahead. Above the conifer-clad lower slopes of this gash in the landscape, a water-streaked headwall blockades the ravine with a massive rockfall tumbling to its right. Kit Carson Peak thrusts skyward to the south of the gorge. This mighty mountain rises amid an intricacy of buttresses and knife-edged ridges. Willow Lake lies well hidden at the foot of the farthest cliffs that you can see from here.

The trail descends briefly and then splits, with a faint track veering right toward the stream. Stay left for Willow Lake.

Willow Creek Park to Willow Lake

The footpath ascends at an eager grade up the left flank of the steep drainage through a thick coniferous forest. Quickly gaining altitude, it leaves Willow Creek to sing its lively tune far below.

Openings in the trees re-veal views to the west. Tiny Willow Creek Park huddles at the foot of the gorge, fringed with aspens. Behind that extends the San Luis Valley—a vast plain 50 miles wide, stretching to the distant La Garita Mountains. Here and there, a road shoots straight as an arrow across this flat expanse of gray-green land, and an isolated farm building sparkles in the sunshine.

The trail switchbacks upward, passing through a talus slope. It dodges huge slabs of bedrock, dotted with colorful patches of lichen and moss. Wild roses and Fremont geraniums bloom among the litter of rocks.

The serrated northwestern ridge of Kit Carson Peak, rising to the south of the drainage, gradually appears more stark and barren. Challenger Point juts above this escarpment. Although topping out at a lofty 14,081 feet above sea level, this subpeak does not rate as a separate Fourteener. The elevation loss between its summit and that of Kit Carson is insufficient.

The trail traverses an area devastated by a landslide. The scatter of logs and rocks testifies to the tremendous power of the avalanche.

Continuing to snake its way up the northern side of the canyon, the pathway ducks back into a forest of subalpine fir and Engelmann spruce. An elbow in the route yields an excellent view of the cataract tumbling down the massive headwall that looms in front of you, with Kit Carson towering high above. The sound of the falls teases, growing louder with every curve.

The trail approaches a second avalanche zone. Uprooted and cracked trees lie higgledy-piggledy over the slope, often bare and denuded of branches. Huge crags tower to the north as the pathway picks its way through this jumble of debris.

Cross the stream cascading to the left of the mud slide area by jumping between the outcroppings of bedrock on either side.

Leaving a band of conifers, you reach Willow Creek. The

The San Luis Valley

The San Luis Valley, 125 miles long and 50 miles wide, is one of the largest alpine valley basins in the world. It lies at an elevation of 7,000 feet between the Sangre de Cristo Mountains to the east and the San Juan, La Garita and Conejos-Brazos mountains to the north and west. The Rio Grande meanders through this flat, brush-covered land, just beginning its long journey to the Gulf of Mexico.

For hundreds of years the valley belonged to the Utes, who hunted and followed herds across the flat plain. The Spanish and Mexicans were next to claim the region. In fact, they may have entered the valley as long ago as the mid-1500s. In 1851, Hispanics established the first permanent settlement of San Luis at its southern tip. The U.S. government built Fort Garland in 1858 to protect the settlers from raids by Utes and other tribes. By 1878, the Denver and Rio Grande Railroad had reached Alamosa, which rapidly became the area's main town and transportation hub. Irrigation canals, dug in the 1880s, turned much of the arid valley into fertile farmland. Today, the green, irrigated fields produce some of the best potatoes in the country.

Sightseeing and outdoor opportunities abound in the San Luis Valley. Its small towns have histories as rich as the mineral deposits, which attracted thousands of miners to the nearby mountains just over a century ago.

Alamosa, lying near the center of the valley 212 miles southwest of Denver, is blessed with

numerous motels as well as a KOA Campground. Roads radiate in all directions, providing an excellent base from which to explore. The best way to reach Alamosa is to drive south on Interstate-25 to Walsenburg, then west on US 160 over La Veta Pass. (800) 258-7597.

Fort Garland features the restored army post of the legendary frontiersman, Kit Carson, who was a regiment commander here in 1866. Exhibits illustrate military life of the period and the Hispanic culture of the

San Luis Valley. (719) 379-3512.

While **San Luis** bills itself as the oldest town in Colorado, it is home to one of America's newest Catholic shrines. Fifteen almost-life-sized bronze sculptures, arranged on a nearby mesa, vividly depict the final hours of Jesus Christ. (719) 672-3321.

The tiny **Jack Dempsey Museum** at Manassa showcases mementos and pictures of hometown hero Jack Dempsey, who became the best American heavyweight boxer of the first half of the 20th century. (719) 843-5207.

The 1880s-vintage **Cumbres and Toltec Scenic Railroad** offers 64-mile trips from Antonito to Chama, New Mexico, through the majestic San Juan Mountains. (719) 376-5483.

At **The Colorado Alligator Museum**, visitors can discover the ins and outs of breeding Rocky Mountain White Tilapia hybrid fish and view alligators reclining in open-air, geothermal-heated pools. (719) 378-2612.

The Carneo Creek Pictographs, consisting of red, painted forms of people, animals and geometric designs, decorate the south face of a rugged, pencil-thin canyon penetrating the foothills to the west of the San Luis Valley on the property of L-Cross Ranch. (800) 258-7597.

La Ventana Natural Arch, a spectacular window eroded in a large volcanic dyke, lies in the foothills six miles west of La Garita. (800) 258-7597.

The Old Spanish Trail was an early-19th-century trade route linking Santa Fe with Los

Angeles. An excellent section of ruts, in some places worn 10 inches into the bedrock, is visible close to La Garita. (800) 258-7597.

The sheer 100-foot cliffs enclosing **Penitente Canyon**, near La Garita, offer world-class rock climbing opportunities. An image of the Virgin Mary, believed to have been painted by the Penitentes, adorns a wall 40 feet above the valley base. (800) 258-7597.

Claiming the largest collection of Native American artifacts in the country, the **Saguache County Museum** occupies the old town jail and adjacent seven-room schoolhouse in Saguache, the valley's northern outpost. A jail cell contains a replica of Alferd Packer, who was charged with murdering and eating five of his prospecting companions in 1874. (719) 655-2870.

Monte Vista is best known for its March Crane Festival. This celebrates the arrival of thousands of sandhill cranes, who, together with a few of their endangered whooping-crane cousins, make a stopover in the Monte Vista Wildlife Refuge during their spring migration north from New Mexico to Idaho. (719) 852-3552.

The Carnero Creek pictographs adorn the wall of a canyon west of the San Luis Valley

best way to cross this rambunctious stream is by way of the large log jammed over the water. Cairns direct the hiker through a thicket of willows and a bog covered with tall chimingbells.

Emerging in front of the headwall, the pathway winds to the right of this massive obstacle blocking the valley. Ahead, a wide sheet of water thrashes down the cliff, bounding over a series of mini-cataracts.

The trail zigzags up the rockfall to the right of the moraine. As it approaches the crest of the rise, wildflowers speckle the increasing patches of grassy tundra. Look for rock primrose, moss campion, alpine avens and sky pilot among the regal Colorado blue columbines. The monstrous crowns of Rocky Mountain thistles nod by the pathway.

The grade moderates as the trail surmounts the headwall and enters the hanging valley. It descends momen-

tarily, fords Willow Creek, then winds through a coniferous forest.

From now until it reaches Willow Lake, it traverses alternately a sequence of level ledges and steep moraines. As the trail crests the final ridge, Willow Lake suddenly appears. Its crystal clear waters reflect the picturesque cascade, which tumbles down a cliff directly into the tarn.

Because the lake lies at timberline, trees decorate its western shoreline. Outcroppings protruding into the water provide good picnic spots for hikers to enjoy this picturesque scene.

The trail winds through the conifers to the left of the lake and climbs over the rock wall at its western end. It continues through the meadows to a second lake. Many "peak-baggers" make this their base camp before ascending Kit Carson Peak.

Reference

Recommended Reading

General Reference

Kennedy, Doris. *Colorado For the 50+ Traveler, An Altitude SuperGuide*. Aurora, Colorado: Altitude Publishing Ltd., 1998.

Kennedy, Doris. *Fun With the Family in Colorado*. Old Saybrook, Connecticut: The Globe Pequot Press, 1999.

Soran, Patrick and Dan Klinglesmith. *Colorado, An Altitude SuperGuide*. Aurora, Colorado: Altitude Publishing Ltd.,1998.

Klinglesmith, Dan and Patrick Soran. *Colorado; A History in Photographs*. Aurora, Colorado: Altitude Publishing Ltd., 1998.

Soran, Patrick and Dan Klinglesmith. *Rocky Mountain National Park, An Altitude SuperGuide*. Aurora, Colorado: Altitude Publishing Ltd., 1998.

Spitsnaugle, Sherry. *Quick Escapes—Denver*. Old Saybrook, Connecticut: The Globe Pequot Press, 1998.

Metzger, Stephen. *Colorado Handbook*. Chico, California: Moon Publications Inc., 1996.

Caughey, Bruce and Dean Winstanley. *The Colorado Guide*. Golden, Colorado: Fulcrum Publishing, Inc., 1997.

Fielder, John and Mark Pearson. *The Complete Guide to Colorado's Wilderness Areas*. Englewood, Colorado: Westcliffe Publishers, Inc., 1998.

Jones, Tom Lorang. *Colorado's Continental Divide Trail—The Official Guide*. Englewood, Colorado: Westcliffe Publishers, Inc., 1997.

Jacobs, Randy. *The Colorado Trail—The Official Guide*. Englewood, Colorado: Westcliffe Publishers, Inc., 1996.

Borneman, Walter R. and Lyndon J. Lampert. *A Climbing Guide to Colorado's Fourteeners*. Boulder, Colorado: Pruett Publishing Company, 1998.

Accommodations

The Complete Colorado Campground Guide. Hudson, Colorado: Outdoor Books and Maps, Inc., 1998.

Kennedy, Doris. *Recommended Country Inns—Rocky Mountain Region*. Old Saybrook, Connecticut: The Globe Pequot Press, 1999.

Crow, Melinda. *Camping Colorado*. Helena, Montana: Falcon Publishing Company, Inc., 1998.

Schlueter, Robyn. *Colorado Camping*. Petaluma, California: Foghorn Press, 1998.

Little, Mickey. *Camper's Guide to Colorado*. Houston, Texas: Gulf Publishing Company, 1990.

Plants

Dannon, Kent and Donna. *Rocky Mountain Wildflowers*. Allenspark, Colorado: Tundra Publications, 1997.

Strickler, Dee. *Forest Wildflowers*. Columbia Falls, Montana: The Flower Press, 1996.

Guennel, G. K. *Guide to Colorado Wildflowers; Mountains*. Englewood, Colorado: Westcliffe Publishers, Inc., 1995.

Guennel, G. K. *Guide to Colorado Wildflowers; Plains and Foothills*. Englewood, Colorado: Westcliffe Publishers, Inc., 1995.

Jones, Foltz Charlotte and D. D. Dowden. *Colorado Wildflowers*. Helena, Montana: Falcon Press Publishing Company, Inc., 1994.

Evenson, Vera Stucky. *Mushrooms of Colorado and the Southern Rocky Mountains*. Englewood, Colorado: Westcliffe Publishers, Inc. 1997.

Little, Elbert L. *National Audubon Society Field Guide to North American Trees, Western Region*. New York, New York: Alfred A. Knopf, 1996.

Emerick, John C. *Rocky Mountain National Park Natural History Handbook*. Niwot, Colorado: Roberts Rinehart Publishers, 1995.

Wildlife

National Geographic Field Guide to Birds of North America. Washington, D.C.: The National Geographic Society, 1996.

Udvardy, Miklos D. F. *The Audubon Society Field Guide to North American Birds, Western Region.* New York, New York: Alfred A. Knopf, 1997.

Gray, Mary Taylor. *The Guide to Colorado Birds.* Englewood, Colorado: Westcliffe Publishers, Inc. 1998.

Gray, Mary Taylor. *Colorado Wildlife Viewing Guide.* Helena, Montana: Falcon Press Publishing Company, Inc., 1992.

Torres, Steven. *Mountain Lion Alert.* Helena, Montana: Falcon Publishing Company, Inc., 1997.

Camp Cooking

McHugh, Gretchen. *The Hungry Hiker's Book of Good Cooking.* New York, New York: Alfred A. Knopf, 1998.

First Aid

Carline, Jan D., Martha J. Lentz and Steven C. Macdonald. *Mountaineering First Aid.* Seattle, Washington: The Mountaineers, 1996.

Tilton, Buck. *Medicine for the Backcountry.* Merrillville, Indiana: ICS Books, Inc., 1994.

Isaac, Jeffrey. *The Outward Bound Wilderness First-Aid Handbook.* New York, New York: The Lyons Press, 1998.

Geology

Chronic, Halka. *Roadside Geology of Colorado.* Missoula, Montana: Mountain Press Publishing Company, 1998.

Hiking and Backpacking

Harmon, Will. *Leave No Trace.* Helena, Montana: Falcon Publishing Company, Inc., 1997.

Meyer, Kathleen. *How to Shit in the Woods.* Berkeley, California: Ten Speed Press, 1994.

Angier, Bradford. *How to Stay Alive in the Woods.* New York, New York: Fireside, 1998.

Helpful Phone Numbers

Road Conditions in Colorado: (303) 639-1111 or (303) 639-1234
Statewide Weather Reports: (303) 398-3964
Colorado Division of Wildlife: (303) 297-1192
Colorado Historical Society: (303) 866-3682
Colorado Travel and Tourism Authority: (800) COLORADO or (800) 265-67236
Rocky Mountain Nature Association: (800) 816-7662
Denver Metro Convention and Visitors Bureau: (303) 892-1112 or (800) 645-3446
Distinctive Inns of Colorado: (800) 866-0621
Bed and Breakfast Innkeepers of Colorado: (800) 265-7696
Continental Divide Trail Alliance: P.O. Box 628, Pine, Colorado 80470
The Colorado Trail Foundation: (303) 384-3729
The Colorado Mountain Club: (303) 279-3080
Blowdown Hotline (for information about the Routt Divide Blowdown): (970) 870-2192

USDA Forest Service Offices
Rocky Mountain Regional Office: (303) 275-5350
Arapaho and Roosevelt National Forests, Boulder Ranger District (for information on the Indian Peaks Wilderness, including backcountry camping permits): (303) 444-6600
Pike and San Isabel National Forests, Pikes Peak Ranger District (for information on the Barr Trail): (719) 636-1602
Pike and San Isabel National Forests, South Platte Ranger District (for information on the Lost Creek Wilderness): (303) 275-5610
Pike and San Isabel National Forests, Leadville Ranger District (for information on climbing Mount Elbert): (719) 486-0749
White River National Forest, Holy Cross Ranger District (for information on the Vail area): (970) 827-5715
White River National Forest, Dillon Ranger District (for information on the Rock Creek Trail): (970) 468-5400
White River National Forest, Aspen Ranger District (for information on the Aspen area): (970) 925-3445
Medicine Bow and Routt National Forests, Hahns Peak/Bears Ears Ranger District (for information on the Steamboat Springs area): (970) 879-1870
San Juan and Rio Grande National Forests, Columbine Ranger District (for information on the San Juan area): (970) 247-4874
San Juan and Rio Grande National Forests, Saguache Ranger District (for informa-

tion on the Sangre de Cristo area): (719) 655-2547

Rocky Mountain National Park

Rocky Mountain National Park Visitor Center Headquarters: (970) 586-1206

For campground reservations: (800) 365-2267

Backcountry camping permit information: (970) 586-1242

Geological Terms

Alpine Glacier

An alpine glacier is a river of ice which flows slowly down a mountain valley that was originally carved by a stream.

Basin

A basin is a depression on the side of a mountain.

Bedrock

Bedrock is the solid rock beneath soil or gravel.

Bench

A bench is a narrow, fairly level terrace cut in the bedrock that interrupts the upward momentum of a slope.

Cirque

A cirque is a scoop-shaped natural amphitheater, located high on the side of a mountain, formed by the erosive activity of a mountain glacier.

Continental Divide

The Continental Divide cuts North America into two massive watersheds. Rain falling on the western side flows to the Pacific Ocean. Water on the eastern side ends up in the Gulf of Mexico.

Foothills

Foothills are low ridges or hills rising at the foot of higher mountains. In Colorado, the "foothills" are the hills located at the base of the Front Range.

Hanging Valley

A hanging valley is a tributary glacial or stream valley whose mouth is high above the floor of the main valley.

Ice Age

An ice age is a period of global cooling characterized by extensive glacial activity.

Ice Sheet

An ice sheet is an extensive glacier covering large land surfaces. Many tongues of ice or glaciers may originate from an ice sheet.

Igneous Rocks

Igneous rocks were formed by the cooling and solidification of molten volcanic rock.

Massif

A massif is a mountainous mass or a group of connecting peaks.

Metamorphic Rocks

Metamorphic rocks are igneous or sedimentary rocks which were changed by extreme heat or pressure.

Moraine

A moraine is a mound or ridge of debris which was carried down the mountain and deposited by glaciers during an ice age. Moraines consist of weathered pieces of rock ranging in size from soil to boulders. A lateral moraine was deposited at the side of a glacier and a terminal moraine was deposited at the end of a glacier. When two glaciers merged, two lateral moraines joined to form a medial moraine.

Pass

A pass is a natural passageway through high, difficult terrain such as between two mountains.

Range

A range is a connected line of many peaks, ridges and their valleys.

Saddle or Col

A saddle or col is a depression in the crest of a ridge between two summits, often forming a pass.

Sedimentary Rocks

Sedimentary rocks are layered rocks created from debris deposited by water, wind or ice.

Shelf

A shelf is a flat, rocky ledge on a slope.

Tarn

A tarn is a small, deep glacial lake lying in a cirque.

Suggested Equipment List

Use this checklist before starting on a day hike or backpacking trip.

Day Hiking

Essentials for Survival
- Day pack or backpack
- Map and compass
- Pocket knife
- Two quarts of water
- Lunch, plus extra food
- Extra layers of clothing (including rain gear)
- Waterproof matches, lighter and other fire starter
- Flashlight or head lamp (with spare batteries and bulb)
- Bivouac gear (space blanket, large plastic bags, insulating pad)
- Sunglasses, sunscreen and lip balm
- First-aid kit (see page 20)
- Toilet paper in waterproof bag; Ziploc® bag to carry TP out
- Whistle, signal mirror
- Metal cup to melt snow and boil water
- Duct tape for general repairs

Clothing
- Waterproof jacket and pants
- Thermal underwear

(polypropylene top and bottom)
- Wool or fleece jacket
- Extra insulation layer of wool or fleece
- Shorts
- Wool or fleece pants
- Sun hat
- Wool hat and gloves/mittens
- Wool socks
- Polypropylene liner socks
- Waterproof gaiters
- Sturdy, comfortable boots

Miscellaneous
- Camera and film (if desired)
- Guidebook
- Insect repellent
- Paper and pencil
- Binoculars (if desired)
- Fishing license and equipment (if desired)

Backpacking

Backpackers should carry the following in addition to the above day-hiking items.

Clothing
- Spare underwear, socks, shirts, vest, down jacket
- Bandanna

Camping and Cooking
- Tent
- Sleeping bag
- Insulating pad or self-inflating mat
- Stove and fuel
- Cooking pots
- Bowl, plate, mug, silverware
- Pot scrubber, biodegradable soap
- Matches in waterproof container
- Rain protection for pack
- Food storage bag
- Spare nylon cord
- Stuff sacks
- Small trowel
- Water filtration system and/or iodine
- Toothpaste and toothbrush

Food
- Coffee, tea, hot chocolate, instant soup, fruit drink

mixes
- Bread
- Peanut butter and jelly in a plastic container
- Instant oatmeal or other cereal
- Powdered milk
- Salt, pepper
- Snacks such as trail mix, dried fruit, nuts, jerky, cookies
- Main course meals (dehydrated food weighs less).

Index

Names and page numbers in bold type refer to the main trails described in this book.

Photography Credits

All photos are by **Christina Williams** except for the following:

Courtesy of the Colorado Historical Society: 40, 43, 60, 163b, 172

Dennis and Esther Schmidt: 27b, 62, 81, 85b, 88, 99, 108, 123, 124b, 128b, 135, 148, 150b, 158, 181b, 196b, 197, 227, 248

Jim Williams: Front cover insets (left and right), 15, 33, 67, 75a, 75b, 77, 80, 107, 113, 116a, 116b, 137, 139b, 142, 143, 147, 153, 154, 155, 160, 173a, 173b, 173c, 175, 181a, 182a, 182b, 188, 195, 198-9, 200b, 205, 207, 210-11, 215, 218, 219, 221, 229, 231b, 234, 240, 244-5, 247, 257, 272

About the Author

The author relaxes en route to Buckskin Pass

Author, photographer and educator Christina Williams was born near London and became an avid traveler, hiker and mountain climber while still a teenager. She immigrated to the United States in 1974 and has lived in Colorado ever since with her American teacher/photograher husband Jim.

Christina holds a Masters Degree in Special Education from the University of Northern Colorado. She worked for many years with emotionally disturbed and dyslexic students in Denver Public Schools while traveling and exploring the Colorado Rockies during the summer vacations. In 1991 she became a travel writer/photographer in order to combine her love of writing and outdoor adventure.

Her articles on hiking and mountaineering have appeared in publications throughout the United States and Canada.

Christina has trekked extensively in the Alps, Andes, Himalayas and numerous other mountain ranges worldwide. She has climbed many of Colorado's 54 Fourteeners and scaled a number of peaks in the Alps.

She is a member of the Society of American Travel Writers, the Colorado Authors' League, the Colorado Mountain Club and the Austrian Alpine Club.

Dedication

This book is dedicated to the following people: To my father, Charles Fryer, who instilled in me a love of hiking and climbing mountains; to my mentors and friends, Doris and Gary Kennedy, who taught me all I know about writing and photography; to my friend and colleague, Sherry Spitsnaugle, who proofread the galleys of this book and shared her expertise as an author; and to Jim, my husband of 28 years, who hiked most of these trails with me and took many of the photographs in this book.